FOOTSTEPS IN THE SNOW

The author on an ice floe in Terror and Erebus Gulf, Antarctica, in February 2020.

FOOTSTEPS IN THE SNOW

JOHN DUDENEY

Whittles Publishing

Published by
Whittles Publishing Ltd,
Dunbeath,
Caithness, KW6 6EG,
Scotland, UK

www.whittlespublishing.com

ISBN 978-184995-539-3

Printed and bound by
CPI Group (UK) Ltd, Croydon, CR0 4YY

FOR HELEN, LIZ, CLARE AND MY GRAND-DAUGHTER KIRA.

CONTENTS

AUTHOR'S NOTE

During my professional life I have been involved with a large number of organizations and projects, many of them with long and complex names. This means initialisms and acronyms – a positive plethora of them. So in this account I have presented these names in ways that I hope you will absorb reasonably easily:

- ⊚ ones such as 'BBC', which 99 per cent of my readers are practically certain to know, I've presented thus and not expanded
- ⊚ those that I judge will be familiar to around 50 per cent of you, I've presented as its initialism/acronym and expanded in a footnote
- ⊚ and those organizations and projects that are less well known I've presented with name in full and initialism/acronym in parentheses, ready for it to appear again shortly afterwards. When the name resurfaces after a longer gap, I've usually shown it in full again …

… and at the end of the book is a reference list with the initialisms/acronyms in alphabetical order, and their expansions alongside.

PREFACE

In the dying days of the last century my aged aunt (in her nineties by then) presented me with a battered old suitcase which she told me contained some documents of her father's. I thought little about it until one day I took a look and was amazed to find a complete typed manuscript – an autobiography that my grandfather had written in his old age, but never, as far as I can tell, even tried to get published. My grandfather was Leonard Dudeney (1875–1956), a very well connected and distinguished journalist. He died when I was just 11, so I never heard much about his somewhat extraordinary life from the man himself. It was therefore a great privilege to read the autobiography in my old age and so get to know him, if at one remove. It was this manuscript that has inspired me to write my own story, not because I necessarily wanted to get it published, but rather so that my family, particularly my grand-daughter, will have an opportunity to have the same insight into my life as I have had into my grandfather's. My life has certainly been unusual, so I hope she – and you, dear reader – will find it equally absorbing. I like to think that Leo Dudeney, who had a fascinating and adventurous life himself, would have found it a good read.

There are lots of folk who have helped and supported me – too many to name them all – but I particularly want to recognize John Sheail, whose enthusiasm for the project has inspired me to complete it. Also my thanks go to Mike Pinnock, David Vaughan and Richard Horne at the British Antarctic Survey for helpful comments on the draft, and to Mike Lockwood for providing important insights. Special thanks go to the family of Kirsty Brown and to Chris Portwine for their dignified approach when asked to review stories which were painful for them. Peter 'Tweaky' Fitzgerald was very generous with his time in helping me digitize several of my original 35mm slides. Acknowledgements are due to the National Archives for the provision of government papers used in drafting this book. Thanks go to the British Antarctic Survey for access to archival material, and its many staff who over the years have provided me with such a wonderful lifetime of fun, excitement and achievement. Last but not least, my heartfelt thanks go to my wife Helen and my daughters Liz and Clare, without whose unending support and love none of this would have been possible.

John Dudeney, Summer 2022
Wilburton

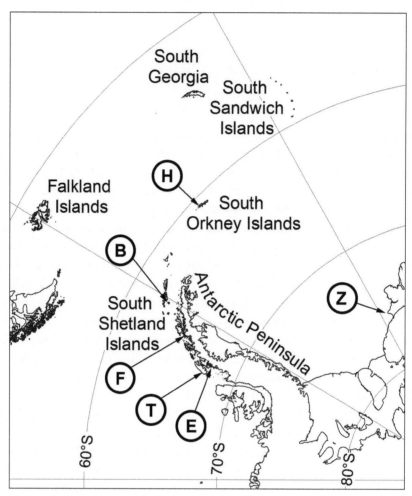

The geographical region in which this book is set. The symbols H, B, F, T, E and Z identify the locations of the British Antarctic Survey Research Stations: Base H on Signy Island (61°S, 45°W), Base B on Deception Island (63°S, 61°W), Base F on the Argentine Islands (65°S, 64°W), Base T on Adelaide Island (68°S, 68°W), Base E on Stonington Island (68°S, 67°W). and Base Z (75°S, 26°W), Halley Bay, is on the Brunt Ice Shelf. In 1976 Base T was replaced by a new station (Base R) at Rothera point, also on Adelaide Island.

1

FIRST CONTACT

Imagine a grey overcast evening, no wind, cold mist curling up from an oily calm sea, the ship rolling gently to a long low beam swell as she creeps forward. Then out of the mist a low white line appears – pack ice!

I will never forget that first encounter with the ice on board the RRS[1] *John Biscoe*. The day had started with the ship bouncing around on the Southern Ocean with giant seabirds wheeling backwards and forwards off the stern and occasionally effortlessly gliding the length of the ship beside us – seemingly close enough to touch. But as the day progressed so the temperature dropped, and then the ocean inexplicably (to us new guys – but not to old hands) started calming down. The ice, brilliant white, shading to a thrilling blue-green below the water in a clear black sea, was suddenly all around us, and there is nothing quite like the feeling I had as *Biscoe* bumped the first floe. All the senses are engaged, the crunch and scrape of ship on ice, the rocking and vibration, the sight of the floe cracking and rolling, the splash and hiss of the water, and the cold clean smell. They all came together in a glorious feeling of just being alive – a symphony in monochrome. It is a sensation that still excites me 50 years on, and one that began my fascination – 'obsession' may be more accurate – with Antarctica.

We had sailed from Stanley in the Falkland Islands just a day or so before, and were on our way to relieve the British research station, Base H, on Signy Island in the South Orkney Islands. In December 1966 Britain had six research stations operating year-round in Antarctica: Base H; Base B on Deception Island in the South Shetlands; Bases F (destined to be my home), T (Adelaide Island) and E (Stonington Island) on islands off the western side of the Antarctic Peninsula; and finally Base Z on the Brunt Ice Shelf. All were completely cut off for most of the year, with only rudimentary radio communications to the outside world. For the island bases access by sea was practical for up to three months in the southern summer, depending on where the base was located. For Base Z, way south, access was for just two or three weeks. For BAS,[2] flying to Antarctica was then an impossible dream – but one that ultimately came to pass.

---

1 Royal Research Ship
2 British Antarctic Survey

RRS *John Biscoe* 'docked' in the fast
ice at Signy Island, in December 1966.
Coronation Island is in the background.

BAS had two ships, the RRS *John Biscoe* and the slightly smaller RRS *Shackleton*; both were ice-strengthened cargo vessels, and their primary role was to support the bases – moving cargo and personnel in and out during the very brief summer period. Base Z was a special case, for which a ship was specially chartered each year from Norway.

Our arrival off Signy Island provided the next occasion in which my senses were flooded to overload by the sheer wonder of the day. With the backdrop of Coronation Island – a riot of ice and rocky peaks with huge glaciers and icefalls – the ship bustled through a flat calm mirror-like sea, pushing floes aside in glorious sunshine, with the sky a deeper blue than I had ever witnessed before. On the floes were crabeater seals basking in the sunshine, whilst between them Adélie penguins porpoised about in gay abandon. Ahead of us was fast ice.[3] The *Biscoe* drove into the fast ice to cut itself a dock. Then we were all quickly over the side of the ship and onto the ice to begin the strenuous task of offloading all the supplies needed to keep the station in operation for another year – and of course the all-important sack of mail, eagerly awaited by the men who had spent upwards of the past year completely isolated from the outside world. Thus I made my first footsteps in Antarctic snow and thus was I introduced to my life's work and my life's passion – my Antarctic journey.

* * *

Even with the benefit of 20:20 hindsight and the passage of more than half a century, I can see that it was a pretty odd thing to do back on that bright May morning in 1966. I was 21 years old, an undergraduate and a bit of a nerd. I weighed in at just under 10 stone, couldn't grow a respectable beard, had virtually no interests other than physics and table tennis, and had shown no previous inclination towards the unlikely – hardly the stuff from which heroes are made. But here I was in Martin Atkinson's office blurting out that I wanted to go to the Antarctic. Martin was the college welfare officer and chaplain,

---

3 an unbroken sheet of sea-ice that was fast to the island

and he had rather taken me under his wing. I haunted his office quite a bit, though in truth this was more because he had a very pleasant secretary for whom I held completely unrequited yearnings and lustful thoughts, but who was more than passing patient with me. Lynn Palmer was her name, and I can still picture her lustrous dark hair.[4]

I was in my final term at the Regent Street Polytechnic, reading for a London University degree in physics. I had already got my life sorted out – or so I thought. A prestigious post-graduate position at Imperial College was mine for the asking, to work at the forefront of plasma physics – then a very sexy subject, which at the time was promising to provide unlimited clean and cheap energy for all within 50 years (at the time of writing it still is offering that promise … in 50 years' time). What actually sparked me to toss this opportunity aside is now lost in the mists of time, but be that as it may, here I was with the object of my dreams looking at me somewhat curiously.

Martin, an ex-military chaplain, was a man of action. He threw me the telephone book barking, 'Look under *Antarctic*.'

I did. Nothing.

A moment's relief, then, 'Well, try *British*, then.'

And there it was – British Antarctic Survey – and with that one name and one telephone call I changed my life completely. A phone call from which stemmed my career (probably 'passion' is a better word) for life, excitement, fulfilment, several heart-stopping moments of truly life-threatening danger, a wonderful marriage, two daughters and a splendid grand-daughter who any man could be proud of. Sadly, Martin was killed in a road traffic accident whilst I was in the Antarctic that first time, so he never knew what a profound and defining influence he'd had on my life that morning.

The young 'Dude' aged 21. The Dude, or Dudes, has been my nickname ever since.

'Are there any jobs going for physicists?' I asked.

'No,' said a pleasant female voice.

'Well, do you have any technical jobs?'

'We still need an ionosphericist,' was the reply.

'What's that?'

'Well, it's to do with radio waves.'

Since that sounded close enough to physics and as the object of my desires was still fixing me with a bright stare, I agreed to present myself at 33 Gillingham Street in London for interview for the post of ionosphericist at the British Antarctic Survey Station – Argentine Islands.

The nerve centre from which BAS was then masterminded turned out to be rather unprepossessing third-floor offices at 33 Gillingham Street, just behind Victoria Station,

---

4 My becoming an explorer did not help my cause with her one jot – but we remained friends, and I was pleased to attend her wedding some years later when I was home from my first trip south.

and it was there that I arrived sweaty-palmed for my interview on one morning in May 1966. And there I met three remarkable men, all of whom in their own ways were to play a profound part in my life story. Sir Vivian Fuchs was then the director of BAS, Bill Sloman was establishments officer, and Roy Piggott was a senior scientist from the Radio Research Station near Slough. I was ushered into the interview by a very elegant lady, Eleanor Honnywill, who had been at great pains to put me at my ease whilst I was waiting. Bill and Roy sat awaiting me, and shortly after the interview commenced Sir Vivian came in from his adjoining office, slumped rather bonelessly in an overstuffed armchair and fixed me with a penetrating look over his pipe – rather unnerving for a callow youth such as me. After all, this was the guy who, less than a decade before, had driven across the Antarctic from the Weddell to the Ross Sea via the South Pole – the first to achieve what Filchner and then Shackleton had set out to do half a century before.

The interview was my first exposure to Roy – and it made quite an impact on me. I got my first 'piggotting' that day – the first of many. A piggotting is a prolonged lecture on a topic (any topic, as I was to find out) delivered with great charm and a constant – slightly manic – smile by one of nature's great enthusiasts. At the height of his powers, a piggotting could extend over more than one working day, with Roy suddenly realizing it was time to go home – often in mid-sentence, apologizing profusely, and then next morning picking up exactly where he had left off.

The topic of the day was the ionosphere – specifically the ionosphere of the Antarctic. Thankfully Roy was constrained by the time limit imposed by the interview and the need to get me to talk. But the piggotting meant that I did not have to tax my rather meagre knowledge of the ionosphere too hard, and obviously what I did say went down well enough. I was able to string together enough basic physics to make a good enough stab at why there was an ionosphere, where it was and what use it might be to humankind. Poor old Bill hardly got a word in edgewise; the only question I can remember him asking me was whether I knew how to mend a wristwatch (it was one of his standard questions at the time). I didn't, but subsequently had to try when mine gave me trouble in the middle of the Antarctic winter. My diary suggests that on 28 October 1968 I was briefly successful at this, but as soon as the relief ship arrived I took delivery of a brand-new Rolex – a watch that still serves me well over half a century on.

Bill was a very urbane man, at first sight a typical civil servant, but one who turned out to be a thoroughly nice man with a wicked sense of humour; I was to get to know him and his wife Peggy very well – in fact they became almost second parents to me. Sir Vivian just looked at me quizzically, saying nothing. Again, I was to know, like and respect Bunny, as he was known to his friends, very well over the coming years.

After the interview came the medical. This had filled me with dread. I was not a sporty type, tending more to being a weed. I just assumed that even if I had convinced BAS of my technical suitability, my physique would let me down. Still, the examination seemed to go well enough, and was actually a lot less demanding than I feared. Even more surprising, there was no psychological testing – or at least none that I discerned.

Even so it was still something of a shock when just a few days later I was invited to spend two years on the Argentine Islands as the ionospheric physicist at the princely salary of £997 per annum all found. I had actually applied for the post of ionospheric technician, but Roy had decided that I had potential as a research scientist and hence had fixed upon the grander title (plus a very slightly grander salary).

Of course all my family thought I was mad – and I think I agreed with them – but I wrote back to accept the offer, and in July 1966 presented myself at the gates of Ditton Park in Slough, home of the Radio Research Station (RRS) – later the Radio and Space Research Station, (RSRS), and later still the Appleton Laboratory – to commence my training in the black arts of the ionosphericist. Here I was introduced to the Union Radio Mark II ionosonde. This was the machine I was expected to look after for the next two years: a wonderful early example of electromechanical automation replete with cogs, wheels, bicycle chains and glowing thermionic valves – very Heath Robinson. Union Radio Mark II might have been its official name, but I soon learnt to love it and hate it under the name of the Beastie – as BAS ionosphericists before and after me have done. I also learnt to answer to the title of Beastieman.

The Beastie transmitted pulses of radio waves vertically upwards and received the echoes reflected from the ionosphere – an electrically conducting layer at the top of the atmosphere, extending from 60 km altitude out into space. As it transmitted its pulses it also swept its transmitting frequency right across the medium wave and high frequency wave bands (300 kHz to 30 MHz). By measuring the time taken for the pulses to arrive back to the receiver, the height of the reflecting layers could be estimated. Also, some basic plasma physics allowed the concentration of electrons at the reflection height to be determined from the radio frequency of the pulses. The normal operating cycle was to make measurements (known as soundings) once per hour, each lasting about 4 minutes. From this a basic picture of the behaviour of the ionosphere could be made. This bit of technical stuff is necessary to understand why the Beastie and Beastiemen got the nicknames they did.

Before spacecraft came along, reflection of radio waves off the ionosphere was the only way to communicate over the horizon. Obviously, the Beastie transmitted at the same sort of radio frequencies as were used for communications – say, between the Antarctic bases and home, and for receiving the BBC World Service. However, while it was operating the Beastie would completely wipe out all other local radio services. Radio receivers would emit a loud and irritating farting noise. At BAS Antarctic bases, where an effective electrical earth was very difficult to arrange, it even found its way into hi-fi systems, which then also broke wind instead of delivering Mozart. Thus it got its name – and we Beastiemen ours.

The Mark II Union Radio Ionosonde at Base F. The Beastie with a young Dude attending to it.

The RRS was a curious mixture of cutting-edge high-tech science and an unworldly throwback to pre-World War II days, with old wooden sheds in the grounds still containing ancient and dusty equipment. There were hallowed names either still walking about RRS or whose influence still pervaded the place – people like Sir Edward Appleton, and J.A. Ratcliffe, who had done much to lay the theoretical foundations of radio physics, and Sir Robert Watson-Watt, who is now recognized as the father of radar, and who with his assistant, Arnold Wilkins, carried out much of the early research leading to that war-winning invention. When I arrived at RRS, Wilkins was still working there, and Ratcliffe was just coming to the end of his time as director, so it was rather special to find myself working there – and actually spending much of my time in one of the famous huts – Hut 20. Ditton Park was (and remains) a splendid area of lush meadow, woodland and lake literally on the edge of Slough, bordered on one side by the M4, and just a couple of miles from the western threshold of Heathrow's main runways. It had remained in this rural state because of the long-term occupation of the site by the combination of RRS and the Admiralty Compass Observatory, which occupied the old moated manor house in its centre. Ditton Park was to play a major role in my life later when I returned from the Antarctic, since it was there that I met and courted Helen, a beautiful young summer student and now my wife of 50 years.

My training at Slough through the summer of 1966 went by in a flash. It was very much a matter of self-help with the occasional bursts of vintage piggotting, and serious but friendly ribbing by the old hands who had just returned from their two years of tending the Beastie. They also pointed out to me that from now on I would be joining the elite band of people known as fids. BAS had originally been known as the Falkland Islands Dependencies Survey (FIDS), and the name now remained as the collective term for BAS wintering staff – 'fucking idiots down south'. In later years I found that there was a semi-official hierarchy to fid-dom. There were fidlets, the new recruits wet behind the ears and of no use to anybody; fids, the salt of the Earth; super-fids, fids who had got above themselves and joined the management; and finally mega-fids, reserved for those few shooting stars who made it to the top of the shop. I was lucky enough to move through all ranks during my career.

Suddenly it was October and a mad whirl of packing and saying goodbyes fell upon me. All my friends and family still thought me mad, but also by and large seemed secretly envious of what I was about to embark upon. For my own part, I was in a bit of a daze, not quite knowing what I had done or why I had done it, but determined to do it nevertheless.

My arrival at the quayside in Southampton was the first rude awakening. The ship I was to sail upon was supposedly waiting for me at the Ocean Terminal, where all the big ocean liners then left for the transatlantic crossing. Across the dock I could see one such enormous vessel – I think it was the *Queen Mary*. But where was the *John Biscoe*? Well, the tide was out, so it didn't really stand out much – in fact only its cream-coloured upper superstructure, red funnel and mastheads were visible at all. In comparison with the wonderful liner it looked little bigger than a lifeboat. It weighed in at a gross tonnage of all of 1,500 tons (smaller than the car ferries that plied between Southampton and the Isle of Wight), which seemed an impossibly small size to me for braving the dreaded Southern Ocean and the even more dreaded southern ice pack. But actually it was a very sturdy and capable little ship, very perky with its red hull and cream upper works, purpose-built for BAS in 1956 and well able to cope with all that the Southern Ocean could throw at it – but comfortable it was not. Having a round bottom, so that ice pressure would lift it out of harm's way rather than crush it, it had a tendency to roll like a pig, and was hence somewhat of a floating purgatory for anybody who did not quickly find their sea legs. Anyway, the scale and finality of the step I had taken finally dawned on me as we gathered pace down the Solent, next stop Montevideo, with my mother, sister and young niece waving frantically from the shore. I realized that there was now no turning back and I would have to make the best of whatever the experience had to offer.

For me the early days at sea were a bit of a physical and emotional challenge. Having been a withdrawn loner with very few close friends, I had to quickly come to terms with being cooped up, with no privacy, with a boisterous group of 30 or so young men – all men in those days of course – from very diverse backgrounds and perspectives on the world. At one extreme came Big Al Smith, a huge man physically who was an ex-rugby professional, ex-professional wrestler and a master builder by trade, and at the other end of the spectrum Richard, a very outgoing young doctor. Big Al was actually a lovely gentle man who could do the work of three normal people, whilst Richard was the only person I have ever met who could recite the whole of 'Eskimo Nell'[5] from memory! There were other scientists, cooks, a serving RAF squadron leader on secondment to fly the BAS aeroplanes, diesel mechanics and a rather awesome Australian mountain expert named Alistair. We all had to learn to live with and work with each other within the confines of that small ship.

---

5 'The Ballad of Eskimo Nell' is a ribald poem in 46 verses recounting the tale of Deadeye Dick, his accomplice, Mexican Pete, and a woman Eskimo Nell, who they meet on their travels on the Rio Grande.

The social arrangement was stratified into three distinct social classes: the officers, the crew, and the fids. The officers lived on the main deck in some luxury, dining in their wardroom, waited upon by liveried stewards. The crew had their cabins and mess aft on the well deck. Their mess was right next to the galley, so their food was always freshly prepared and hot (unlike that of the officers, which journeyed some distance from galley to tummy). Us fids occupied the forward section of the well deck and had our own mess-room, bar and facilities, which we were expected to keep spick and span ourselves. We took it in turns to clean and to acquire and serve our meals under the watchful eye of the King Fid. King Fid did what the title suggests – he was in charge of the fids and was our liaison with the ship's officers and BAS headquarters. He was almost invariably somebody who had travelled with BAS before and hence knew the ropes.

Communal ship's toilets are generally not the sweetest of places at the best of times, and at any other time – maybe when the ship is in heavy weather – they are anything but. So my first turn on the cleaning rota was a challenge to say the least. Doing the cleaning and food service job was known in Royal Navy slang as doing gash. There were two gashmen each day, their duties starting at 6.00 am with cleaning up the fids public areas and toilets before serving breakfast. Then came 'smoko'[6] in mid-morning, followed by the service of lunch, afternoon smoko, service of dinner and finally cleaning up and mopping anything that conceivably looked as though it should be mopped. My first turn as gashman came on a bright morning in the Bay of Biscay but one with a fairly lively sea. It is one thing to not suffer the *mal de mer* when you can sit down when you need to; quite another cleaning toilets recently visited by mal de mer sufferers and then serving up bacon and eggs from large metal dishes in which the contents are sliding back and forth in slowly congealing fat. That takes a stomach of a different order all together! I can proudly say that I did not actually throw up into the porridge on that morning, but my green complexion undoubtedly put several diners off their stroke. However, there are always those irritatingly hearty souls for whom sea-sickness is incomprehensible and for whom 'it's all in the mind, old boy' as they gleefully slurp greasy bacon in and out of their mouths to wind the sufferers up before finally swallowing it with a smack of their lips. I managed to hold what was inside me in its rightful place, and got through the day without disgracing myself. But it was a serious learning exercise for a soul as innocent as I was then.

Perhaps now is the time for a short digression that will help set the context of why I was such an innocent when I set sail for Antarctica. I was the youngest of three children with a brother three years older and a sister six years older. My parents were not happily married, and parted company when I was 11. This left my mother to fend for herself, my brother and me, my sister having run off in disgust with a man some years older

---

6 naval slang for coffee break

than her. To say that we were disadvantaged would be an understatement, though I was not really conscious of it at the time. We were ignored by my father and his rather grand family, and left to fend for ourselves. There was no other father figure in my life, and with precious little spare money for recreation of any sort I became a rather solitary introverted figure; the municipal library became my refuge and lifeline. With no radio or television in the bed-sit where we lived, books became my life. Unsurprisingly, perhaps, I had failed at the age of 11 to get a place at grammar school, and it seemed that I was condemned to pass through secondary school without learning much or gaining any qualifications. I did not make friends easily (I still do not), but had one close school friend, David Selwood, who was a stabilizing influence for me through those difficult teenage years. Sadly, we lost contact after I went south, only to rediscover each other much later through the good offices of social media. But around the age of 14 I discovered maths, and more to the point discovered that I was good at maths – in fact better than anybody else in the school at maths. With that discovery and a couple of very dedicated teachers, my life was transformed. Although it was a struggle to keep going in education in the face of unremitting poverty, in 1966 I arrived at BAS with a first class honours degree in physics from London University, thinking that I was the most important person around as a result, but completely unworldly otherwise, and socially inept. And with this background I was thrust into a bunch of mostly extroverted young men from all walks of life, who quite rightly didn't give a toss about my physics degree – they just cared about whether the bog was clean and the coffee was hot when they wanted it to be hot. So my early days with BAS were a trial as I came to terms with being a team player and being judged by how I performed for the common good rather than whether I could solve second order differential equations before breakfast (I could then – but not any more!).

The gash rota on the ship served two purposes as far as the BAS hierarchy was concerned: firstly the obvious one of maintaining civilization amongst the fids, but secondly, and just as important, it provided a testing ground to see how (or sometimes whether) people fitted in, and hence whether they were likely to be successful wintering in Antarctica or not. Back then there was no compunction about saying to somebody 'we don't think you're going to fit in so we're sending you home'. This was before sophisticated labour relations required formal warnings and counselling, appeals and tribunals. No doubt decisions were sometimes arbitrary and occasionally unfair, but the alternative – trapping unsuitable people in Antarctica – would have been much worse. In later years as I ascended the greasy pole at BAS it became my duty on occasions to pass that sad message of rejection to youngsters.

Life on board an ocean-going vessel on a long passage such as ours – from Southampton to Montevideo – quickly settles down to a much slower pace than normal. The ship ploughs steadily on at around 12 knots, setting the pulse for the day, aiming at the empty horizon but never reaching it. The watchkeepers stand their watches, the navigating officer takes his sun-sight at noon (long before the wonders of GPS had been dreamt of), and meals come and go exactly on time. The menu marks the passage of the days and weeks as it rotates around its short list of offerings – fish on Friday, steak on Saturday, curry for Sunday lunch, roast for Sunday dinner. Sunday morning brings Captain's Inspection where everything (including the tops of cupboards and door jambs) were inspected for cleanliness, and woe betide any fid who was (a) still in his bunk or (b) whose bunk was not made with military precision. Twice a week we would get the ship's projector out and have a movie. In the tropics when the weather was good, we could set this up on the afterdeck and enjoy the film under the stars. Otherwise when we fids were not on gash, there was little for us to do except read, play board games, watch the ocean go by, and of course drink alcohol. The provision of alcohol on board was a private business run by the captain and his chief steward. It was all duty free and stupidly cheap even after the captain's profit had been made. It was thus very easy to drink far too much. Getting plastered regularly was definitely not a good thing to do – all part of the test of whether one was suitable or not – but the temptation for young men sometimes enjoying their first release from parental control was strong, so drinking could be a real problem. I quickly learnt either to win or not to participate in such games as liar dice, where to lose a round was to be required to drink the designated tot. There was generally no way back from a couple of unfortunate rounds of the dice. I am consequently to this day a consummate liar where dice are concerned. The chief officer would occasionally find us some work to do around the ship – perhaps paint chipping, caulking or even standing wheel watch. The latter required one to steer the ship for an hour at a time – unutterably boring, as there was never any need to change course, and the only fun to be had was to try to see how far off course a bit of 'left hand down a bit' could achieve before the captain noticed the sun's shadow doing odd things and put a stop to the fun.

Thus we spent the three weeks or so on passage to South America getting to know each other and slowly browning in the tropical sunshine. The only significant disruption to the steady beat of our lives was when the ship allowed King Neptune and his acolytes on board to do unmentionable things to the poor souls who had never crossed the line before. This entailed us being anointed in some really horrible glutinous brew produced by the galley, ritually shaved, and then be required to kiss King Neptune's foot, adorned itself with a rather smelly flying fish that had been unfortunate enough to make a hard landing on the ship's deck that morning.

Our first inkling that land was approaching came when the beautiful deep blue sea began to develop a dirty brown tinge, heralding the outflow of silt from the mighty River Plate. As the day wore on and low-lying land appeared on the horizon, plus the low hill that is the 'monte' of Montevideo, the water around us turned a deeper shade of brown until for all the world we could have been steaming through milk chocolate. The air became thick and humid, with a smell which lay somewhere between compost heap and drains, and all too soon our long voyage was coming to an end with the excitements of Montevideo now to be a reality, rather than the lurid talk of the old hands aboard. The pilot boat raced alongside, and we were on our way along the roads into the port with the old hands convincing us that the wreck we could see sticking out of the water was the infamous Nazi battle cruiser *Graf Spee* – it was not, though; it was actually the *Calpean Star*, a whaling support ship that sank in suspicious circumstances (rumoured to have been scuttled as an insurance scam in June 1960) on its way from the whaling grounds of South Georgia. The next excitement for us was the appearance of the customs and immigration officials on board to clear the ship before we could be released ashore. These gentlemen came aboard with empty holdalls, to be met obsequiously by the chief steward who conducted them to his cabin. Some time later they arrived back at the gangway with alcoholic grins and much heavier holdalls that clinked as they walked. The ship thus cleared, we fids were free to taste the delights of Monte, having been lectured by the doctor on the dangers of wine, women and song – especially women. But coming from a guy who was word-perfect in Eskimo Nell this seemed to be a laying it on a bit thick.

With the doctor's warnings ringing in our ears we were released for a run ashore in the early evening of a warm early summer Sunday evening. The crew and old hands had been filling our heads with the wonders to be had in the bars and restaurants of the town – basically cheap but gorgeous women in the bars and wonderful steaks in the restaurants. However, first impressions were not promising, for the bars that clustered in the streets leading from the dock gates were all locked and silent, whilst what restaurants that were open seemed to be having a meatless day. So we wandered as a bunch rather disconsolately through the empty streets until suddenly a window was jerked open in an upper floor of one of the terraced line of bars and a voice shouted with some alarm and a heavy Spanish accent '¡*John Beesco?*' It turned out that the bars had not been expecting us until the following morning, so hadn't bothered to open, but as a result of good weather we had arrived just in time to be cleared into port that evening. With remarkable speed all the bars began to open and soon the streets had taken on a very different character. This was my first taste of such an environment, and to a young and impressionable chap the women were indeed extremely attractive, dressed appropriately to snare clients and very (*very*) friendly. I was far too scared of them and the hellfire that would follow to indulge in their services even though the scuttlebutt had it that an issue fids silk scarf would be sufficient to obtain an all-nighter, and the peso rate, when converted into a hard currency, was derisory to us (though not to them).

Monte was a real eye-opener to me. It was my first taste of exotic South America, and it didn't disappoint: from the ornate and classical style of the architecture, somewhat dog-eared and down at heel, and the chocolate soldiers guarding the presidential palace, to the ancient vehicles (quite a few Ford model Ts and American cars made familiar by 1920s American gangster films), the elegant women, the outstanding steaks and the men sucking on their silver strainer/straws to drink from their mate[7] gourds. We did manage to get a steak the following day; we were lucky, because it was at a time when most Uruguayan meat was going for export so there were several meatless days each week. And we had to make a pilgrimage to Mario's the leather shop, where Mario would ply us with 'free' beer while his very comely young sales assistants would model some of his garments.

In later years I discovered the Monte meat market, which stood –still stands – just across the road from the entrance to the docks. This is just what its name suggests, a butchers' market, but it is also a wonderful collection of barbecue stalls attached to the butchers' stalls where a *bife de lomo* (fillet steak), *ensalada mista*, *papas fritas* and an *iced cerveza* could be purchased with crusty bread for virtually nothing – and what a bife de lomo! A meal to die for. It became my favourite first stop over many years of arriving in Monte after months south in a ship that by the time we reached port had run out of almost all but the bare essentials as far as food went. The joy of the steak and the beefsteak tomatoes and that iced beer will stay with me to my grave.

Leaving Monte we set off across the mouth of the River Plate for the four-day passage to Stanley in the Falkland Islands. Those four days were a time machine to take us back 30 years or more to a unique, almost feudal, society of hardy folk who happily lived in glorious isolation from the rest of the world with almost none of the trappings of modern civilization. The Falklands are a wild windswept archipelago of peat bogs, coarse grassland and rocky crags – and sheep and Land Rovers. No trees or shrubs except for a few evergreens that cling to life in the city, and (then) no roads except for those in Stanley itself – hence the need for the Land Rovers.

There was then no airport in the Falklands and just one ship sailing per month – the RMS[8] *Darwin* – which plied between Stanley and Monte. No television, no bus service, no restaurants or cafes, only one general store, a town hall that was also the post office, dance hall and cinema; and a good selection of pubs. Most houses in Stanley – and in the camp[9] for that matter – used peat fires for heating and cooking, so over the town hung the evocative haze and scent of peat smoke. Still to this day the smell of peat smoke crowds my mind with memories of my first, almost wholly positive, impressions of Stanley.

Stanley climbs up the steep south shore of a long narrow natural harbour which has a very narrow gap on its north side out to Port William and the open sea – this gap imaginatively called the Narrows. On a clear day, the view as you came in on a ship

---

7 Mate is a traditional South American caffeine-rich infused drink made by soaking dried leaves of the holly species *Ilex paraguariensis* in hot water. It is sucked through a metal straw from a container typically made from a calabash gourd.

8 Royal Mail Ship

9 All the terrain on the islands that is not a settlement.

through the Narrows was stunning, with the town and its highly colourful corrugated iron roofs and red brick cathedral set against a superb background of wild bare mountains in the west with names now familiar to many people in Britain – Mount Tumbledown, Mount Kent, Mount Longdon, Wireless Ridge – but then magnificently unknown to us, and the harbour wonderfully blue with white horses driven by the ever-present westerly wind. Riding in the harbour were a motley collection of old sailing ships – relics of the days when Stanley had done a roaring trade in providing refuge for clippers rounding (or failing to round) Cape Horn. These ships were by then abandoned and mostly used for storage, though some had been turned into the ends of jetties. Across Port William, in Sparrow Cove, lay a particularly famous hulk – Isambard Kingdom Brunel's ship *Great Britain*, later to be epically salvaged and returned to its home port of Bristol for renovation and display.

Stanley's population in 1966 was around 1,000 people, with a further 800 or so scattered across the camp in isolated sheep farms or in the few small settlements, one which was to become famous some years later – Goose Green, the site of the first significant land battle of the Falklands Conflict. The only means of travelling around the islands overland were on horseback – most shepherds travelled this way – or by Land Rover. There were more Land Rovers then per head of population in the Falklands than anywhere else in the world – and there probably still are. The terrain tested even these vehicles to the limit, but they were ideally suited to it, although a journey of 50 miles would routinely take all day for a highly skilled camp driver. There were also two de Havilland Beaver single-engine seaplanes that formed the Falkland Islands Government Air Service (FIGAS). These used Stanley Harbour as their runway and provided a reasonably regular link to the outlying settlements. There was also a small inter-island coaster that carried provisions to the settlements and collected the wool – then the main output of the islands. The islanders' diet was pretty basic: overall very little fresh fruit and vegetables, though most houses would have a thriving vegetable garden, and mutton, known to all as 365 for obvious reasons.

Stanley was then a significant forward base and communications centre for the BAS operation with a dozen or so staff. Our few days in Stanley were very full. Firstly, it was here that we were issued with all our polar kit, then there was quite a bit of cargo shifting to do – stuff off the ship and stuff onto the ship; I remember in particular a day of back-breaking work loading sacks of sand and gravel. And there was the formal reception at Government House where the governor – Sir Cosmo Dugal Haskard – and his wife Alicia held court for us young explorers, and where we tried to get as much food and drink down our necks as possible in the regulation 75 minutes. But soon it was time to say goodbye to this small haven of Britishness, to set sail again on our grand adventure.

2

HOME FROM HOME

The Argentine Islands are a small archipelago of rocky islands surmounted by permanent icecaps rising to a maximum elevation of around 60 metres. They sit in the Southern Ocean about 5 miles from the west coast of the Antarctic Peninsula, separated from it by the Penola Strait, at 65°15'S, 64°16'W. They were named by Jean Baptiste Charcot (leader of the French Antarctic Expedition 1903–05) in recognition of the help he had received from the Argentine Republic. The islands had first been occupied in 1935 when

Base F at Marina Point, on Galindez Island, one of the Argentine Islands. In the background are Booth Island (left) and Mount Scott (right) on the mainland; between them is the southern entrance to the Lemaire Channel. From left to right: the diesel generator shed, the main fuel tank, the coal store, the main living hut, and a radar installation for tracking weather balloons. Just visible on the far right is the dog span with a team of huskies.

they provided the wintering base for the British Graham Land Expedition, building a hut on Winter Island. This hut was destroyed, probably by a tsunami, in 1946, and a new hut had been built there in 1947 by the FIDS, named Wordie House after the polar explorer Sir James Wordie. This marked the commencement of permanent occupation of the islands, first in Wordie House and then in a larger building (named Coronation House to mark the Queen's coronation in 1953) on the neighbouring Galindez Island from 1954.

The base was formally known as Base F, a wonderfully unimaginative name which harked back to the origins of FIDS in Operation Tabarin[10] in World War II, when a multi-departmental government committee was charged with establishing a permanent British presence in Antarctica, and each station was assigned a code letter in alphabetical order. Base F was operated as a static base to carry out observations of the weather, geophysical measurements (geomagnetic field, solar radiation and atmospheric ozone) and ionospheric measurements. None of these studies required significant field journeys – hence the 'static' label. That is not to say that the station lacked the equipment to make unsupported journeys; just that they were not a requirement and hence were only done for recreation when time allowed. The station complex was situated on a relatively flat promontory named Marina Point, close to the shore and about 3 or 4 metres above sea level. It was here that I was destined to spend two years in the company of 10 or 11 other men.

I finally moved ashore to the station on the first of March 1967, just a few days before my 22nd birthday, having spent the previous few months first on the *Biscoe* and then on the *Shackleton*, visiting other bases, assisting in oceanographic research in the Southern Ocean, and even getting a visit to the Chilean port of Punta Arenas. With me came Chris, the other half of the two-man Beastie team. We had been travelling together since Southampton but had not yet forged a good working relationship. We were somewhat like chalk and cheese: me a young new non-smoking graduate, he an older chain-smoking technician who had already done one winter previously as a beastieman at the southern station of Halley in 1963. Not an ideal combination to be thrust together.

Coronation House was a long single-storey wooden building with a central corridor which ran its length. In it were three bunk rooms each with five bunks, a kitchen, dining room, lounge, surgery and what was euphemistically referred to as the bathroom. There were also several science rooms, a radio office, an office for the base commander and a drying room. There was also a tiny room – more of a cupboard, really, that we used as

---

10 A secret British operation during World War II to establish a permanent presence in Antarctica. Contrary to popular myth, it had nothing to do with the prosecution of the war but was to bolster Britain's territorial claim. See Dudeney, J. R, and D.W.H. Walton (2011) From Scotia to 'Operation Tabarin': developing British policy for Antarctica, *Polar Record*, 48, 342–60; and Haddelsey, S. (2014) *Operation Tabarin*, Stroud: The History Press.

Coronation House, the main living hut at Base F; the window next to my bunk is the one to the right of the ladder.

a darkroom. The hut was roughly oriented east–west with airlock-style doors at each end, and at the eastern end there was an external balcony which had a magnificent view of the mountainous spine of the Antarctic Peninsula. That view was to be mine for two years because the windows of the Beastie room also looked out in that direction. We had electric power provided by diesel generators, but heating (such as it was) was provided by small coal-fired stoves, and we cooked on a coal-fired range. The diesel generators had their own hut some way from Coronation House (primarily for fire safety) and there was also a large coal store – about 25 tons – which was replenished once a year. The western end of the hut had some utility areas – a workshop, a room we called the doggy room because it was there we kept all the paraphernalia needed to support our 12 huskies, and a coal store which held the running stock of coal needed to keep the fires burning.

The observant reader will have noticed that I have not yet mentioned a toilet. To talk about that and other matters of a plumbing nature we need to talk about the problem of water. The Antarctic ice mass is truly stupefyingly large. The continent has an area of 14 million sq km and rises to over 4,000 metres elevation. It is the largest mass of ice on our planet by far; 90 per cent of all the Earth's ice is contained within it, and it is all made up of lovely fresh water. So you would think that water would be the least of the worries confronting your Antarctic explorer. But not so. Indeed, there is water, water everywhere, but also there is not a drop to drink. Sucking ice is not very habit-forming, nor is rubbing oneself down with snow, no matter what some strange folk may claim. Every drop of water that is consumed has to be made in one way or another. These days there is lots of technology to help, and also lots of energy kicking about to assist in the process. At coastal stations it is normal now to desalinate sea water using reverse osmosis, while inland a variety of clever and energy-efficient melters are used to turn the ice into useable water.

But in the 1960s things were not quite so easy, at least not for the British Antarctic Survey, where money was in short supply and energy was also in short supply. So water was a precious commodity that was always in short supply. Every drop of water we used for drinking, cooking, washing, cleaning and flushing had to be melted. For a couple of months in the summer there would sometimes be a pond of meltwater outside Coronation House which, depending on exactly where it formed, could be used directly to give us water. This we could pump into the building using a hand pump, but we had to be careful to only use water that came from an (relatively) unpolluted pond. There was always the danger that lurking in the depths would be old seal meat, dog turds deposited by our husky dogs, bits of dead penguins, or run-off of greywater from kitchen or bathroom, or even nasty chemicals from film processing or the production of hydrogen for use in met balloons. Even so, a melt pool meant relative plenty.

Otherwise we had to shovel snow and melt it. The process was crude. In the building we had several large copper tanks (around 500 litres each): one in the kitchen that used heat from the cooking range to keep the water warm, and two in what we called the bathroom, one nominally for hot water and the other for cold. The hot tank was heated by a little coal-fired 'pot-boiler' stove located in the carpenter's workshop next door. The basic system was to bring snow blocks in from outside and put them into the copper tanks – always remembering not to let the tanks themselves become too empty, as ice melts much better if immersed in warm water. This was the system that had been supplied by our lords and masters. It had the great advantage of simplicity – there was nothing to break down and little to get frozen up. But it was messy and did not produce much water when considered against the daily needs of 12 men. The base members had therefore built themselves a rather basic water melter. This was a glorified electric kettle that consisted of a large galvanized metal tank in an insulated wooden box with a kettle heating element in it. It was kept outside and would produce sufficient for our needs if used wisely, which could then be pumped into the indoor copper tanks. In winter it would become buried in the snowdrift that accumulated around the hut. This accumulation would become sufficiently impressive that we would excavate a cave around the melter, using the diggings to feed the kettle. So every day it was somebody's task to make water – one of the several domestic jobs that had to be done each day.

Apart from the pipes linking the copper tanks to the stoves, Coronation House had no plumbing of any sort. No hot or cold running water piped around the building,

Making water in summer (upper panel) and winter (lower panel).

no flush toilets, no sewage system and definitely no central heating. The bathroom did have a bath in it, but this was never to my knowledge used for its primary purpose. It did serve a vital function, which was to provide the means for rewarming somebody suffering from hypothermia – a basic rule is that anybody apparently dead from hypothermia is not declared dead until they are *warm* and dead – but thankfully we never had to use it in that way, an undertaking which would have sorely taxed our water resources if we had ever had to do it in earnest. Otherwise it provided the bathroom drain. Its drainhole had a short vertical pipe that went through the floor and then stopped. All waste water went down that pipe, where it vanished out of sight and mind to add to an artificial glacier that flowed down the rock on which the hut was built into a gully which ended up in the sea.

Hence water was strictly rationed. Having a shower was a real treat that was rationed to once per week and to 5 gallons (22 litres) per man. The rationing was enforced in a very simple and effective way – we had a 5-gallon drum which had a watering can rose with a tap fitted at the bottom. To take a shower one simply filled the drum from the copper tanks – mixing from the hot and cold tanks to get the required temperature – hung it on a hook above the bath and stood under it. Showers were usually reserved for Saturday evenings when tradition required that we dress for dinner. It was a real joy to have that one evening of the week when one felt clean. The only other occasion when an extra shower would be allowed would be when the coal store in the hut needed replenishment. This was a task that all participated in, chaining coal sacks in from the dump outside to the coal hopper – but there was one particularly mucky job, which required an individual to empty the sacks into the hopper and rake the pile. For doing that job the prize was a shower.

So, returning once again to the subject of the toilet. There was a small unheated room by the western entrance, and in this stood a large galvanized bucket with a nice wooden toilet seat on it. In this we would put a small quantity of water and a shot of a chemical called Elsan Blue. Hanging on the wall next to this was another, smaller, bucket, the urinal. These two buckets were emptied once a day into the sea when there was no sea ice, or into the tidal crack between the sea ice and the land ice when the sea was frozen.

Thus it was in this somewhat spartan but actually quite comfortable home that I settled down to spend two years. There were 11 of us in total; in command was Brian 'Speedy' Swift, an RAF sergeant on secondment. As base commander, Speedy was a sworn-in magistrate for British Antarctic Territory[11] (BAT), the BAT sub-

11 By 1966 the Antarctic Treaty provided the overarching governance of Antarctica. There were then 12 treaty nations: Argentina, Australia, Belgium, Chile, France, Japan, New Zealand, Norway, South Africa, the Soviet Union, the United Kingdom and the United States of America. Seven of these retained territorial claims, which although not generally recognized internationally, were acknowledged within the treaty and administered for their own nationals with various forms of government. BAT had its own legal system, its own postal system and tax regime. We fids paid BAT tax, which at that time was just 7 per cent.

postmaster, our doctor and our dentist. He was also the radar technician whose job was to track the weather balloons we launched once per day. Then there was Grahame the diesel mechanic, Robin the radio operator and Dave the cook. This group formed the blackhand gang. The scientists were Peter Mitchell and Peter Morgan (known as Gobbler and Gonker respectively, as befitted their habits of eating and sleeping), the observatory physicists; and Phil Cotterill, Richie Hesbrook and Ian Tyson, who were the meteorologists, known as Phil (he never got a nickname), Big Rich and Wink. Richie got his nickname for the obvious reason – he was 6 foot 6 – but the origin of 'Wink' I don't think I could make understandable to anybody. It had to do with the fact that he only had one eye (that patently wasn't true) and it was too close together (which might have been). Rounding off the team were Chris Jefferies and me. Poor old Chris being somewhat older (a relative term) and somewhat careworn, collected the unfortunate appellation of Scrotum (the wrinkled retainer) while I finally collected the nickname 'The Dude' or 'Dudes', which has stuck with me throughout more than half a century of Antarctic adventures. These were my companions for the next 12 months or so, much of it in complete isolation from the outside world. We all had our specialities, but we also all had to share in the routine tasks of running the community.

The wintering team at Base F for 1967. Left to right: Back row, Phil, Peter Mitchell, Richie, Chris. Middle row, Peter Morgan, Speedy, Robin, Me. Front row, Grahame, Wink, Dave.

Life was organized around a rota of jobs: gashman, waterman, second cook and night-watchman. Each job was rostered on a weekly basis. Gashman was the general skivvy who did the housework of sweeping (no vacuum cleaner.) mopping etc, keeping the fires burning and emptying the gash (kitchen waste, general waste and toilet waste). Waterman mined for water, but also had a vital role in keeping all doors and windows clear of accumulated snow – an essential fire precaution when living in a tinder-dry wooden box. Waterman also got to do his washing using a twin-tub washing machine in the bathroom, as did the gashman. The duties of second cook were to generally assist the cook as needed, lay the tables for meals, make tea and coffee for the morning and afternoon smokos, and do the washing up. The latter was a pretty horrible task given the limited amount of water available. It certainly gave me a lifetime dislike of washing up – thank god for dishwashers! Night-watchman was shared between the metmen and the physicists who had to do the three-hourly met observations through the night, and it involved a regular inspection tour of the base to ensure all was safe while the rest of us slept. The cook got Sunday off, and the other ten of us each took a turn in cooking. This was initially a daunting task because standards were high, but I found that I had an aptitude for it and it is something I have continued to do throughout my life.

Food was very important to us. But our diet was severely circumscribed by a complete lack of fresh food, and during my first winter also of frozen food. We lived on tinned and dehydrated food, with the one exception that we had an abundance of flour for baking, so always had a variety of freshly baked bread and cakes each day. The recently signed Agreed Measures for the Conservation of Antarctic Flora and Fauna[12] has banned any foraging for food off the local wildlife except *in extremis*, but back then we would occasionally supplement our diet with seal meat when we had been hunting for dog food, and also collect Adélie penguin eggs from a nearby rookery early in the breeding season, on the basis that the birds would lay a second egg. The eggs could be kept for several months if stored in sawdust, and made a very welcome change from powdered dried egg. They were somewhat different from hen's eggs, both in size and appearance. If fried, the white would not turn opaque but remain translucent, while the yolk was somewhat orange with a greenish tinge – not necessarily the most attractive sight on one's breakfast plate. But they did make very good scrambled egg and meringues. The big social event of the year was midwinter (rather than Christmas), and for that in my first year the cook had kept a large joint of 'fresh' beef in a snow hole for our midwinter feast. For some time after that I became quite taken by horseradish sauce sandwiches since they reminded me of the beef feast.

In the 1960s, bases in the Antarctic, British or otherwise, were physically cut off from each other and the outside world for the duration of the Antarctic winter – and here winter was not measured in practice by the passage of the seasons, but by the

---

12 This measure was signed in 1964 within the Antarctic Treaty. It was the first step towards environmental protection of Antarctica.

length of that period of isolation before the environment relented sufficiently for ships and aeroplanes to arrive from warmer climes. For us at Base F the winter lasted from mid/late March until around the New Year, or normally a little over nine months. Within that time our only contact with the outside world was by HF radio. In 1967 this meant a radio link to the Falkland Islands using Morse code. From there official messages for HQ were sent by telex to London. Between the bases both Morse and voice communications were possible, dependent on the vagaries of the ionosphere and the operating cycle of the Beastie. Personal contact with the outside world was strictly rationed to 100 words once per month out, and 200 words once per month in between the base member and one nominated member of his next of kin. Think about *that* when you next pick up your smartphone to txt, email, skype, zoom, phone or use social media! We 11 men were a very enclosed group, and forging an effective team was paramount to our safety and sanity.

My first few months on base as we headed into the winter were not easy. It takes time, effort and considerable self-reflection for anybody to learn how to succeed in such a strange isolated society and alien environment, where there is no chance of physical escape and no real privacy, and where all are reliant on each for their health and wellbeing. The team is not necessarily going to contain anybody that one would naturally choose as a friend. I was a young, arrogant and self-important graduate, and I soon learnt that I had to earn the respect of my companions pretty quickly, and that I was anything but the most important being on base. The diesel and electrical mechanic (DEM), radio op and cook were far more important than me. I had no previous experience of teamwork, or really even of work of any sort on which to fall back; I lacked practical skills, and had no confidants to whom I could turn for advice. What I did have – though I would not have recognized it in myself at the time – was a very well-developed sense of self-reliance, an obstinate determination born out of my troubled childhood, and a strong belief in fair play. I quickly found the best approach was to be first to step forward to volunteer when Speedy asked, and to try always to question my motives, rather than criticize others, when the potential for conflict or rivalry arose. The diary that I kept during that first winter is fascinating to read now, being filled with very critical self-analysis of my weaknesses. However, I slowly found my feet within the community, found my place within the working group and gained the respect of my colleagues. But I found it best for me, and for the best functioning of the group, to keep my inner emotions to myself, and not to form close friendships with any individual. That is not to say I did not gravitate more to some than to others, but close emotional intimacy I shunned. Some years later I discussed this period with Sir Vivian, by then retired from BAS and working on a history of BAS; I ended up as a case study in his book for how the experience of wintering shaped young and impressionable people.[13]

---

13 Fuchs V.E. (1982) Of Ice and Men, Oswestry, Anthony Nelson.

In fact, my most difficult relationship was probably with Chris. There was anyway friendly rivalry between the blackhand gang and the scientists, and Chris saw himself more allied with the former than the latter. I, of course, had been given the title ionospheric physicist (rather than technician), which not only meant higher pay but also gave me airs and graces as a research worker – something encouraged by my mentor Roy Piggott – which put me firmly in the scientist camp. Nonetheless Chris and I had to work together in analysing the relentless flow of data produced by the Beastie, and in keeping it operational, and there I was arrogantly certain of my intellectual superiority, which cannot have been easy to cope with. But I like to believe from the distance of more than half a century that by the end of the year we were both more inclined to identify the strengths in the other than dwell on perceived weaknesses. If I had any individual with whom I formed any sort of bond, it was Big Richie; he (along with Wink) shared both my winters with me, and it just seemed often the case that we would pair up for tasks outside or for recreational jaunts, but it never blossomed into a friendship that continued once we were home.

We were of necessity a hard-working community, each with our own full-time job as well as each taking turns with the domestic duties, and with various levels of commitment and enthusiasm for the one-off jobs that forever arose for a community surviving in such a hostile environment. But we also found time for recreation. There was of course no TV and we did not even have a cine projector to show films. We could listen to the BBC World Service when the ionosphere (and the Beastie) allowed, but mainly we listened to recordings (on 78 rpm records) of BBC comedy shows – the Goon Show, Round the Horne, the Navy Lark – in these we would become word-perfect. We also had a good selection of books and music LPs. Board games were popular: chess, mahjong and uckers,[14] along with card games of various sorts, and of course the dreaded liar dice. Photography was very popular, not surprisingly, and the little darkroom was often busy with folk carrying out quite complicated chemistry to process their 35 mm colour slides. These would then be shared in slideshows to the accompaniment of much barracking but also honest appreciation. Given the limitations we worked with, I am amazed how well my own slides have stood the test of time. We would also occasionally have fancy dress parties. We had a very large collection of newspapers, periodicals and magazines which were sent down from the UK each year, and a selection of these would be issued each Saturday as close as possible to a year out of date.[15] These covered the whole range from serious periodicals like *New Scientist* and *The Economist* through women's magazines like *Woman's Own*, to girly magazines such as *Playboy*

---

14 the Navy's version of Ludo

15 This was a tradition on all BAS bases at the time, and was probably first introduced by Jean-Baptiste Étienne
    Auguste Charcot (1867–1936) on his second expedition in 1908 to 1910. He wintered at Petermann Island,
    a few miles north of the Argentine Islands, on his ship the *Pourquoi-Pas?* and is reputed to have had an
    excellent wine cellar aboard.

and *Penthouse*, and were avidly read, dissected and discussed by us all. We particularly liked the agony columns in the women's and girly magazines, which provided endless entertainment – I remember the one about the young lady, very worried about the calories involved in oral sex, who was reassured that it amounted to the same as a small salad. We were young and testosterone-fuelled, so the *Playboy* centrefold of the Pet of the Month was of more than passing interest.

Then there was skiing (our main means of getting about – we were each issued with a pair of skis) and exercising the dogs, either individually or as a working team. Apart from being our heavy draft animals, for we had no mechanical transport, the dogs were a joy to have as companions. They would live for the most part outside in all weathers chained in a line on what we called the dog-span. They were each attached to the span by a short length of chain that just kept them out of reach of their nearest companions, as they liked to fight. In bad weather they would curl up and allow themselves to be buried in drift snow and seemed perfectly content except on those few occasions when the temperature went above freezing and their coats became wet. Though they were vicious with each other they never were with us. They were always pleased to see a human and would all jump up, running round and round in circles until it was their turn to be petted. In this they provided a very valuable service for folk for whom life was getting a bit tiresome. If one needed cheering up, a quick stroll along the span was a sure way to do it.

The dogs of course also needed feeding. Their diet was almost exclusively seal meat; a 3-kg chunk every other day was their ration. But that meant we needed to hunt and kill around 70 or so seals each summer to feed them. This was done using a small dinghy with outboard motors to get to (mostly) crabeater seals lazing about on ice floes or bay ice. The boat would come alongside, and the hunter armed with a Lee Enfield .303 rifle would leap onto the ice, and shoot all the seals at close range, and then he and a companion would gut them and tow them back to the base, where they would be stored on the aptly named seal pile. It was then a rostered job for folk to cut up the carcasses as required and feed the dogs. The cutting process would involve a saw and axe, as the carcasses were usually well frozen. When I first encountered sealing shortly after arriving at base I found it a nauseating experience, both physically (the smell was indescribably bad, particularly if the stomach or bowel was ruptured in the gutting process) and emotionally. But by my second and third summers I saw it as a great excuse to get out and about on a sunny day.

Well-rotted seal meat has an aroma unique unto itself, and the dogs seemed particularly to favour meat that had been through a few freeze/thaw cycles. Their farts were something to be experienced to be believed, and I swear that on some occasions they were actually visible. So sealing, and feeding the dogs, was a very messy business for which we each kept a dedicated set of windproof clothing and gloves which quickly became well saturated in various glutinous and smelly substances. I remember one

Springtime sledging with the dogs, on Petermann Island with the southern end of Lemaire Channel in the background. The wheel attached to the back of the sledge was our means of measuring distance travelled, using a counter to determine the number of revolutions.

occasion when on seal chop in my second winter, I was using a felling axe to cut up a frozen carcass with frozen shards of meat flying in all directions like wood chippings. Once we had finished and were walking back to the hut to clean up for Saturday dinner (shower night) my companion complained of a horrid smell of seal meat. He was still complaining when we sat down to dinner having had our showers and got dressed in our best. In fact, the smell, he said, was getting worse and worse, and then he blew his nose ... and out popped one of my shards, now nicely defrosted!

We had no need to make overland journeys for work purposes. But that didn't stop us from enjoying the environment by skiing, man-hauling a sledge or driving the dog team whenever we had free time and the weather was good enough. However, we were pretty constrained, unless the sea was relatively free from pack ice in the summer to allow boating, or it had frozen solidly enough to allow us to travel on it in winter and springtime. There were periods when neither were the case and we would chafe at the bit, waiting for cold calm weather to get the sea freezing or a good wind to move the pack. Then we would be off exploring the nearby islands and the Antarctic Peninsula across Penola Strait. During the wintertime there would be no wildlife to amuse us, but by springtime we would have penguins returning to their nesting sites, Weddell seals pupping on the sea ice, terns, skuas, cormorants, gulls, giant petrels, diminutive Wilson's petrels and the beautiful snowy petrels. In summer we would also have the crabeater seals and the occasional leopard seal, but almost never did we see whales. They had almost been exterminated by the commercial whalers, who had only stopped their gruesome trade when there were no whales to catch.

As winter turned to spring, I had turned from a callow youth unsure of my place in the community to a fully functioning professional well fitted to the Antarctic life and – at least, with many decades of hindsight – thoroughly enjoying the experience. But I wonder now how I would have felt had I known what I would have to face in my second year and how that would shape my life.

The role of base commander (BC) of a fids base in the 1960s was a very unusual and demanding one. Upon him[16] fell the ultimate responsibility for the safety and wellbeing of all on the station and for the completion of that year's work programme. But he also had a political and legal role as the magistrate who upheld the law in British Antarctic Territory. On top of that he was the sub-postmaster in charge of the base post office (itself a clear statement about British sovereignty). Then on those bases where BAS had decided in its wisdom not to provide any medical officer, he was both doctor and dentist to the men in his charge. He had to be able to inspire and lead, but also act as a shoulder to cry on. The role had a lot in common with that of a military officer, but with two very big exceptions: the BC did not have the military discipline or sanction to fall back upon, and once winter had begun he was essentially on his own, with no way of moving on any troublemaker.

On Monday 4 December 1967 I was happily at work in the ionospherics laboratory preparing data for analysis, when in walked Speedy. 'They want you to be BC next year.'

I was dumbstruck. It was not something that had even crossed my mind as a possibility. 'Christ,' I thought, 'I can't even grow a beard.' There were only three of us staying on for the next winter – Richie, Wink and me – and my first thought was 'What would they think?' My thoughts at the time are succinctly put in Sir Vivian's book:

> Years later Dudeney told me that he was appalled and frightened when he had been told that he had been chosen to take charge of the base. He could not believe that anyone should think him an appropriate choice. Yet having been offered the appointment he was damned if he was going to refuse the chance.[17]

I took a few days to come to terms with the offer, not the least because it came on the day that two big events in BAS life were unfolding – a volcanic eruption on Deception Island, which caused the Chilean, Argentinean and BAS bases to be evacuated, and a medical evacuation from our most southerly base – Base Z – where the base doctor had been seriously injured in a fall over an ice cliff. We were avidly following the radio chatter about both of these as they unfolded. So I mulled over the offer and had a quiet

---

16 In those days the base personnel were all male. In due course, as you will see, BAS became gender-blind.

17 See p. 321 of Fuchs V.E. (1982) *Of Ice and Men*, Oswestry: Anthony Nelson

word with both Richie and Wink, since I decided that I could not take on the job if they expressed any doubts. Finally, the choice was made by the thought that if I turned it down I would probably regret it for the rest of my life. I treasure, somewhat immodestly perhaps, Sir Vivian's view, expressed later on, that I had proved myself 'one of the best we ever had under the most testing conditions'.[18] The evacuation from Deception Island, performed by the Chilean Navy, involved amongst others our incoming cook – Ken Portwine – who had been just put ashore there for the summer season. Poor Ken was subsequently to play a central role in those 'testing conditions', as was the closure of Deception Island base for the coming winter.

So the next couple of months were very busy for me, trying to keep on top of the day job, while understudying Speedy for the BC role and generally making certain that everything around the base was in good order for the coming winter. An incident in late January involving a seal hunt caused me to get Speedy to use his military skills to teach me the rudiments of safe use of our firearms. The base had quite an arsenal: two Lee Enfield .303 rifles that dated from World War I, a 12-bore shotgun, a .45 revolver, a .22 rifle (for recreation) and an American 30-30 rifle for which we had no ammunition. On the day in question the party had gone off seal hunting with one of the .303 rifles, but Robin, who was not noted for adventurous activity, had decided to go along as well and had armed himself with the .45 like some character from a Western movie. They came across a leopard seal basking on a floe a few hundred yards from the base. Grahame shot at the seal from the boat, but sadly did not make a clean kill. Now Robin was not much enamoured of leopard seals, so when this one demonstrated its irritation at being woken up so rudely by a bullet grazing its head, Robin opened fire with the .45. Unfortunately, the relative positions of floe with seal, boat and base had changed, so as Robin emptied the chamber not all the bullets found their way into the seal. Several ricocheted off the rocks around the kitchen end of the base, causing folk to hide behind the cooking range and for one joker to wave a white flag. So I had my session of gun training, which included trying to hit a close-by iceberg with the .45 – I failed – and thereafter during my tenure as BC I kept strict control of the main weapons (the .303s and the .45) and did all the seal hunting myself. I only ever used the .45 once – and that was to dispatch an aged and infirm husky at very close range. For sealing I only ever used a .303.

I also had to get to grips with the large influx of new folk joining us for the coming winter: nine new faces who would make up the team. David (Brav) Bravington was the new DEM, having wintered the previous year at the BAS Base on Signy Island. Paul Burns – very unusually at that time – a married man, was to take over from Speedy as radar technician, whilst Bob Davidson was a radio technician whose role was to assist both Paul and our new radio operator, Tony Feenan, a wonderful Irishman who by

---

The 1968 Base F wintering party. Standing left to right: Richie, me, Paul, Brian, Dick, Brian, Bob. Sitting left to right: Brav, Wink and Tony. Inset: Ken.

his own admission was not a practical chap. He was however an outstanding operator, cool calm and collected in some very challenging situations which were to arise. Then there were the two new observatory physicists, Brian Gilbert and Brian Gardiner. Brian Gardiner was to follow my footsteps with a lifelong career in BAS, along the way being one of the three BAS scientists who discovered the ozone hole over Antarctica – he also had a wickedly dry sense of humour and a razor-sharp mind. Dick Kressman was to replace Chris as my ionospheric sidekick. He also ended up making a career in BAS, playing a very major part in supporting my own career, as an outstanding software and hardware engineer with a unique skill for technical problem solving. Then came Lewis Philp to join the met team, and finally there was Ken Portwine, an ex-Youth Hostel warden and the oldest on base at 31 (I was nearly the youngest, becoming BC a few weeks before my 23rd birthday). So this year we had an extra hand in Bob, BAS management having concluded (rightly) that the station was undermanned with just 11 men.

My diary entry for 26 January records my preliminary impressions of them. Only one stood out: 'I have lurking doubts about Ken which I can't quite put my finger on – oh! just his general attitude.' I had to choose a deputy BC; in the best of all worlds I

The visit of the Chilean Navy – 'Scrambled Egg' heads back to his ship.

would have chosen Big Richie, but realized that with such a large incoming group that might be seen as incestuous, so chose instead Paul, who had already impressed me with his cheerful attitude and his appetite for hard work.

I formally took over the job of BC from Speedy on Tuesday 6 February, but hardly looked the part. Slim and fresh-faced, still unable to produce even a smudge of a beard, I could probably still have passed for half-price on the buses at home. And this was to lead me into some interesting moments with visiting dignitaries. The Antarctic tourism industry was in its infancy, and one of the first tour ships to venture down the Antarctic Peninsula visited our base on 15 February. The ship was Chilean, the *Navarino*, and had approximately 100 tourists on board, led by Sir Peter Scott making his first visit to Antarctica. Having so many folk – including young stewardesses – invading our home was somewhat overwhelming, and I cannot say that I warmed to Sir Peter when I gave him a tour of the base, but my lasting memory was of one passenger asking me, 'And what do you do, sonny – make the tea?' That sort of disbelief was to occur again with potentially more serious consequences when the Chilean naval vessel, the *Piloto Pardo*, paid us a visit – well, at least its helicopters did. It was my week to be on gash, so I was dressed in rather shabby clothes and was sweeping the corridor as the helicopters landed a short way from the hut. Out of one got two smartly dressed officers – one with a great deal of scrambled egg on the peak of his cap. They marched into the base where I was sweeping and demanded to be taken to be taken to my leader. I explained that

I was the leader, which they patently could not accept. Things were heading towards a diplomatic incident, but luckily the rest of the team had rushed in to find out what was going on and formed a semi-circle around me. I invited them to point to the base commander, and thus old Scrambled Egg had to accept the reality of the situation, and we repaired to the base lounge for an alcoholic welcome. Inspection visits by one Antarctic Treaty nation on the facilities of another are enshrined in the treaty. This visit was not a formal inspection, more of a social visit, but even so Scrambled Egg would have had to have written a formal report – I have often wondered what he had to say about the strange British who let children command their bases.

Our last ship visit was in mid-March 1968, and our next scheduled one would not be until early January the next year. It was the RRS *John Biscoe*, and it departed through a pack-choked channel on a grey, unprepossessing sort of day. I remember to this day standing on the ice edge by the base, watching it slowly disappear northwards for home. The awesome weight of what I had ahead of me hit me with gut-wrenching force. I, just turned 23 years old, was totally responsible for the lives and wellbeing of 11 other men and the successful operation of the base for the next nine months. My abiding thought was 'What the fuck have I let myself in for?' Little did I know how things were going to turn out in the coming months.

The *John Biscoe* heads home in March 1968, leaving me in charge of the base and wondering what I had let myself in for.

3

A DIFFICULT WINTER

We did not have anybody with any medical training amongst the team. BAS, in its wisdom, had rationed the number of medical doctors it recruited in the late 1960s to three stations, and sent them to the stations they considered most difficult to access. That meant that Base Z on the Brunt Ice Shelf, and Signy Island in the South Orkneys, both got one. The latter was at relatively low latitude, but was a small island often surrounded by pack ice with no feasible landing strip. The third doctor was sent to the most southerly station on the Antarctic Peninsula – Base E on Stonington Island – and the theory was that if the need arose at any of the other peninsula stations, separated by hundreds of miles – Base F, Base T, on Adelaide Island or Base B on Deception Island – he could make house calls using the aircraft that was left (with a pilot) at Deception Island for the winter.

At the best of times there were a number of serious flaws in this plan, and these were not the best of times. Two events had made this plan completely irrelevant. First, the volcanic eruption had forced the closure of Base B. That in itself would not have rendered the plan completely useless, because the one serviceable BAS plane – a Pilatus Porter – was operating out of Adelaide for the summer and would now have to winter there. Sadly, however, towards the end of February 1968 it suffered terminal damage attempting to take off in Palmer Land, and three men had to sledge 130 miles to a small hut on Alexander Island, there to spend the winter. So the doctor would not be making house calls in 1968.

Initially this did not concern me. I felt, perhaps naively, that we were all young and healthy, and barring major accidents I would not be called on to serve as doctor. But several minor incidents showed me that might not necessarily be so. Paul managed to gouge his wrist with a sealing hook which required me to give him large doses of penicillin in his bum, a novel experience for both of us. Then Brian Gardiner lost a filling, requiring me to demonstrate my dental prowess – which amounted to not a very great deal. He survived the encounter but I cannot vouch for the filling. In all things medical my guide was a worthy tome kept in the BC's office – the *Ship's Captain's Medical Guide*. This was a comprehensive volume designed to allow non-specialists to

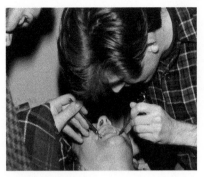

A little light dentistry – the patient survived!

have at least some hope of doing some good (and certainly no harm) no matter what the condition, until expert help was available. However, I quickly found not to idly browse because there were all sorts of nasty terminal illnesses described in graphic detail. It was but a short step of imagination for a minor hangover to simulate all the symptoms of a deadly terminal illness for which there was no cure.

With the ships on their way north we settled down for the coming winter with the new folk steadily shaping up both in their professional roles and as base members. There was the same banter between the blackhand gang and the scientists, and we also had a new split between the giants and the diddy men, based on our weight. Once a month we would each weigh ourselves, and the results were plotted on a graph on the base noticeboard. There were five giants at around 200 lbs (90 kg) or more and seven diddy men at less than 160 lbs (72 kg). The graph generated much ribald comment, but also had a more serious point in keeping an eye on our health, as in winter it was easy to eat too much and do too little exercise.

Generally, the group settled in well and we were a harmonious team. However, I continued to have some doubts about Ken, who clearly was not comfortable with me as base commander, having been in a position of authority himself as a youth hostel warden. He also had a habit of taking everything left over from breakfast, liquidizing it, and adding it to the lunchtime soup – including the scrambled (dried) egg, which made for some unusual lunchtime offerings.

Fairly early on, I realized that all was not well with someone. On an Antarctic base there is very little, if any, privacy; even the contents of our bowels were available for inspection every day, if one was so inclined, given the nature of our toilet. The bog bucket had to be emptied once a day and it was from this process that my attention was drawn to the appearance of blood in it. I also noted that we were consuming toilet rolls far faster than normal (though I didn't link the two immediately). Nobody had come to me with a medical problem, so I found myself having to snoop in and out of the bog to build up a picture of who the unfortunate individual might be. I narrowed it down to two likely candidates: Richie and Ken. Richie was adamant that it wasn't him, so I tackled Ken. He admitted to a problem, which, he opined, was piles. So we had an R/T session (a 'sked') with the doctor at Stonington Base – Dr Mike Holmes – who decided that a rectal examination was necessary. Thus I was instructed over the R/T what was involved, and quickly found myself sticking my finger up another man's bottom! This was the first of many indignities that Ken had to suffer at my hands. There was indeed some indication of the symptoms of piles, so Doc Holmes decided to wait to see if things resolved themselves. But as midwinter approached Ken's behaviour was becoming erratic; he was clearly losing weight and not eating. On 15 June he had another consultation with Holmes, and it was then I think that Holmes started to realize this was not just a case of piles. Things came to a head on 19 June, just before midwinter, when Ken appeared so unwell that I told him to go to bed, and for the first time was able to grasp the seriousness of his illness. Ken had been firmly in the giants camp, though there had been some indication that his weight was declining – however we quickly discovered that he had actually lost around a quarter of his body weight. He was also having up to 30 bowel movements a day, the outcome of which I now had to describe in detail to Doc Holmes each day. It was now obvious that Ken's illness was not going to resolve quickly; indeed I was giving serious thought to what I might do if I found myself with a body on my hands – a macabre but necessary precaution. It was obvious that the normal routines could not continue; we needed 24-hour nursing cover and we needed to organize a cooking rota as well as attempt to keep as much work ongoing as possible.

I got a small team together to help with the nursing rota – Bob, Dick, and the Brians. Bob also took on the job of the daily bake (for bread and cakes). A further sked on 22 June with Mike Holmes and Dr Murray Roberts at Halley resulted in a tentative diagnosis of ulcerative colitis, a condition that we did not have the resources to manage. I informed London that day of the tentative diagnosis[19] and Mike followed up[20] the next day with a much more detailed analysis and a request for specialist advice from the leading authority in the UK on this condition – Professor Golligher at Leeds University. Golligher responded by telegram to Mike, copied to me, on Friday 28 June:

ON THE INFORMATION AVAILABLE DIAGNOSIS ALMOST CERTAINLY ULCERATIVE COLITIS AND QUITE SEVERE AT THAT. PROGNOSIS WOULD APPEAR VERY GUARDED IN THE ISOLATED CIRCUMSTANCES OF THE PATIENT. IDEALLY THE PATIENT SHOULD BE IN HOSPITAL IN INTENSIVE CARE.[21]

Apart from our obvious lack of medical expertise on base, we lacked even the most basic of drugs, and were also quite limited in such essentials as hypodermic syringes. I had already rapidly started using what drugs and syringes we did have. The reason for our developing shortage of toilet rolls had now become abundantly clear.

Back in London, given the very guarded prognosis, Sir Vivian began to investigate possibilities for getting help to the base, and on 28 June we received a message from him:

19 Message FHQ/063/68 BAS No 108 222140Z

20 Message BAS No 107 232100Z

21 Message 849/68 from London dated 28/6/68 1000Z

AM INVESTIGATING POSSIBILITY OF FLIGHT FROM SOUTH AMERICA TO DROP DRUGS SUGGESTED BY GOLIGHER [sic] AT ARGENTINES. A LANDING WOULD NOT, REPEAT NOT BE MADE.[22]

Sir Vivian had contacted the Foreign and Commonwealth Office (FCO) on the same day, generating an urgent telegram to the British embassies in Argentina and Chile, asking them to investigate whether either country was willing and able to carry out such an airdrop in the depths of winter, with a response required by 9 am on Monday.[23] I was not aware of the details of the FCO involvement until many years later, when it became possible to access government files at the National Archives (TNA), but am now able to provide missing parts of the story from that source. Both embassies replied on 1 July and both were initially positive about possible airdrops or shipborne helicopter evacuation.[24]

Things now got somewhat complicated, as I was contacted by radio on 3 July by the Chilean Gonzáles Videla base with the proposal that the Chileans planned to send a ship. I immediately signalled London for guidance and received an immediate reply telling me not to agree to anything but to provide all the medical information requested and also up-to-date sea ice information, which of course we were already doing.

Whilst this high politics was under way we got on with the essential task of keeping Ken alive. Mike had, more in hope than expectation, asked whether it would be possible to do some basic blood tests. Here is where Dick, my ionospheric sidekick, really showed his mettle. He had studied the odd combination of electronics and physiology at university. We discovered that our library contained a copy of a renowned text book by Samson Wright entitled *Applied Physiology*. We also discovered under the bed in the 'surgery' an old Royal Naval blood transfusion kit. Armed with these and a microscope, Dick taught himself first how to do red blood cell counts, and subsequently the more subtle differential white cell counts. Once I had sorted out how to get blood from Ken without being too much of a vampire we were quickly providing a full routine path lab operation as far as blood was concerned. It was not without its funny moments, however; when I read Dick's first effort at a differential count over the R/T to Mike, he responded, 'Well done, John, that's really good – but of course he's dead!' Dick had made a mess of staining the samples, but he learnt from his mistake, and away we went so that by 3 July our path lab was delivering a pretty complete picture of Ken's medical state.

Back in London that day Sir Vivian, having understood from Golligher the very serious threat to Ken's life, asked the FCO to enquire whether either Chile or Argentina could carry out a shipborne helicopter evacuation either as well as or instead of an

22 Message 850/68 from London dated 28/6/68 1010Z

23 Telegram number 432 on file FCO7/1000 *UK Activities 1967*

24 Telegram 399 from BA and 197 from Santiago on FCO7/1000

Argentine Navy DC 4 aircraft, 5-T-3, swoops low over the
Winter Island drop zone to deliver its vital cargo.

airdrop.[25] By 5 July, however, the Chileans concluded that given the location, ice
conditions and weather they could not carry out either.[26] The Argentine Navy was,
however, giving both options serious consideration, using the airdrop also to survey
ice conditions in preparation for the possible medevac attempt. So now we were having
also to deal with technical questions to help them frame their operation in the safest
manner.[27] On 8 July the Buenos Aires Embassy signalled London:

> ARGENTINE NAVY WILL ATTEMPT FLIGHT AS SOON AS POSSIBLE. REQUEST DRUGS
> BE SENT IMMEDIATELY PACKED FOR FREE DROP.[28]

By 10 July the drugs etc were on their way to Buenos Aires (BA) with quantities
enough to provide five months' cover, with the quantity then doubled against losses
during the drop. Having realized that on the station we now had a developing toilet roll
crisis I requested a supply of these be included. This was disregarded (I never found
why), so we had to severely ration the supply. To determine the daily ration we had a

25 Telegram 440 dated 3 July to Embassies in Buenos Aires and Santiago, file FCO7/1000

26 Telegram 204 dated 5 July from the Embassy in Santiago to London, file FCO7/1000

27 Telegram 426 dated 5 July from the Embassy in Buenos Aires to London, file FCO7/1000

28 Telegram 433 dated 8 July from Sir Michael Cresswell (ambassador) to London

toilet roll party at which – with a few drinks at hand – we unrolled a toilet roll down the corridor to count the number of sheets and then carefully rolled it up – having added sagacious messages at various points along it, to be brought out later in the year. We determined the ration to be five sheets per man per day – and remember this was the shiny stuff, not the soft quilted luxury product we're all used to today. Just take a moment to think about that when next you visit the loo – remembering, too, that we could only shower once per week. Later in the year we also ran low on the Elsan and had to switch to using dilute creosote. Take it from me – you don't want to have any splashback from creosote even when it is diluted.

So the airdrop was on, and the Argentine Navy plane – a DC4, call sign 5-T-3 – was positioned to Rio Gallegos[29] in Patagonia on 13 July to wait for suitable weather. On base, as well as maintaining our 24-hour nursing schedule, the met team now switched into an intensive operation of hourly synoptic weather observations and twice-daily balloon flights, the results of which were radioed through to the Argentine station, Almirante Brown, and then to the flight crew at Rio Gallegos. The need for around-the-clock radio contacts meant that poor old Tony got very little sleep. We also had a very large number of empty 45-gallon (200-litre) oil drums to paint in day-glo orange to be the markers for the two drop zones, each to be 300 metres long. The latter were laid out roughly at right angles to each other on two adjacent islands (Skua and Winter). For four days the weather was against us, and we all felt the pressure. A comment in the base diary for 15 July sums it up 'Ken is at present being injected with syringes that you could roll marbles down, and is as anxious for the drop as everyone else.' Ken's state of health was actually starting to go backwards as we ran out of essential drugs that were to some extent holding the fort.

Finally, on 17 July the weather was deemed good enough for the plane to depart under the command of Commander Jorge Irigoin with a crew of seven. The departure time was chosen so the plane would arrive overhead around noon, to have daylight. As the flight proceeded so the weather at base started to go downhill, with cloud and lightly falling snow. It is important to note that navigation was a much more rudimentary affair then – no GPS to guide the plane to an exact point overhead. All we could provide was an NDB[30] to allow the plane to home in roughly on the site. But remember that just a few miles away was the Antarctic Peninsula rising to an altitude of 2,000 metres. (Some years later, for reasons which will become apparent as this narrative unfolds, I gained a private pilot's licence, and learnt to carry out NDB approaches, so I know they are not easy to do, particularly in such extreme circumstances.) But after an hour of anxious waiting while the plane would have been circling, its pilot looking for a break in the cloud, we heard the roar of powerful engines and suddenly there it was

---

29 Later infamous in every UK household as one of the bases from which the Argentine Air Force attacked the British Task Force during the Falklands Conflict.

30 Non-directional beacon, aka radio compass

– seemingly impossibly low – thundering over us, down our primary drop zone, and the first package came tumbling out. This was a ranging shot which contained fresh vegetables, newspapers and magazines. Then round went the aircraft three more times, dropping the medical packages, before a final pass during which I was able to talk to Irigoin on the R/T to thank him and his crew for their daring mission. We learnt later that the safety plan required two Albatross amphibian aircraft patrolling off Cape Horn, and the ill-fated battlecruiser ARA[31] *General Belgrano* positioned in the middle of the Drake Passage to provide navigational assistance.

The day after the drop was a chance for folk to catch up on sleep – particularly Tony – and for us to gorge ourselves at lunchtime on the amazing produce that had arrived in the first package dropped – carrots, tomatoes, onions and lettuce – plus pumpkin pie for dinner the next day. There had been a bit of initial confusion regarding the pumpkin – it was taken to be a melon, so sliced and served for breakfast. Our first taste gave the game away, though, and we were quickly on the R/T to the American base – Palmer Station – for a recipe for pumpkin pie. Things then settled down to something of a routine. With the new broad range of specialist drugs, Ken's condition started to improve somewhat, and I was more confident that we might keep him alive for the winter. We had maintained regular radio contact with Almirante Browne Station, and on 22 July learnt unofficially from the commander there that the ARA *San Martin* (the Argentine Navy icebreaker) was expected to sail for an attempted rescue at the beginning of August. Since Fuchs was unaware of this, I immediately signalled this information to him.[32]

An Argentine Air Force DHC Beaver arrives at Base.

31 Armada de la República Argentina
32 My signal to London F/219/68

But then on Monday 29 July events took a very strange turn indeed. Out of the blue (actually, out of a very grey and overcast sky) there appeared a small red single-engine plane flying low over the base, which then appeared to land on Skua Island. I set off on the sea ice up Stella Creek in the direction of Skua, only to meet four folk coming the other way. The plane was an Argentine Air Force Beaver based at the Argentine station, Teniente Matienzo, on the other side of the peninsula from us. The four were Capitan Julio Lujan, Teniente Oscar Posé (both pilots), Dr Eliseo Iturrieta (a medical doctor specializing in haematology) and an aero-mechanic, José Diaz. They led me to understand that they had come to evacuate Ken. But as their plane was totally incapable of actually doing that I invited them to stay – the doctor particularly welcome. Lujan suggested that they could fly Ken north to the Argentine station of Esperanza on the north-east tip of the peninsula, where it would be easier for a ship to collect him. I never did fathom out by what authority they had come. I strongly suspect that it was on their own initiative, completely separate from any official arrangements being made in BA and London. There is nothing in the Foreign Office files suggesting that their visit was officially sanctioned in BA, and the first Sir Vivian knew of it was when I signalled him that day. His response:

NO OFFICIAL RESPONSE YET FROM FO. YOU SHOULD FALL IN WITH ARGENTINE PROPOSALS BEARING IN MIND THAT AS FAR AS I KNOW THE OPERATIONS ARE IN THE HANDS OF ADMIRAL VARELA. IT MAY BE OF USE TO HAVE PORTWINE FLOWN TO ESPERANZA WHEN THE ADMIRAL SIGNALS HIS PLANS EITHER TO YOU OR TO LONDON. THANK AIRCRAFT PARTY FOR THEIR VALUABLE SUPPORT WHICH IS HIGHLY APPRECIATED.

And that is how matters stood. The doctor took one look at our medical/nursing regime running under Mike Holmes' remote direction, and decided to leave it alone. In fact, he confided in Mike that he was

VERY IMPRESSED BY STANDARD OF NURSING FROM ARGENTINE BASE PERSONNEL AND RANGE OF DATA THAT THEY HAVE MANAGED TO KEEP TRACK OF.[33]

His expertise did however come to the fore in providing Ken with several blood transfusions from the walking blood bank. One consequence of the disease is serious anaemia. Until the doctor arrived we had been combating this with regular intramuscular injections of a rather glutinous brown iron-replacement drug called Imferon. This had to be administered with a large-bore needle, which was not pleasant for either me to attempt or Ken to receive. But now, as several of us (myself included) had appropriate blood groups, with a few pints of our blood inside him, Ken started to perk up somewhat.

---

33 Signal from Holmes to London, E/217/68 dated 5 August

The Argentine folk fitted in very well, taking their turns at cleaning and cooking – and thereby introducing us to homemade spaghetti and to *dulce de leche*, made by putting a can of condensed milk in a pan of boiling water for several hours until it turns into a delicious caramel-coloured dessert. They arrived on base to witness on their first night a strange fids tradition. Some fids leave sweethearts at home, who of course swear undying love. For the fid the relationship is frozen, but for the girl at home life goes on. Often by the middle of the second year, when she is either married or about to get married to someone else, she finally plucks up courage to send a message. Just such a message had arrived that day for one of us. It was called getting chinged (why I do not know), and the message was always referred to as a 'Dear John'. We had a ching board on the wall in our lounge on which a pithy quote would be inscribed – my memory is that on this occasion it was 'Love is no basis for marriage'. The unfortunate recipient is invited to tear up and bin all the letters from said girl, and is assisted in getting absolutely blotto while throwing darts at the Dear John mounted on the dartboard. He is then gently put to bed. On this occasion, he needed a pee in the small hours. After stumbling around for a while in the bunkroom, opening and closing cupboard doors, he happened upon the waste bin, which he mistook for the pee bucket. Next morning, in a moment of remorse, he decided to recover his letters … need I say more? Quite what our Argentine guests made of this process is hard to tell. They had relatively little English, and we even less Spanish.

I was by now feeling the strain of the situation, which was exacerbated by Ken's understandably deteriorating mental health. But Mike was alert to my stress, and on more than one occasion when we were doing our daily medical sked he would suggest I throw everybody else out of the radio shack, put on headphones, and just have a quiet session of what would now be called counselling with him. This was very important in keeping me functioning effectively no matter what new crises hit me. Only once did I lose my cool. I'd had a particularly difficult session with Ken and had just got things cooled down when I was handed a message from London in which one of the officials there questioned why I had ordered a new fuelling hose. Since it had been that particular official who, the previous summer, had told me to order one, I lost my temper – but worse than that, I shot off an immediate angry response. I got a stiff reaction from Sir Vivian, so immediately responded by resigning as BC. Luckily for everybody my resignation was intercepted by BAS staff in Stanley who quickly sent a little message saying 'calm down – we all love you'. That day I learnt a very powerful message: never answer anything in anger.

Lujan was in more or less daily contact with various folk at Argentine stations and also in Argentina itself, and at one point I was called to the radio room to find myself being broadcast live across Argentina by their radio station, Radio El Mundo. I have no idea now what I said, but was certainly full of fraternal thoughts and thanks to the Argentine people. For the next few days we got on with our lives, awaiting developments.

With Mike's support I agreed with Lujan's proposal to move Ken to Esperanza once I had definite information that the *San Martin* had sailed. There were two problems with this plan: firstly the landing site on Skua Island was too short to allow a safe take-off with a full load, and secondly we did not have any Avgas to refuel the aircraft. For the first problem we decided that the sea ice next to the station provided a sound enough runway of around 350 metres, so this was carefully surveyed and marked out in readiness. For the second problem the only solution was to make a short flight to the American station – Palmer – on Anvers Island, which had a supply of Avgas. The confirmation came via Almirante Browne on 30 July that the ship would sail on 7 August, and I let London know.[34] I also reported that I would probably accompany Ken on the flight and then be flown back. Ken, even though he had found it very difficult to come to terms both with his illness and my handling of it, effectively made it a condition of his flight that I accompany him.

So we again waited for a suitable weather window; 8 August dawned clear and cold – ideal flying weather – so the plane was moved to the sea ice runway with Brav getting a jolly in it, taking (as it turned out) a rather crucial aerial photograph of an iceberg. Then Lujan flew to Palmer with Lewis, Brav, Paul and me as passengers. There we refuelled while our American cousins filled the plane with all sorts of goodies including frozen milk, cigars, frozen turkey, sausages and a 1000-sheet service roll soft absorbent toilet roll – enough for 12 days or so of luxury at our five-sheet ration. The weather looked set fair for an attempt to make the flight the following morning, so the plane was left parked on the sea ice overnight.

Come the morning we were greeted with thick freezing fog with visibility under 200 metres, and an air temperature of minus 12° C, with the fog depositing rime. Not promising, but the fog was quite thin, and later in the morning the sun could be dimly seen. Having at the time precisely zero expertise in matters aviation, I had to rely on Lujan's expertise, though it was my decision to accept the flight. By early afternoon the fog was thinning. Posé (who was to be pilot in command) spent some time with Diaz preparing the plane – sweeping rime from the wings and running the engine – while Ken, carried out to it on a stretcher, was strapped to its floor on an airbed. Because I was to travel with Ken, Diaz remained on the station. With photographs taken, emergency kit stowed and Eliseo and I sitting (without harnesses) on it, we began our take-off.

At first the take-off seemed okay, except on lifting off we did not seem to be gaining much height. But then the engine note started to rasp and vary in pitch, the plane began to pitch and yaw, and out of the window I got a glimpse of very black water. Lujan and Posé started to yell at each other rather desperately, and we hit something – not hard, but this was followed by a more severe impact, at which point the plane began to rotate about its vertical axis. The thought flashed through my mind that the next

---

34 Signal FHQ/122/68 dated 30 July, file FCO7/1000

Ready to go – but what about the freezing fog?

An ignominious end to the medevac attempt.

time I hit that bulkhead would be my last. I have an abiding memory of being certain that we would not survive. I was thrown back against the side of the cabin as a further impact arrested the rotation, followed almost immediately by another, which brought the plane to a rest. The starboard door burst open, and I saw what I took to be a large ice floe or bergy bit.

My next conscious thought was of standing on the ice looking down at the plane, having somehow got up there (probably) by stepping on blocks of ice in the water. I had no real idea where we were, but quickly realized that it was the ice foot of an island, with the plane settling in the tide-crack between the land and sea ice. My next act was to get Eliseo throwing the emergency kit out, and once done I helped him ashore and asked him to start an emergency fire to make smoke. Posé climbed over his seat into the cabin and made a human bridge by holding onto the rim of the door with me holding his feet, so we could guide Ken across his back. Once the three of us were safely on the ice, we got Ken into a sleeping bag, then Posé helped me remove my sodden and rapidly freezing boots. I am unapologetic to say that I then got Ken's boots off him, while Posé stripped to his underclothes and began running on the spot to get warm. After that Lujan exited the plane. As he did I called to him that Posé was somewhat upset, but he just held up his arms in a gesture of resignation to me, and said, 'No problems – it's only his third crash; it's my seventh. No problems.'

With all safe there was nothing more to do but wait, so I sat on an ice block taking photos. Posé pointed at an isolated iceberg and shuddered. I did not understand then what he was getting at. The realization of how close we had come to complete disaster was to dawn on me later.

By now the fog was rapidly clearing, to give a glorious clear sunny day. The base members were quickly alerted to what had happened, both by Diaz's sudden concern at the sound of the plane and then by a radio call from Lujan. They soon arrived with a sledge on which Ken was ferried to base – a distance of about 1 km. Leaving Eliseo to deal with Ken, who was in a state of shock, I was immediately on the radio reporting what had happened to the BAS office in Stanley, then talked to Holmes and dispatched a signal to HQ. I took a short moment to rest, before having a more comprehensive talk to the Stanley office by R/T. As well as reporting the facts I was very keen to make certain that all next of kin were told what had happened and that all of us were safe before garbled accounts could appear in the press. By evening Radio El Mundo had the story. By then I had received a message from Sir Vivian telling me that the next of kin was being informed, and a further message from Sir Cosmo Haskard, expressing support.

As magistrate, it fell upon me to carry out a formal inquiry and write a report on the accident. Given the political sensitivities I did not actually do this until our Argentine guests had departed. But the next day Richie, Brav and I walked the route of the plane and were able to get a pretty good idea what had happened, and this is

The fog clears – the wreck revealed.

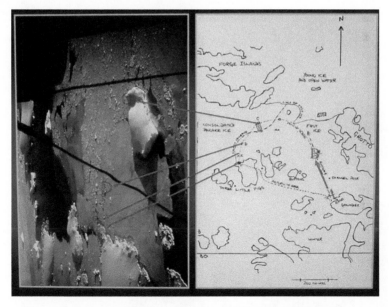

The crash site mapped for the accident report. The letters indicate the
skiway (A&B), impact with the iceberg (C) in its gulley, impact with
the sea ice (D), with the bergy bit (E) and the final stop (F). (Credit
for the map UKRI/BAS, credit for the image D.N. Bravington)

Above: The chopper arrives to evacuate Ken to the icebreaker.

Left: Talking to the UPI press photographer, Anibal Pastorino.

when Brav's iceberg photo came in so useful, since it showed pretty well the whole accident site. It transpires that on take-off the carburettor had iced up, as had the wings. Realizing this, and that the good sea ice came to an end ahead, the pilot banked to the left in an attempt to return. In doing so the plane lined up on a collision course with the berg, which now loomed out of the fog. He took evasive action, attempting to fly over the berg. He was partially successful, getting the plane into a gully. However, the port wing struck the berg, as was evident from the furrow we could see, flecked with red paint. The impact broke the wing, so a crash-landing became inevitable. The plane impacted on the fast ice beside the berg on roughly an even keel, but the port side ski broke through the ice and was ripped back, so it was attached by the rear pin only. This caused the plane to rotate through 90 degrees as it skidded across the ice towards open water. But the tail now hit a bergy bit set in the ice, which stopped the rotation. Travelling broadside to its direction of motion, the plane slid across the ice, coming to rest in the tide-crack on the second of the Three Little Pigs – a group of islands about 1 km from the base.

The question arises, should we have attempted the flight in that fog? There was a time constraint, because we needed daylight at Esperanza to land, but perhaps the flight should have been aborted that day. I subsequently heard from a senior Argentine Air Force officer, but cannot independently confirm, that Lujan had been advised not to attempt the flight that day. One consequence of the accident was that I developed a phobia about flying a few years later, and partly to confront it I learnt to fly myself, gaining my licence in 1979. During my training I learnt that Posé had broken the basic rule for engine failure on take-off; it was drummed into me that in those circumstances you should not attempt to turn because the likely outcome is a cartwheeling impact; instead, just land straight ahead. But had Posé not broken that rule we would all have ended up in very cold water, with an outcome much more serious, if not tragic. As Eliseo said to me later – we were all reborn that day.

So we all settled down to wait again. But we also made serious efforts to salvage what we could of the aircraft, first by removing the wings and remains of the tailplane. Then Brav devised an ingenious set of sheerlegs from radio mast sections, with which we were able recover the fuselage onto the island and ultimately remove the engine, which we then put on an improvised sledge made out of the skis of the plane. Nine days were to pass before the *San Martin* got close enough to launch its two helicopters to effect the medevac. They arrived in mid-afternoon, and Posé – ever the showman – was adamant that he would act as marshal to guide them to our preferred landing zone. This he did with great aplomb, stepping slowly backwards as the first chopper came in to land. As the chopper landed a great cloud of snow was blown up into which Posé disappeared, as the dust settled – no Posé! He had stepped backwards over the edge of the island – an ice cliff about 4 metres high, done a double somersault and ended up spreadeagled in a snowdrift – luckily with only his dignity injured.

Lujan and Diaz were immediately transferred to the ship by helicopter. But Iturrieta stayed on base with Ken, and we were joined by a press photographer from UPI[35] – Anibal Pastorino. He had also been on board 5-T-3 for the airdrop. The weather then turned sour, which brought flying to an end for the day, stranding him, Eliseo and Ken on base until the following morning. Anibal was amazed to learn just how young we all were; only Bob and Ken were aged over 30. He spent most of his enforced stay filming pretty well everything he could. Just after 11 am local time on Monday 19 August a helicopter arrived, and we sledged Ken out to it. He was able to walk the last few yards and climb aboard himself – a testament to the care he had received over two long months. Eliseo and Anibal went with him. A second flight removed Ken's personal belongings. I had expected the ship to attempt to salvage the wreck, but the decision was made to leave it until the summer. The atmosphere on the base was strange. The base diary for the day best describes the mood:

> A somewhat hysterical hilarity prevailed on base after the relief, and the contents of Ken's last bedpan were ceremonially piped into the og [sea]. The good old happy family is now settling down to normal, and we doubt if morale on base has ever been higher than it is tonight.

I felt a great weight lifted from my shoulders; in fact I almost felt so light I was hovering! Of course I had to make a formal report to London to announce that the medevac had been completed successfully. Only very recently did I find a copy of that signal, to discover that, though worded in the usual terse and professional style, its first line captured the mood on base precisely: 'YIPPEE (EXCLAM)'.[36] I hope that brought a smile to various faces around the world – in the FCO, in BAS, in the British Embassy in BA and in Government House in Stanley.

I imagine that having reached this point in the story you, dear reader, are looking for that happy ending. Ken arrived in Ushuaia on 23 August and was flown to BA, arriving on the 24th. The plan, as I (and Mike) understood it, was that he would be flown to the UK as soon as possible and put under the care of Professor Golligher. That did not happen. Instead he was hospitalized in BA, where he underwent major surgery in early September. He seemed to recover from this but required further surgical intervention on 23 September. His brother flew out to be with him, and very sadly on 10 October Ken died in BA of post-operative pneumonia. His funeral took place in BA, then his brother returned to UK with his ashes, which were scattered in Coniston, a place Ken had loved. A very sad end.

---

35 United Press International

36 FHQ/149/68 dated 19 August 1968

Recd. 19·8·68

FFFR

NR 34 PRIORITY 191534Z

FHQ/149/68

FM BASE COMMANDER ARGENTINE ISLANDS

TO LONDON HQ

INFO STANLEY OFFICE

    BASE COMMANDER STONINGTON FOR DR HOLMES

F/268/68

YIPPEE (EXCLAM)

PORTWINE SAFELY EVACUATED BY HELICOPTER AND NOW ABOARD SAN MARTIN

WHICH IS STEAMING NORTH . ALL ARGENTINE CONTITDENT ALSO ABOARD .

MEEE   FOR REASONS UNKNOWN IT WAS DECIDED TO LEAVE THE BEAVER

UNTIL THE SUMMER .

    PLEASE EXPRESS OUR HEART FELT THANKS TO THE ARGENTINIAN

GOVERNMENT AND ARMED FORCES . HAVE NOTHING BUT PRAISE FOR THE

MANNER IN WHICH THE OPERATIONS WERE CARRIED OUT .

    ALSO THANKS TO YOU FOR PROMPT AND SUCCESSFUL ACTION WITH

OUR PERSONAL MAIL .

                DUDENEY

My exultant telegram to a waiting world. (Credit UKRI/BAS)

4

THE AFTERMATH AND HOMECOMING

We then settled down to complete our winter, now including a regular turn at cooking in our menu of base tasks. We also attempted to catch up with the scientific work that had taken second place during the months of intense activity supporting Ken. We were a pretty happy bunch by and large, and the weather became much kinder – good sea ice, low temperatures and some fine sunny weather in spring. This allowed us to have a few recreational forays off base, though only for a few days at a time.

We finished dismantling the Beaver, and in the process discovered that it appeared to have been made up of three planes: the plaque on the dashboard giving the aircraft's radio call sign identified the fuselage as P-06 and the tailplane was P-03, whilst the wings were P-05. Clearly at some point two aircraft had been sacrificed to keep a third operational. I have only very recently learnt that the one remaining aircraft had been operating as a crucial lifeline between Matienzo and Esperanza stations; Matienzo had not had a proper resupply by sea for two years because of impassable pack ice, so was being resupplied regularly by Beaver flights. With the loss of the Beaver it was necessary to carry out an overland traverse between Esperanza and Matienzo to deliver supplies to keep the station operating safely until the following summer.

My turn on cook. Making ice cream using the natural freezer, and for those who want to try it – evaporated milk, sugar and cocoa powder!

The remainder of the winter was uneventful, but we did have one problem – our freezer holding our precious stock of meat decided to die. We were unable to repair it and as, with the approach of summer, we could not guarantee the air temperature to be continuously at or below minus 17° C, some lateral thinking was needed. The radar system that we used for tracking weather balloons – a Wind-Finding Radar Mk 2 – had begun its life at Christmas Island and so was equipped with a self-contained air-conditioning unit, something that served no purpose in our environment. So, using

The springtime return of the wildlife. A Weddell seal and her
pup on the sea ice in October 1966 – a joy to see.

some rather well-crafted wooden packing cases in which the radiosondes had been
delivered, and the A/C unit, we built ourselves a new freezer. We didn't really expect it
to work, but having completed it on a Saturday we put a radiosonde in it, switched it on
and, clutching pre-dinner drinks, repaired to the met lab to see what would transpire.
We were stunned as the temperature of our contraption quickly plummeted to below
minus 20° C. We had ourselves a freezer again! It served the base well for several years
as an overflow freezer once the main one had been repaired the following summer. This
was one of the better fids' bodges that I have been involved in during my many years of
Antarctic activity.

I have talked about how rudimentary our communications with the outside world
were compared with today, but there was one strange sophistication: we were furnished
with a highly restricted naval cypher system based on what were known as one-time
pads. This was something that the BC had under lock and key but never otherwise
concerned himself with. So imagine my surprise and excitement when a cypher message
arrived for me from none other than the governor of the Falklands himself. What could
be so secret and so important that the cypher was necessary? The deciphering process
was slow and laborious, requiring a lot of subtracting of four-digit groups from other
four-digit groups with pen and paper and then converting the resulting numbers into
letters of the alphabet. And what was so important? 'Please secretly destroy the code
books without opening them and signal the word MINIMOKE when done.' Well, dear
reader, have you ever tried to secretly burn a book whose pages are gummed together?

Hard enough – but outside on an Antarctic winter's afternoon? Secretly? With the rest of the team watching and giggling at the lounge windows? I suppose one of them could have been a soviet spy, but perhaps not. The job of BC was definitely a bit weird sometimes.

As a little footnote to the Portwine story, in December 1968 the Royal Navy's new ice patrol vessel HMS *Endurance* (affectionately known as the Red Plum), on its maiden voyage south, delivered us a new cook – Allan Wearden. He arrived by helicopter at 4 am along with a gift of fresh cabbages, eggs and cauliflowers from the governor's vegetable garden, and a bottle of scotch for me from the ship's captain, plus our first mail. All of these seemed more important than Allan – until he cooked his first meal for us. He was a superb chef, and went on to serve BAS for many years. But I repaid him in advance by sending him off with a guide across the sea ice to collect penguin eggs before he'd even had time to unpack – a rather extreme introduction to life on base!

Back in the FCO there was much head-scratching over how to properly thank the Argentine authorities for the assistance they had given.[37] The cost of the operation would have been considerable, but there was already a precedent amongst Antarctic Treaty nations that such help would always be provided without the expectation of recompense. Some thought was given to replacing the Beaver, but that was not followed up. The foreign secretary of the day, Michael Stewart, did however write formally twice to his opposite number, Dr Costa Mendez, to express the appreciation of the British government, once for the airdrop and then again for the medevac. It seems also that six of the Argentine personnel involved were honoured with Queen's Commendations, presented by the British Ambassador in BA. And the following year three of them were invited to the UK for a visit. I was invited as well, but sadly was overseas at the time.

We had an unseasonably cold spring and early summer, allowing us to celebrate Guy Fawkes night in style on the fast ice, where we built a splendid bonfire. This was mainly made of old wooden packing cases and had a fine Guy upon it. But it had a special extra ingredient to hasten Guy's departure into the heavens. We had a load of 15lb tins of butter that had turned rancid with age. Several of these found their way into the fire, where they exploded in a most satisfactory manner.

But we had an even more spectacular detonation that night. I can claim to have participated in the only detonation of a hydrogen bomb in the Antarctic. We had to make hydrogen on base to fill our weather balloons, using a rather Heath Robinson device called the Gill. This worked by mixing aluminium filings with caustic soda in the presence of water in a reaction chamber; the resultant (barely controlled) chemical reaction generated hydrogen. So we put some caustic soda and aluminium filings in

---

37 Various documents on FCO files FCO 7/1000 and FCO 7/1001

Guy Fawkes Night, November 1968, our main bonfire – before the tins of butter rearranged it! The hydrogen bomb is out of picture, yet to detonate.

an old oil drum and suspended a plastic bag full of water above the chemicals in the drum – which was then sealed. A second fire was built around this, and then a very dog-eared stuffed giant petrel (we called him Fred) was placed on top of the drum. We retreated to a safe distance. The result was spectacular: a mighty *Womph!*, a beautiful ascending smoke ring, and a gentle rain of feathers as Fred spread himself liberally around. I should say that such silliness does not happen these days; the provisions of the Environmental Protocol see to that.

Our isolation was ended in early January 1969 with the arrival of the *Shackleton* cutting itself a harbour in the fast ice. There was then a hectic few weeks of handover and packing. And so came my time to leave Base F, homeward bound.

I left with mixed emotions on 27 February 1969, a very different person from the one that had arrived just two years before. As Big Al was to say to me many years later at my retirement do, 'You arrived on station as a boy, but you left as a man.' He meant it as a compliment, and I took it as such. The man now leaving the base was a self-assured professional who had weathered some pretty traumatic events and for whom the Antarctic had become home – a challenging home without doubt, but home in which he was comfortable nonetheless.

* * *

I had a slow introduction back into civilization, with a voyage south into Marguerite Bay on the *Biscoe* to help resupply the southerly bases at Adelaide Island and Stonington Island, visit Horseshoe Island, and assist in hunting 250 seals to provide winter food for the dog teams. Then it was to Deception Island, where just a few weeks before, on 21 February, a second major eruption had resulted in a lahar[38] which had destroyed the station, amazingly without loss of life. Here the two ships *Shackleton* and *Biscoe* rendezvoused, and we fids assisted in recovering what we could from the devastation. Then I transferred to *Shackleton* en route to Stanley. The passage was hardly comfortable, with a full-blown Southern Ocean storm which had the ship hove to and rolling 40 degrees back and forth while I tried, only partly successfully, to wedge myself in my bunk, where I listened to the deck cargo of 45-gallon drums of petrol banging against each other, acutely aware that in the ship's forepeak there were two tons of TNT also being thrown around. Amazingly the ship's cook, Eric,[39] was still able to serve up fillet steak and chips for Saturday evening dinner – for those few hardy souls (me included, as it happened) who yearned for it.

The ship was heading south again, but I managed to wangle a shore posting. The BAS office in Stanley was looking for somebody with electrical skills to wire up a new

The remains of Biscoe House at Deception Island shortly after the lahar had flowed through it.

---

38 A violent type of *mudflow* or debris flow composed of a slurry of pyroclastic material, rocky debris and water resulting from a volcanic eruption. At Deception the eruption took place underneath a glacier behind the British station, so in addition to mud and boulders it contained ice.

39 Eric Heathorne had a distinguished career with BAS as chief steward on the *Biscoe* and then on the *Bransfield*. I sailed with him on several occasions subsequently.

warehouse. I had received from my mother a 1969 pocket diary which just happened to be themed as an electrician's diary, and it told me all I needed to know about ring mains etc. So, armed with that, I boldly offered my services. It is hard to credit now, in our safety-conscious and litigious society, but my offer was taken up and I installed myself, along with my electrician's mate (Wink) in the Ship Hotel,[40] where a room could be had all found including laundry for £1 per night. So I had a rather enjoyable reintroduction to society. This is actually not a small matter when one has been living such an isolated life when issues/problems are generally simple and solvable (or, rather, final and not), and where the complications of relationships etc do not impinge. Having spent two years without any female company, that was the first of the big shocks and adaptions that had to be confronted. The first big shock was how nice women smelt after two years of male company, rotting seal meat and smelly socks. Also, while I had been away hemlines had risen rather dramatically. I am told by those who saw it that Wink's and my faces when we strolled into the BAS office in Stanley to find some very attractive young ladies in mini-skirts was a moment never to be forgotten – motionless with jaws at half-mast and eyes out on organ stops would best describe us. And it was there that I met 'quarter speed' Jacqui – so named because she operated the Stanley end of the quarter speed HF telex link that had kept me in touch with the outside world during the Portwine crisis. Jacqui and I had an intense but largely innocent relationship for the month I was in Stanley, and that, with some fishing for migratory trout in the Murrell River, and labouring all day at wiring the store, made my stay in Stanley very enjoyable while I waited for the *Shackleton* to return for its final (as it turned out) voyage home for BAS.

Over the years several homecoming fids have not got any further than Stanley before ending up married and settled. This could have been my fate too, as Jacqui and I were getting quite close – but then a message from home told me that my mother (who had been claiming she had a touch of flu) actually had a growth in her lung that needed urgent attention. So when the *Shackleton* finally returned in mid-April I boarded it northbound. Another significant turning point in my life had arrived, and I have an abiding memory of a lone figure standing on the public jetty, growing smaller and smaller as we headed for the Narrows to leave Stanley Harbour, and finally disappearing from view as we turned to starboard in Port William and headed for the open sea.

Rather than leave me to make the nearly four-week voyage back to Southampton by ship, BAS had me flown home from Montevideo, so I was back just after my mother had undergone major surgery. The prognosis had apparently been poor, but she was a tough and determined lady, who made certain that she was with me when I met the

---

40 The hotel started life as the Eagle Hotel in 1854, renamed The Ship in 1875, and then its modern name, The Upland Goose, in 1969, just after I stayed there. It stands on the seafront road, but is now closed and converted into apartments.

Shackleton in May to collect my luggage at Southampton. And she went on to survive for another seven years – for the most part very active and fulfilling years.

So in May 1969 I found myself suddenly back in the midst of the hustle and bustle of modern life, with a nice nest-egg of nearly two years' salary in the bank, which meant there was no rush for me to earn a living. I could catch my breath and decide what I wanted to do. I had a reasonably firm place at the University of Wales to do a PhD with Sir Granville Beynon – an old colleague and pal of Roy Piggott. I also had a tentative offer from BAS of a year at Halley Station as base commander. I thought of training as a Navy helicopter pilot (the fear of flying had not yet appeared), but my eyes started to play up, requiring me to wear spectacles, which put paid to that idea. BAS in its munificence offered me a short-term contract (one year in the first instance as far as I remember) to train new beastiemen and work up some of the data I had collected – to be based at the RSRS in Slough under the guidance of Piggott. This I gladly accepted, as it put off the evil day when I would have to make serious long-term decisions about a career.

Without me realizing it, however, I had become a small pawn in a much bigger picture, in which the whole future of BAS was in the balance. From just post war, FIDS, then BAS, was primarily serving a political purpose by providing the physical presence and administration of Britain's territorial claim in Antarctica; the UK had always used scientific exploration and research as the acceptable (and affordable) public face of that activity, rather than maintaining a military presence there. The Antarctic Treaty, which had come into force in 1961, had put the territorial disputes to sleep, so the Treasury immediately turned its attention to the BAS expenditure, and specifically whether, with the Antarctic Problem apparently resolved, BAS needed to exist any longer. BAS was under the control of the Colonial Office at the time, but the latter was in its death throes – to be swallowed up by the Foreign Office as part of the then new FCO. Much debate was generated in government in the early 1960s on whether expenditure on BAS could be justified on the grounds of science alone. A cabinet-level committee – the Advisory Council for Science Policy[41]– was asked to study the matter and report back. It decided that BAS could and should be justified, for the quality of its science.

The next question was under whose control should it be placed. There was a broader debate at the time about how to fund and manage government science, one strand of which was to bring together several different entities under one umbrella to create a big enough organization to match the weight of the Medical Research Council in seeking funds from Treasury. The main organizations in question were the Institute of Geological Sciences, the Nature Conservancy and the National Institute for Oceanography. These were given a home in a new research council – the Natural Environment Research Council (NERC), in 1965. After much argument BAS also

---

41 The Advisory Council was renamed in 1965 under the auspices of the Department for Education and
     Science, becoming the Council for Science Policy.

became part of NERC in 1967 with a dowry from the Colonial Office of £1 million and the requirement to maintain the same size footprint in Antarctic affairs as hitherto. So I left the UK in 1966 as an employee of the Colonial Office and returned home as an employee of NERC.

You may wonder why this digression is necessary – well, J.A. Ratcliffe was a member of the Advisory Committee, the director of RSRS, and a colleague of Roy Piggott, so the importance of ionospheric research in Antarctica had been highlighted within the committee's deliberations. BAS did not then have its own programme in ionospherics; we beastiemen were a bit of an afterthought, doing our work on behalf of RSRS, essentially on behalf of Piggott. It now seems pretty apparent that Piggott was able to influence BAS to establish its own research programme, and he saw me as a possible founder member.

But all I knew at the time was that I had a year at RSRS, where I turned up in the summer of 1969. And here another encounter took place which profoundly altered my life. Roy Piggott liked to employ undergraduate students for work experience during their long summer vacations. In 1968 he had employed a young physics student, Helen Mason, who had done a pretty good job but who had also had her head filled with stories about this young Antarctic hero and his derring-do at Base F. That clearly didn't put her off, because she came back the next summer. So I strolled into the big shared office at RSRS to be confronted with Helen. The rest is history – we were married on 5 April 1972. She told me many years later that after that first encounter she went home and told her mother she had just met the man she would marry!

During that year I was offered the opportunity to develop a research programme and was told that BAS would be happy for me to register as a part-time student, so that my work could go towards a PhD, whilst paying me a full-time salary. Thus I found myself registered at University College London in the department of physics with Professor Sir Robert Boyd as my titular supervisor, but in practice being supervised by Roy Piggott. Helen obtained a first in physics from London the following year, and started a PhD in the same department in atomic physics applied to studies of the sun. At the time RSRS was a world-leading centre for ionospheric research, so I had access to such major figures as Henry Rishbeth, Joe King and Lance Thomas, who all gave of their time and expertise with great generosity. Meanwhile I was building a little group which took over the training and support of the BAS field ionosphericists, and began developing a purposeful research strategy. The first recruit was Dick Kressman, who developed into a highly innovative systems engineer as well as a valued scientific colleague with an outstanding capacity for problem solving. By the mid-1970s he was joined by Alan Rodger, another beastieman, who in due course became a world-recognized scientist.

Major developments were under way for BAS in the 1970s. Having found a home within NERC, with the assurance of funding to maintain its historical level of presence in Antarctica, the question of organizational structure and strategy came to the fore as well as the need for a permanent home. Sir Vivian Fuchs retired in 1972 to be replaced by Dick Laws,[42] a biologist who had wintered with FIDS at Signy Island in the 1940s and made an international reputation for his studies of large mammals (whales and seals in the Antarctic and elephants in Africa). BAS did not have a permanent integrated headquarters. There was a small administrative and logistics team housed in an office in London, and then a marching army of folk scattered all over the country lodging in university departments and government labs, most of them like me on short-term contracts, but with a very small group of more senior folk who had formal civil service gradings. NERC's other institutes all had integrated campuses (sometimes more than one), so it was decided that BAS should likewise have a home where the many strands of research could be brought together with the administration and logistics groups.

But where should it be? BAS already had a presence at Edinburgh and Birmingham Universities as well as a glaciology team housed at the Scott Polar Research Institute in Cambridge. Various offers were made and considered, all with advantages and disadvantages. One great advantage of Edinburgh would have been access to a port for the BAS fleet – but in the end Cambridge won the day, possibly because both Bunny and Dick were Cambridge men with their homes close by.

It was not obvious that my little developing empire at RSRS would be included in the grand plan. But Dick Laws had also embarked on reorganizing/creating a robust management structure for BAS. He decided the science should be organized around three main themes – life sciences, earth sciences and atmospheric sciences – and that three structural divisions would be created, each headed by a senior scientist with a civil service grading of senior principal scientific officer.

As Roy Piggott was about to retire from RSRS in 1975, he was invited to join BAS as the head of the Atmospheric Sciences Division, to bring together the meteorology and observatory physics work at Edinburgh led by Joe Farman, the whistler[43] work based at Sheffield University under the guidance of Professor Tom Kaiser, and the work on the ionosphere led by me at RSRS. Thus the new laboratory and logistics facility came together on the western outskirts of Cambridge in the spring of 1976 with my group included.

My position had been made a bit more formal by my being given a two-year appointment in 1972, and Helen and I had both gained our PhDs in early 1974 – actually having our vivas in the same department of the same university in the same week! Dick Laws now offered me a permanent civil service graded appointment as a higher scientific officer (HSO) to lead the work on ionospherics.

By the end of that year I was promoted to senior scientific officer (SSO) and was hence nearly up to super-fid eminence! I had by now started on my first independent

---

42 Richard Maitland Laws, CBE FRS

43 Whistlers are VLF electromagnetic waves generated by lightning. More about them in Chapter 5.

research collaboration – the beginning of a long-term association with Professor Tudor Jones at Leicester University. Our first joint experiment was a study of atmospheric waves in the ionosphere over the Antarctic Peninsula, using a technique which Tudor had developed relying on small Doppler frequency changes in fixed frequency radio transmissions from a network of spaced transmitters around a central receiving station. Waves showed up as variations in the received frequency, and their direction of travel could be determined by triangulation. Before establishing a fully operational system in Antarctica it was prudent to carry out a pilot study, and as we would have to rely on bases operated by the USA and Argentina to site some of the transmitters, there was some negotiating to be done. Also I was now responsible for the ionospheric programme at three bases, two of which (Halley on the Brunt Ice Shelf, and King Edward Point on South Georgia) I had never visited, so it was time for me to head south once more.

5

SOUTH AGAIN: MY LOVE AFFAIR WITH HALLEY BEGINS

With my newly minted PhD figuratively, if not actually, shining bright on my chest I set off for Antarctica again on 4 December 1974. But this was a very different departure than that in 1966. Now I boarded a jumbo jet at Heathrow to fly to San Francisco, and from there via Rio and BA to the Falklands, with various meetings on the way. It was on this flight that I had my first intimation of problems with flying, as I found myself gripping the arms of my seat very tightly before we had even departed from the gate.

The trip occupied well over four months, and as well as it being my first chance to visit my southern empire, it was my first real outing as a professional scientist, visiting and negotiating with a number of different research groups in North and South America. As such it marked the start of my independent professional career. Not only was I charged with doing my own work, but also I had a wider brief from Roy Piggott to cover the work of the embryonic Atmospheric Sciences Division. But the trip didn't go entirely as originally planned because the new BAS ship, RRS *Bransfield*, only in its fifth season, ran into a very serious storm in the North Atlantic while heading south via a call in the USA. The buffeting it received exposed issues with the installation of its rudder, requiring emergency dry docking for repairs in the USA – and thus throwing its whole schedule into disarray. My planned visits had been carefully arranged to get me to Stanley to meet the *Bransfield* before Christmas, but in the event it did not arrive there until 6 January.

My first stopping-off point was San Francisco to visit Professor Helliwell's group at Stanford University. I spent a little under a week there, but met several folk who became important one way and another for my developing career over the years: Bob Helliwell himself, Chung Park (who sadly died quite young), Don Carpenter and Juan Roderer, an Argentine polymath who had been forced to leave Argentina because of his opposition to the dictatorship there. The meetings allowed me to widen my horizons away from just using the data from ionosondes. The beginnings of a more strategic view of what was important in the developing field of what became known as geospace physics began for me there.

From the USA I travelled on to BA. My visit there took place while the British government was engaged in talks with the Argentine government over the future of the Falkland Islands. In the late 1960s there had been very secret negotiations on a possible transfer of sovereignty, but this had become public in 1968, and the outcry from the islanders and in Parliament was such that the British government had to guarantee that nothing would happen against the islanders' wishes. Argentina would not accept that the islanders could have any say in the matter – indeed, they did not (and still do not) accept that there is a population of Falkland Islanders. Instead, the Argentines see the islanders as representing a colonial occupation, and they won a major diplomatic victory in the United Nations with Resolution 2065 in 1965, when Britain and Argentina were invited to negotiate an agreement which only took account of the *interests* of the islanders but not their wishes. The intractable issue of sovereignty was temporarily parked, and an attempt was made – by both sides – to win over the hearts and minds of the islanders and make them see their future as aligned with Argentina. This was enshrined in the 1971 Agreement on Communications between the Falkland Islands and Argentina. As part of this, Argentina provided an air service to the islands, became the supplier of fuel oil and postal services, and offered opportunities for education and health care in Argentina. The only other way in and out of the islands – the RMS *Darwin* which had sailed monthly between the islands and Montevideo – was withdrawn from service, and Britain agreed to build

The infamous White Card that allowed me to travel from Argentina to and from the Falklands in 1974–75.

an airport in the islands for the Argentines to use.[44] One particularly upsetting aspect of the agreement was the requirement for all travellers to the islands to hold a white card issued by the Argentine government – effectively a sort of passport. My first act on arriving in BA was to apply for and receive my white card.

It was against this background that I found myself engaged in a series of meetings with Argentine government scientists and various government/military officials. To begin with I had the support of Bill Sloman, who was on his way home from a visit to Stanley – but then, when my stay was extended because of the problems with *Bransfield*, I found myself on my own and considerably out of my depth, especially as I was not aware of the broader geopolitical issues which in retrospect I can see were driving the Argentine agenda. I spent just over a week in BA, and it was very full on. Here was me, a young scientist still wet behind the ears, mixing with the acting director of the Argentine Antarctic Institute (IAA),[45] the head of the Ionospherics Laboratory of the Argentine Navy (LIARA),[46] the head of the National Council of Science and Technology (CONICET)[47] and sundry other military and civilian worthies. And not just mixing, but being expected to negotiate over their desire to have a grand collaboration between the UK and Argentina on ionospheric research, bringing together RSRS (by now renamed the Appleton Laboratory), BAS, LIARA and IAA, and apparently involving Argentine experiments sited in Stanley! The avuncular head of LIARA, Victor Mesterman, played host to both the business and the social sides of my visit – the latter including three charming young secretaries (Nora, Gabriela and Anna Maria). They were delightful company, but their role was never quite clear to me; thankfully I had the sense not to be put in any potentially compromising positions with any of them. Both LIARA and IAA were under military control, and so I felt very uncomfortable getting into discussions on matters that were clearly above my pay grade, particularly when the suggestion arose of writing to Brian Roberts, the British expert on Antarctica at the FCO, to elicit his support for the Grand Collaboration. I managed to head that off temporarily by agreeing to raise it with Roy, who they were hoping would be visiting them.

Meanwhile, I had my own more mundane agenda; to gain agreement to use the Argentine station, Almirante Brown, for the site of one of the Doppler experiment transmitters. I also gave two seminars to a joint IAA and LIARA audience – my first overseas scientific presentations. I had lots of informal discussions with the staff of both institutions, finding myself cast in the role of wise overseas expert. There was a lunch at the Air Force club, which became rather jolly when my hosts realized that I had crashed in one of their aircraft. With the alcohol flowing quite freely, there were some quite

---

44 This opened in 1979, but the runway length was limited to 900 metres. This meant that all connections with the outside world had to go via southern South America – effectively via Argentina.

45 Instituto Antártico Argentino (IAA)

46 Laboratorio Ionosférico de la Armada de la República Argentina (LIARA)

47 Consejo Nacional de Investigaciones Científicas y Técnicas (CONICET)

A LADE F27 Fokker Friendship taking off from the temporary runway at Stanley in 1975.

disparaging remarks bandied about regarding the then Argentine president Isobel Peron's[48] relationship with her close advisor José López Rega, who was apparently into the occult.

I was pretty relieved to get away from BA unscathed, and with agreement in principle to use Almirante Brown. My next stop was a godforsaken place called Comodoro Rivadavia[49] in Patagonia; it was a coastal town of grey dust, tumbleweed and oil wells, but it also had an Air Force base from where the airlink to the Falklands operated. This was provided by the State Air Lines, LADE,[50] using Fokker F27 military transport planes, landing on a temporary prefabricated runway installed by Argentina just outside Stanley. I spent a very unpleasant weekend in Comodoro, with just the writing up of my notes and Tolkien's *Lord of the Rings* to sustain me, before flying to Stanley shortly before Christmas. And there I waited for the *Bransfield* to arrive.

As the ship steamed through the Narrows into Stanley Harbour a very large L plate was unfurled from the conning tower by the fids on board. This was aimed at the young captain – Stuart Lawrence – who was in his first season of command, and, according to them, had already broken the ship. It was my first encounter with Stuart; he was a consummate mariner, only two years older than me, excellent company, but could be a pain in the arse to management – as I discovered as I approached the top of the shop in later years. I travelled with him often during my career, and he served BAS with great skill and dedication, remaining captain of *Bransfield* until it was paid off in

48 Isabel Martínez de Perón was president from July 1974 until March 1976, then deposed by a military coup. The malign influence of José López Rega over her was one factor in her downfall. She has the distinction of having been the first woman to hold the title of president anywhere in the world.

49 Along with Rio Gallegos, this was an operational base for the Argentine Air Force during the Falklands Conflict.

50 LADE – Líneas Aéreas del Estado – is an airline based in Comodoro Rivadavia, Argentina. It is state-owned but operated by the Argentine Air Force to provide domestic scheduled services, mainly in Patagonia.

1999 and went off to the breaker's yard, much to his disgust. He then transferred to its replacement, the RRS *Ernest Shackleton*, for a few years before retiring in 2003.

We sailed on 7 January for the Antarctic Peninsula, calling at the American Palmer Station to do a resupply, where we also installed a Doppler transmitter for our pilot study. Then to Base F to install the Doppler receiver and to Adelaide Island to install another Doppler transmitter; I had installed yet another on the stern of *Bransfield* as part of the test. The ship was also resupplying the BAS stations at Stonington Island and Adelaide Island before returning briefly to Stanley. And then it was off to pastures new for me – South Georgia, the Weddell Sea and the Brunt Ice Shelf.

We made a quick call at South Georgia – just three days – and as it was my first visit to this fabulous island I found it to be a place of astounding beauty, incredible wildlife and fascinating industrial history, being the home of Southern Ocean whaling from 1904 until just a few years before my visit. However, if the weather is poor – and it often is –it can be a grim and unpleasant place. The BAS station was at King Edward Point (KEP), just across the bay from the Grytviken Whaling Station, which had been mothballed in the hope that the whale population would recover sufficiently for whaling to restart. South Georgia has a sub-Antarctic climate, so KEP was unlike any other BAS base. It was housed in a large three-storey building (Shackleton House), originally used as a dormitory for the whalers, standing on the edge of the former government settlement from which the whaling had been managed by the Falklands Islands government (FIG).

King Edward Point, South Georgia, with two young bull elephant seals having a set-to in the foreground.

With the demise of whaling BAS had taken over the administrative role from FIG as well as carrying out a substantial research programme – including the ionospherics work for which I now had responsibility. From there we headed south into the Weddell Sea, bound for the Brunt Ice Shelf and the BAS station (Halley Bay) at 75°S, 26°W, where another new chapter in my life and work was to begin.

Ice shelves are a defining characteristic of Antarctica. There are minor ones in the Arctic, but nothing there on the scale of Antarctica. They consist of thick flat platforms of floating ice attached to the coastline, and are created by the ice flow off the land under gravity. At the coastline (the grounding line) they can be as much as 3 km thick, whilst at their seaward edge perhaps 200 to 400 metres. The ice slowly flows seaward, and a kind of equilibrium in size is established by pieces episodically calving at the seaward edge as icebergs. These icebergs – known as tabular icebergs because of their shape – can be many kilometres long and sometimes thousands of square kilometres in area, so are very different from the smaller, much more irregular, bergs that break off from tidewater glaciers. Much of the coastline of Antarctica is fringed by ice shelves, the biggest being the Ross Ice Shelf (500,000 sq km, about the size of France) and the Filchner-Ronne Ice Shelf (430,000 sq km).

The Brunt Ice Shelf, on the south-eastern side of the Weddell Sea, is a baby compared with these giants, but still covers many hundreds of square kilometres, with a seaward edge about 80 km long, consisting of an unbroken ice cliff around 30 metres

The cliffs of Brunt Ice Shelf, the bay ice, and in the distance, the ramp up onto the inland ice. The flags mark the surveyed safe route for vehicles.

high. These cliffs offer no easy access inland from the sea, except at a point where a sea mount interrupts the flow of the ice seaward, causing its edge to split into a number of creeks, which although moving with the shelf and changing shape, offer a fairly stable path inland from the sea. In winter they freeze over, and then wind-blown snow forms drift slopes to provide relatively easy access from the sea ice onto the shelf. When in 1956 the Royal Society set up a research station on the coast of the Weddell Sea as its contribution to the IGY,[51] it was one such creek (named Halley Bay at the time) that provided access to establish the station. By the time I first arrived there Halley Bay had disappeared, but new creeks now provided access, and the station was by then operated by BAS as Base Z, or Halley Station.

By any stretch of the imagination Base Z and its environs are mighty strange and challenging. The ice shelf flows roughly westwards at about 1 to 2 metres per day, taking with it anything put on the surface. Not only that, but wind-driven drift snow gathered over a vast fetch[52] continuously builds up on the surface, giving around 1 metre of accumulation per year. But because the shelf is afloat and is scoured by the tide on its subsurface, the surface altitude stays roughly the same. So objects placed on the surface will seem to disappear downwards and westwards into the shelf, ultimately to break off, entombed in an iceberg. The IGY traditional wooden hut was quickly buried, becoming unsafe in the mid-1960s. It was replaced by a reinforced wooden structure, intended to be buried, but this also suffered severe stress from the pressure and movement of the ice. In the early 1970s a new approach was adopted for what became known as Halley III. The station was still built from wooden modules, but these were erected inside corrugated metal (Armco) tubes, themselves assembled on the surface, but which as they became buried over time would protect the buildings from being crushed. Halley III had been in operation for two years when I arrived, but was already well below the surface, so there was little to be seen except antenna masts and access shafts. Otherwise there was just a flat featureless snow plain marching away into the distance. On a clear sunny day it was, to my eyes, incredibly beautiful in its own very one-dimensional way – but when the wind got up and the sky was overcast it became a menacing and potentially very dangerous place. Odd, then, that I became fascinated with Halley, and that it dominated my career both as a scientist and as an administrator from then on with BAS.

Access by sea to the Brunt Ice Shelf is not easy; there is only a short window in the summer when the Weddell pack ice allows a passage. Normally this window occupies January and February, with the minimum sea ice cover in late February. Attempting the passage too early will just mean spending a lot of time and fuel bashing ice; too late

---

51 The International Geophysical Year (IGY) was a very major international research programme held in 1957 and 1958, during which 12 nations established research stations in Antarctica.

52 Fetch, or fetch length, is the length over ocean or icefield over which the wind can build up ocean waves or drifting snow. The longer the fetch, the bigger the waves or the denser the drift for a given wind speed.

Above: Unloading supplies for the station from the ship 'docked' at the ice foot in Mobster Creek.

Right: Frost smoke in Mobster Creek heralding the start of the winter sea ice formation.

and there is a risk that the creek ice will have broken out, making access inland difficult. Also by late February the temperature will be plunging and new sea ice will be forming. The ideal time to arrive is early January if possible.

The *Bransfield*'s rudder problem meant a big delay, and it was not until 8 February that we arrived off Halley. The creek ice had pretty well disappeared, and the temperature was around minus 10° C, dipping below minus 20° C at night. So the annual resupply became very difficult, as the ship had to go alongside the unstable ice foot at the head of the creek – known as Mobster for reasons I have now forgotten. After a few days Mobster was abandoned for an area some distance away, where the shelf height was much lower – about the same height out of the water as the main deck of the *Bransfield* – still not very stable, but flat, with the illusion of a quayside. The big disadvantage was that it was now 60 km across the shelf from the station, making the remainder of relief very slow indeed.

The ship stayed for about two weeks endeavouring to complete the resupply while I spent time at the station assessing my ionospherics programme and at low-shelf assisting with relief and running the test Doppler transmitter. By late February the temperature was routinely below minus 20° C, the sun was setting each night and the sea was starting to freeze with characteristic frost-smoke.[53] So it was time to be heading north, leaving the station for the long Antarctic winter. By then I was smitten by the 'Halley bug'. I was starting to see the scientific opportunities that might unfold there, and I was also captivated by the unique engineering required to successfully live there. But mostly it was the sheer austere majesty of the environment that caught hold of me.

From Halley we headed for the South Orkneys to Base H, then to South Georgia, before heading to Argentina, making landfall in the coastal resort of Mar del Plata. We docked in the naval dockyard, which was somewhat uncomfortable given that the ship was registered in Stanley and there were extremists wishing to make a fuss over Argentine claims to the Falklands. Consequently, we had an armed guard on the gangway searching folk arriving and leaving the ship. The main purpose of the visit – apart from R&R for the ship's company – was to host a reception on board for the staff of the IAA and local naval dignitaries. Here I saw for the first time the power of champagne cocktails (a sugar lump dosed with brandy in a glass of champagne) to loosen the tongues of folks who didn't really have a common language. There was also a huge casino to be visited. From Mar del Plata we headed back to Stanley, where I started my journey home via Comodoro Rivadavia, BA and North America.

I spent a little under a week in BA, visiting the IAA to give another seminar and hold more discussions on the Grand Plan. The same three young ladies were in attendance, apparently to meet my social requirements – I had received a letter from one of them while in Mar del Plata suggesting a two-week trip together to the mountain resort of

---

53 Frost smoke looks like low-lying fog; it is caused by cold air passing over warm (relatively – around minus 2° C) ocean, picking up moisture which then condenses out and freezes.

Bariloche. I decided that the letter was best 'lost in the post' and made no mention of it. I remain very unsure of quite what was going on, whether I was being set up or whether it was just over-enthusiastic hospitality on the part of the IAA. In retrospect it was definitely very odd.

From BA I flew to Washington DC for my first encounter (of many) with the Office of Polar Programs (OPP)[54] which oversaw the US programme in Antarctica. I was able to get a firm commitment from the OPP to host our experiment at Palmer Station and generally get familiarized with how the US programme was funded and what its priorities were. Contacts were made that served me well for the rest of my career. My final port of call was to Dartmouth College, Hanover, New Hampshire. This was the home of Professor Millett Morgan, for whom BAS had for many years run a whistler programme in Antarctica – indeed I had looked after some of his equipment during my time at Base F. I had arranged for Trevor Thomas, a beastieman who had spent two winters at Halley, to do a PhD with Morgan using the data from the programme, so my visit was a chance to catch up with him as well as generally discuss the future of the work with Millett. And from there it was home, finally arriving there on 13 April 1975.

My homecoming coincided with big developments at BAS. Construction was under way on the new building on university land about 2 miles west of the centre of Cambridge, and my little group now had space allocated in it. So I was heavily involved in planning for that, both professionally and personally. I was now on an established open-ended career track, with the financial stability it provided. Helen, meanwhile, was starting to build an academic career in solar physics as a post-doc at University College London, but with no assured long-term employment. So we faced the dilemma which strikes most young professional couples at some point: how to meld marriage and careers in a mutually sensible manner. We didn't want to live apart, and with my financial security we could afford to get on the housing ladder. But it meant moving to the Cambridge

WHISTLERS

Whistlers are naturally occurring very low frequency radio emissions which are generated by lightning but get channelled by the Earth's magnetic field to travel from one hemisphere to the other. On transit their spectrum is dispersed by the charged gas (plasma) in the near-Earth environment through which they pass, to give them a characteristic whistling tone with the higher frequencies arriving before the lower ones. The exact spectrum received is a diagnostic of the plasma they have encountered.

54 The Office of Polar Programs (OPP) (at one time the Department for Polar Programmes, DPP) is part of the National Science Foundation (NSF) of the USA. It has responsibility for running the logistics of both Arctic and Antarctic science programmes and for awarding grants to fund the science activities.

area. Luckily Helen was able to move her post-doc position to Cambridge University, but she then spent many years on soft money and short-term contracts until finally being awarded a long overdue tenured position, having by then built up a very strong international reputation and become senior tutor of St Edmund's College (and now one of its very few life fellows). So we bought our first house in a small village just outside Cambridge, and I commenced work in the new integrated BAS headquarters.

1976 proved a momentous year for me in several ways. I was awarded my first Polar Medal and was promoted yet again – now to principal scientific officer (PSO), regarded as the career grade: the level a competent research scientist could expect to reach and then stay at for a career. I reached it at the unusually early age of 31. But very sadly my mother died at the end of February before I learnt of my medal and my promotion, and indeed before Helen and I had found our first house. It was also the year that I started having my first (of several) 'big ideas' about what direction the BAS ionospherics programme should take.

In the autumn of 1976 BAS appointed its first computer manager, marking the beginning of an organization-wide computing service. He was a larger-than-life Ulsterman – G.L.M.H. (Grahame) Hughes, five years older than me, and from a background of technical service with the Ministry of Defence. Grahame was a big man both physically and in his appetites, but very forward-thinking and committed.

The investiture at Buckingham Palace for my first Polar Medal. An emotional day, made more so by the kind personal comments made to me by her Majesty the Queen!

He was not, on the face of it, somebody that I would find kinship with. But oddly we became very close friends and also very close colleagues – framing BAS computing and data-handling policy for the next 25 years, until his untimely death aged 60 in 2000. I do not make friends nor find confidants easily – in fact almost never – so my relationship with Grahame was all the more surprising and important to me.

As a bit of an aside, back in the early 1970s there was an exclusive dining club amongst the senior staff of BAS organized by Bill Sloman. I decided that BAS beastiemen should also have their own such society, so Dick and I set up the very exclusive TIDsoc. This was, and still is, reserved for only those fids who have wintered as beastiemen looking after Union Radio ionosondes. It has some very odd rules: each attendee at a feast must cook one course; each course must be different from any previously presented; and each must be made out of raw ingredients. Dress is formal, and the venue is provided by one of the members. The name of the society is a play on words, standing for Travelling

The TIDSoc meeting in Wales in April 2000. From left to right, Stuart Broom, Mike Pinnock, me, Alan Rodger, Grahame Hughes, Dick Kressman, Jim Turton and Peter Fitzgerald. Quite why we were toasting a pair of carpet slippers is now lost in the mists of time. Sadly, just five months later Grahame passed away.

Ionospheric Disturbance (a major topic of research early in my career) but also for Thrasonical[55] Ionosphericists Dining. The society occasionally invites a distinguished guest, known as the Gastronomer Royal, whose sole function is to eat heartedly and regale the company with boastful (thrasonical) stories. In the past we have numbered up to seven, which has produced some pretty wonderful feasts, but now we are only six. Grahame was not one, but he was an excellent Gastronomer Royal on more than one occasion, well up to the task of eating mightily and boasting magnificently.

Grahame died as he lived. He had not been treated well by NERC; he had an unfortunate habit of speaking the truth to power even when it was not welcomed, and an even more unfortunate habit of being right. He was consequently passed over for promotion, and decided to retire early. He got himself a very idyllic smallholding in

---

55 Thraso was a blustering old soldier in the comedy *Eunuchus*, a play written by the great Roman dramatist Terence more than 2,000 years ago. Terence is generally remembered for his realistic characterizations, and in Thraso he created a swaggerer whose vainglorious boastfulness was not soon to be forgotten. Thraso's reputation as a braggart lives on in 'thrasonical', a word that boasts a history as an English adjective of more than 440 years.

Wales, with a new young wife and a baby daughter. So his last years were spent in paradise, where I would occasionally visit him to enjoy his lifestyle.

On the day he died we had spent a fine day out and about, and in the evening he had to give a report to the local hunt club, of which he was treasurer. Typically, he had chosen a country pub in the middle of nowhere and was standing in its garden in the summer evening sunshine with a pint in his hand belabouring the committee over financial issues when he simply dropped dead. I (with others) spent quite a while administering CPR but to no avail. It turned out that his left ventricle had ruptured, so nothing would have helped. His funeral a few days later had a lovely element of farce which he would have enjoyed. The funeral was in Newcastle Emlyn, but the cremation was quite a long drive away, in Narberth. At some point on the journey the hearse started speeding up, as the slot time was approaching – but the vicar clearly realized he should get there before the coffin. So a race developed with the hearse zooming ahead, the vicar's car chasing to overtake it, and the rest of the cortege desperately trying to keep up. I imagined Grahame rolling about in his coffin, laughing his head off. I still miss him sorely more than two decades on.

6

DEVELOPING MY
SCIENTIFIC IDEAS

In the summer of 1976 I attended the International Symposium on Solar Terrestrial Physics (ISSTP) in Boulder, Colorado, and was also able to visit the Space Environment Laboratory (SEL) located there; it was part of the National Oceanographic and Atmospheric Administration (NOAA). Here my eyes were opened to new possibilities, and I quickly came to the conclusion that the BAS programme of ionospheric research, based as it was on three ancient electromechanical ionosondes, would never amount to much. It was here that my ideas started to form about the aims and methodology that would carry my group through the next three decades. It was embryonic then, but ultimately would be condensed into the question: 'How does energy flow through geospace?'

The term 'geospace' was not then in the scientific lexicon, but now it is used to describe the region of the local solar system in which the Earth's upper atmosphere (ionosphere and magnetosphere) is coupled to the Sun's atmosphere – the solar wind. You may well ask why would humanity be much interested, apart from the pure scientific challenge of understanding such a complex system? Well, one of the most striking manifestations to most people are the Aurora Borealis and Aurora Australis. Ancient humans would have been overawed, and probably sacrificed various animals to ward off the evil. Victorians, too, would have been awed but would have tried to understand them, although they did not impinge on their way of life. Not so, however, for our modern technological society, for whom electrical power is fundamental – as now is global digital communications, essential to our wellbeing. Sudden loss of either would be catastrophic. Our Sun is an active star, and when it has disturbances they disrupt local geospace – sometimes severely enough to crash power grids and communications – a phenomenon now known as space weather. So understanding and predicting such disturbances has high strategic significance, and consequently much money and effort now goes into it. In fact, space weather impacts now figure in the UK government register of strategic risks to the UK. Of course I wasn't prescient enough then to have any of that worked out, but I was embarking on a path towards it.

But then you ask, 'What has Antarctica got to do with all this?' And that is a very good question – one that Roy Piggott could wax lyrical about for hours on end, and one about which he and I published a seminal paper in 1977.[56] The simple answer is that the continent not only provides a good platform on which to site experiments to study geospace from the ground, but also has some unique geographical properties. The most important is that the Earth's magnetic field is not aligned with its rotation axis – that is, the geographical and the geomagnetic poles[57] are not co-located – and since geospace is influenced both by the sun directly and by the magnetic field that threads it, behaviour varies as a function of longitude at a fixed latitude. But even more than that, the offset of the Southern Geomagnetic Pole versus the South Geographic (or Rotation) Pole is about twice as large as that at the northern poles, which provides some very stark contrasts, both between Antarctica and the Arctic, and within Antarctica itself. And, even more interesting to me, the location of Halley turns out to be a uniquely exciting place to site experiments – which is one of the reasons why, back in 1956, the station was established there by the Royal Society in the first place.

At NOAA I met an engineer who was to play a big role in what I did next. His name was Dick Grubb, and he was masterminding a whole new concept for sounding the ionosphere, which would potentially provide a means of studying it in three dimensions with very high time resolution and in fine detail. To do this he was marrying traditional radio physics with digital techniques, which allowed for powerful signal processing in real time, using a mini-computer. He was working with two colleagues, one American – J.W. (Bill) Wright – and one British – Mike Pitteway – to design a practical digital ionosonde. I immediately latched onto the possibilities that placing such a system at Halley would offer – it would propel my group into the forefront of the science in one step. The issue was – how could I acquire one? I made initial enquiries to see whether NOAA would be prepared to enter into a collaboration with BAS to build one for Halley, and at what sort of cost. The NOAA seemed to be open to the idea, but raising the money was another issue entirely. However, it was from here that the seeds were sown for what was to become known as the BAS Advanced Ionospheric Sounder (AIS) programme.

During that same visit, I realized that to make any real progress in understanding how the complex coupling and energy flow in geospace worked; ground-based measurements would be insufficient on their own. I also needed access to *in situ* measurements made by a variety of current and planned research spacecraft aimed at exploring the various key regions of geospace, from the solar wind through the magnetosphere

---

56 Dudeney, J.R. and W.R. Piggott (1978) Antarctic ionospheric research. In *US Upper Atmospheric Research in the Antarctic*. Eds. L.H. Lanzerotti and C.G. Park, *Antarctic Research Series*, 29, publ A.G.U., 200–235

57 The points on the Earth's surface where the magnetic field is vertical

and into the ionosphere (which constitutes the lower boundary to geospace). So I embarked on a second strand – engagement with the various leaders in that field, with the aim of getting my foot in the door of the spacecraft missions. All of my emerging ideas I put in a letter to Roy while I was still at the conference.

Once home I began the campaign to convince people to provide the necessary funds. This seemed at first a monumental task: BAS had never put any significant money into this area of research previously, and more to the point NERC did not fund space research, the latter being firmly in the remit of the SRC.[58] But my letter from America fired up Roy, who enthusiastically badgered Dick Laws – who was prepared, in principle at least, to listen. Also, though I didn't know it at the time, BAS had been encouraged to start a programme of ionospheric research in the mid-1960s so maybe Dick had been waiting for something he could push. But it wasn't sufficient for me to convince Dick – an outstanding biologist, but no expert in my field. He needed to be convinced that the UK research community saw the plan as of high importance.

The rest of the UK community was at the time much taken up with trying to get the money for British participation in a very large European initiative called EISCAT.[59] That community was, apart from my small operation in BAS, dependent on SRC for funds, and the figurehead pushing this was Sir Granville Beynon at the University of Wales. He was cautious about any other initiative that might distract from delivering a leadership position for UK in EISCAT, so there was no chance of getting any funding for the AIS out of SRC. In fact, our only hope was that any BAS project would be funded by NERC and hence not be seen as a rival. But that meant convincing NERC to put up a considerable sum in a field which it otherwise had no business funding. The instrument alone would cost in the region of £100,000.[60] The key was getting Sir Granville to endorse our project and putting his considerable influence behind it. Luckily, he was an old pal and colleague of Piggott. Also he had been my external examiner on my PhD, when I had drawn heavily and very positively on some of his early work in radiophysics, so he looked more benignly on me than he otherwise might have. But it was still necessary to get him onside, so Roy decided the best approach was to beard him in his lair.

We set off in Roy's car to Aberystwyth to spend a couple of days doing that. It was a hair-raising drive, as Roy drove at high speed, talking all the way (a classic piggotting) mostly looking at me to emphasize a point rather than at the road ahead. But we survived and had a pleasant time, being entertained at Sir Granville's house – and more important, coming home with his support assured. But probably it was

---

58 Space research in the UK in the 1960s was funded by the Science Research Council (SRC); reorganizations had it placed in the Science and Engineering Research Council (SERC) in the 1980s, then in the Particle Physics and Astronomy Research Council (PPARC) in the 1990s, and finally today in the Science and Technology Facilities Council (STFC) – and, ironically, NERC.

59 The European Incoherent Scatter Radar programme, which would see several huge facilities built in the Scandinavian Arctic.

60 That was in 1976; at the time of writing, about £800,000.

not my scientific eloquence that made the case; we had come with a secret weapon – an offer of a trip south with BAS to write a review of BAS activities. This offer Sir Granville took up with great enthusiasm the following season. But much more formally, there were national scientific committees under the auspices of the Royal Society that had to be brought into the picture – the British national committees for Solar Terrestrial Science, for Radio Science and for Antarctic Research. A special joint working group of these committees, chaired by Sir Granville, was convened to make the case and develop a national plan for exploiting the system. They endorsed it wholeheartedly.

Things then moved quite rapidly, as NOAA was planning to have a small production run of instruments and were prepared to build one for BAS at the cost of parts and labour if it was included in that run (six were actually built). The proposal was therefore brought urgently before the NERC Council in January 1978. With that approval in our pocket, Bill Sloman and I set off in mid-January 1978 to Boulder to negotiate the deal. It was a successful if rather cold and snowy visit, with my abiding memory of being in the bar of the Holiday Inn with Bill being plied with 'fiery fuzzy fuckers', an evil drink: tequila in a shot glass on which a slice of lemon is placed with some burning sugar on it. The victim is required to lick the lemon and down the tequila in one go! After a few of those I found myself in the small hours in the hotel pool, which spanned the warm inside of the hotel and the icy outside. It was a surreal experience swimming from the hot brightly lit pool inside through a low opening out into the freezing night, where the hot pool water created its own fog and the pool surrounds were deep in snow. But the project was up and running.

Getting the instrument itself was but a small part of the project. There was the matter of how to install it on a floating ice shelf and maintain it there successfully for a significant number of years. This needed some very innovative systems development and snow engineering, to which I will return later. I also needed a team of scientists, engineers and field operatives to effectively run the project. Dick Kressman was the obvious choice as project engineer because of his excellent software and hardware skills. Alan Rodger was developing into a very effective research scientist and so could be relied upon to help develop the science programme. These two became the core team. But we also needed someone experienced to help with the installation and to lead the first wintering campaign. So now we come to another important name in my career, Mike Pinnock. Mike had been appointed as a beastieman to spend 1977 and 1978 at Halley. He was a very likeable but very bright and practical engineer with an HND in electrical and electronic engineering. He was a natural leader, and a very successful field engineer. I appointed him as lead field engineer when he came home in 1979, and he will figure more in my story throughout my career. I was also fortunate enough to convince my masters that I needed a further professional scientist on the team. Thus it was that Dr Martin J. Jarvis joined us in 1979 from the Post Office.

We planned to put a very sophisticated system into a challenging and hostile environment. It was much more complex than anything that BAS had deployed previously and would incorporate the first computing system anywhere in the BAS field programme – possibly the most complex system deployed by any nation in Antarctica up to then. It required an antenna system that was an order of magnitude bigger than anything that BAS had built before, which we planned to erect on a floating ice shelf, and which consequently several knowledgeable folk assured us was impracticable. The whole system needed to be commissioned in the USA, further tested in the UK, and then delivered and installed at Halley, where hitherto it would have ended up buried with the rest of the station within the ice shelf. It contained a high-powered radio transmitter which would be routinely transmitting complex pulses whose impact on the base communications and other systems in operation had to be minimized. Radical thinking was needed. The solution was to containerize the equipment, but even more radically we would mount the container on a ski base so that it could be dragged from the ship to its operational site, and we would keep it on the surface by jacking it 2 metres above the snow and devising a way to keep jacking it up as the snow built up.

This then created the need for office space and a power supply. The solution was to make ourselves operationally independent of the main station by having diesel generators also housed in a shipping container jacked above the snow surface, and likewise an office container. This approach naturally helped reduce radio interference as there need not be any electrical connection between our container village and the main station, and we could physically separate the two within the constraints of safe winter access between them. So the concept of the surface Halley village was born.

Much of 1978 was spent on preparation – designing the containerized facilities using half-ISO containers and getting them constructed. This also needed innovative thinking, particularly for the AIS container, which had to provide a comfortable working environment for personnel and equipment at the low winter temperatures (as low as minus 55° C) but not overheat on a 'warm' sunny day in summer (as high as plus 4° C) while the AIS itself was dissipating upwards of 5 kW of heat inside it. The solution to that (refined over the first couple of years of service) was to pump in cold air from outside. There was also software development, procuring ancillary equipment and developing our plan for the installation and commissioning the system in the USA, which involved further trips to the USA and elsewhere. On top of all that, I also had a research group to run, a developing involvement in national and international science coordination and research programmes, and a need to continue my own personal research, both in studies of geospace and in the other line I had developed of devising empirical models[61] of the ionosphere. So 1978 was a busy year. Then on 31 December Helen gave birth to our first child, Elizabeth Amy (Lizzie) which added a whole new dimension to our lives.

---

61 This work produced six peer-reviewed publications between 1973 and 1986; surprisingly, the techniques described are still being cited and used by other researchers in 2020s.

1978 had also been the start of a difficult decade for me careerwise. Roy was approaching 65 and would have to retire in 1979. There were two obvious contenders to replace him within the division: Joe Farman and me. Joe was somewhat older than me and had also wintered at F, but in the late 1950s. He had then run the BAS observatory physics unit at Edinburgh University throughout the 1960s and early 1970s. Other things being equal, he might have expected to have been given the job of head of division when Dick Laws created his new structure, but had been passed over in favour of Roy. Joe was a very fine observatory physicist, but a difficult man to work with, and did not suffer fools gladly – or even at all. He also lived in a permanent smokescreen of evil-smelling pipe smoke. But he was destined to have a truly global impact on the future of humanity, as we shall see in a later chapter.

At the time, permanent government service posts had to be advertised and filled from within the government or civil service. Only if no suitable candidate could be found would they be advertised more widely. In the event, there were four candidates interviewed on 10 August 1978, Joe and me, and two from outside BAS. I was considered rather young for such a senior post (SPSO),[62] and I think that Roy had been scheming, because an individual merit SPSO from RSRS, and a mentor of mine during my PhD work, was one of the two external candidates. He was close to retirement, and I believe – but without firm evidence except my memory of conversations with Roy – that he was seen as the stopgap, giving me another chance at the job a few years later. However, that scheme fell at the first hurdle because the chemistry between Dick and him went badly wrong in the interview. I was told afterwards that I had passed the board, but that the post would be trawled outside government first, before making an appointment. Very few folk from the UK community applied, with a lot of gossip at the time that there was no point because they saw the job as Dudeney's. Just one external candidate was interviewed – and was offered the job: Dr M.J. (Michael) Rycroft, a lecturer from Southampton University.

I believe that I made an honest and sustained attempt to welcome and work with Michael while focusing on all the other opportunities open to me. But it was not to be, and it was the start of a very uncomfortable and combative decade for both of us, before he departed and I finally got the job in 1990. I do not intend to dwell on the details of our differences, and my judgements of Michael's strengths and weaknesses do not need to be aired here. Dick Laws softened the impact on me by establishing beforehand that I was content with the policy of the division before he signed off on it, which I suspect Michael found difficult. Dick also made an effort to give me challenging policy work over that decade, as will become apparent. After he retired Dick told me that he regretted having not just appointed me, but with 20:20 hindsight I feel it was probably better that I didn't get the job in 1979, because the 1980s were

---

62 Senior principal scientific officer. Equivalent military rank, colonel; equivalent academic rank, professor.

very productive in spite of the frustrating managerial problems I felt I faced. But it was a long and tedious wait.

On top of all that, in 1978 I decided to confront my ghosts hanging over from the Antarctic plane crash, so started taking flying lessons. For this I turned to Marshalls Aerospace, based at Cambridge Airport and run by the formidable Sir Arthur Marshall. The company was a major aerospace contractor, but Sir Arthur decreed there would always be a flying school on the premises. In fact there were two: one, the Cambridge Flying Group, offered flight training using two Tiger Moth biplanes, and the other, run by Marshalls itself, using the more modern Cessnas. For the latter the instructors provided the training as a sideline from their day jobs as professional pilots for the company. I opted for the Cessnas, though I did later fly the Tiger Moths for a short period. I started training in April with a short air experience flight over the Cambridge countryside, and I can still summon up the elation I felt about it – I was hooked! Helen indulged me, so over the next year or so I worked hard, both in the air and in ground school, to achieve my private pilot's licence in June 1979. Apart from the sheer joy of flying I was privileged to be trained by some highly professional pilots, one of whom had been a Lancaster bomber pilot during the war and had some hair-raising stories to tell. Helen has never been comfortable with flying, so it was a remarkable testament to her faith in me and her commitment to us that she volunteered to be my first passenger just a few days later for a 30-minute joyride around the sights of Cambridge. I flew actively for the next eight years, gaining an IMC[63] rating and doing a bit of gentle aerobatics, but finally work and financial pressures brought that interlude to an end. Well, not quite, because later in my career I did have some rather splendid flights in the right-hand seat – and from time to time in control of – BAS Twin Otters[64] over Antarctica, some of them in IMC. But I never felt it was appropriate to actually formalize them by having an entry for the hours flown in my pilot's logbook.

The next step on the path with the AIS was to take delivery of the system and commission it. Having got the containerized lab completed we shipped it to SEL, and in late February 1979 Dick and I set off there, accompanied by Helen and two-month-old Liz, plus a rather large cheque made out to me. In those days, life was much simpler; I opened a bank account in my name, from which I made stage payments (and the final payment) for the system, covered all the ancillary costs for the installation and commissioning, and paid Dick and myself our travel and subsistence costs. Such a simple arrangement would be looked upon with horror now, possibly even as fraudulent, particularly as the only record of how the money was dispersed was a little

---

63 The Instrument Meteorological Conditions (IMC) rating was the elementary (and strictly limited) instrument rating; it allowed flight in cloud etc outside commercial airways.

64 The Otter is a high-wing two-engine STOL utility plane with a range/payload in normal operations of 500 nm (926 km) carrying a payload of 1,000 kg, with an all-up take-off weight of 12,500 lbs (5,670 kg) and a cruise speed of 120 knots (with the ski/wheel conversion).

notebook in which I recorded all the expenditure, and which I handed into BAS when we got home. All based on trust, but it got the job done in a highly efficient and effective manner. We took a short-term lease on an apartment in Boulder, and Helen was able – at least part-time – to carry on with some of her research collaborations while nursing Liz. It took us two months to install and commission the system into our container. This required the hiring of cranes and low loaders to move the system out to a field site some distance out of town where there were antennae we could use. I also got to do some more flight training, with the flat view of the Fens replaced by the magnificence of the Rocky Mountains.

Liz had been born just on the cusp of the revolution in nappies – moving from towelling ones, requiring endless soaking and washing, to disposable ones. The USA was ahead of the UK, and we found that there we could get Huggies, a rather marvellous diaper with elasticated legs which kept all the 'flavour' in, unlike the best of British at the time – which did not. We had a lot of equipment and spares to be packed in the AIS container, so Helen and I bought a somewhat sizeable stock of Huggies, which we used as soft packaging in the container, listing them thus on the customs manifest. They gave us quite a few months of squirt-free living once the container arrived home. Helen and Liz headed home a little before us via Washington DC, as Helen had been invited to visit the Naval Research Laboratory (NRL) there to give a seminar. This led to two rather bizarre occurrences: the first, the convening of a special meeting of the NRL Security Committee to decide whether Liz posed a security threat (Helen already had clearance), and the second, the (then extraordinary) sight of an attractive young scientist giving her talk to an attentive audience while her baby slept, blissfully unaware, in her carrycot by the lectern.

Dick and I left the AIS, now snug in its container, to be shipped home slowly by sea. It arrived back in the summer, and after a period of commissioning at BAS was moved to the Appleton Lab, where we were given access to large antennae. Here we could test the system, and train ourselves and the first wintering team to exploit its capabilities effectively, ready for its planned deployment to Halley in the 1980/81 summer season.

There was a great deal of planning, training and preparation ahead of deployment at Halley. Almost everything that we planned to do was new and untried. There was scepticism that the AIS caboose could be successfully moved from the ship's side over the sea ice up onto the shelf ice. It weighed over 9 tons, and doom-merchants claimed it would just drop through the ice – and even if it didn't it would bog down and be impossible to tow. Then there was erection of the antennae which required two 45-metre masts and a 30-metre mast – all to be built on ice foundations and needing to be very precisely positioned relative to each other. At the time these masts would be some of the tallest structures ever erected in Antarctica, so I and my team have probably had bigger erections than anybody else ever in the whole continent! And all this had to be done in a very short summer period (just six weeks) which would undoubtedly include a good measure of bad weather. Preparation occupied us pretty fully from when Dick and I got home in spring 1979 to the late autumn of 1980. Dick concentrated on getting to grips with the software and hardware of the AIS itself, and Mike planned and organized the field deployment, while Martin and I started developing a suite of analysis programs.

It was expected that the AIS would be a national facility with the data available to all. It was seen as a big data project – but this was in the days when the data were recorded on half-inch magnetic tape and 'big' meant megabytes, not the terabytes we routinely bandy around today. The web/internet had yet to be invented, and the concept of online databases was unknown. Research was starting into relational databases,[65] and there were embryonic ideas of linking databases across platforms, but what now we take for granted on a daily basis in the manipulation of data was a pipedream at the beginning of the 1980s. Even so the NERC computing service (NCS) bravely offered to construct a relational database to our specifications that would be magnetic tape-based. NCS and my team spent quite a bit of effort trying to specify a system, and a prototype began operating in May 1984 on the NERC central computer, accessible via the Joint Academic Network (JANET).[66] But the sophistication and complexity of what we wanted was beyond the computing/networking capabilities of the day, and it also fell foul of a less than perfect relationship between BAS and NCS, and more generally between BAS and NERC. Then, as technology was leaping ahead, Dick was quickly involved with upgrading the computing systems and the data storage to new media. As a result, there never was a readily accessible database from the early tape data.

The summer season at Halley would be short, and there was a lot of basic groundwork required to prepare the site, so we tried something else new: Dick and Mike would be flown into Halley three weeks before the ship was due to arrive with me and the AIS. There would then be a further three weeks or so to complete the installation before the ship had to leave. This required the *John Biscoe* to take them from the Falklands to a summer air facility called Damoy in the Palmer Archipelago, and from there fly via Rothera Station to Halley – a long flight. Alas, the best-laid plans of mice and men came to nought. First, *John Biscoe*[67] suffered a major propulsion failure en route to Damoy and had to return to Stanley. Damoy passengers were then transferred to *Bransfield*, which made an unscheduled voyage to deliver them, arriving on 11 December. But then a combination of aircraft problems and bad weather meant that finally Dick and Mike only arrived at Halley on 7 January, just four days before I did. My arrival at Halley on 11 January was also later than scheduled, because of having to take over

---

65 A relational database is a set of formally described tables from which data can be accessed or reassembled in many different ways without having to reorganize the database tables.

66 JANET, a very simple forerunner of the internet, allowed British academic institutions to share data.

67 *John Biscoe*, which had recently undergone a major refit, had one of the blades of its new high-tech propeller fall off while transiting Drake Passage. It limped back to Stanley, and was then towed by HMS *Endurance* to Montevideo (some 864 nm or 1,600 km) to undergo temporary repairs sufficient to get it home.

from the crippled *John Biscoe*. So, given its planned date of departure from Halley of 28 January our window of opportunity for the deployment had now contracted to just 21 days in total from what had originally been expected to be six weeks – hardly an auspicious start to our campaign.

The enforced delay in Stanley did have one noteworthy side-effect: Grahame Hughes and I, along with others, were invited to a reception and dinner at Government House with Sir Rex Hunt and his wife Mavis. This event turned out to be both surreal and somewhat sobering. Surreal because Mavis appeared to lose the plot and had to be reminded by Grahame to put down her G&T to get on with serving dinner – Grahame being a chap who never wasted a good opportunity for a feast. Sobering, because the Falkland Islanders present were all very gloomy and anxious about their future. They believed that the British government had no real interest in protecting them, and this wasn't helped by the announcement of the withdrawal of HMS *Endurance* from service as their patrol vessel. They feared what the junta in BA might be planning – and as it turned out they were right to be worried, since it was only a little over a year later that Argentina invaded. Another curious moment was a trip in a Land Rover with David Attenborough who was to sail with us to South Georgia to film king penguins for the BBC. We went together to Cape Pembroke lighthouse to look at seals, and as we bumped along I discovered in my pocket a packet of chocolate buttons stashed there at some time in the past for my daughter. These I shared with David. Some years later, when Liz was engaged in a project at school, she wrote reminding David of this and requesting some information for her project. He replied most graciously with all the material she needed.

My notes from the time show that I was getting very anxious myself as the ship ploughed sedately to Halley via calls at South Georgia and the South Orkney Islands.[68] The aeroplane was stuck in Punta Arenas because of bad weather day after day, and when it finally did make it to Rothera, suffered hydraulic problems. For me on the ship it was frustrating watching the days slip by, knowing that even with everything on our side the deployment was going to be very difficult, but there was little I could do except wait and worry. So when we finally got tied up alongside the fast ice in Mobster Creek it was a huge relief that at least we could get going.

For the next 36 hours we worked almost continuously with just a few short rest breaks to achieve the first major task – to get the AIS caboose and the generator caboose safely across the sea ice, up the snow ramp and onto the shelf ice. We knew there were risks because of the weight, but we planned to tow the cabooses separately

---

68 The visit to the South Orkney Islands was an attempt to reach the British base on Signy Island. At the end of the previous summer pack ice had stopped the ship making its final call to pick up homebound personnel. This meant that several folk who had thought they were there just for the summer, and others who had completed a two-year tour, found themselves having to do another winter with inadequate supplies. An early attempt by *Biscoe* and *Bransfield* to relieve the station had failed because of heavy pack ice. Our visit was also thwarted by the ice, but we finally reached the station in February on our return from Halley.

The AIS caboose on its way from the ship (visible in the background) up the snow ramp, pulled by a bulldozer. The black oil drums mark the safe route across the sea ice from the ship.

across the sea ice using an IH[69] bulldozer, with a rope weak link between the dozer and the caboose, and me walking beside it with a very sharp knife. If either dozer or caboose looked like breaking through, my job was to cut the weak link and get out of the way asap. Also the dozer's cab had been removed, so hopefully the driver would just end up, if need be, bobbing in the watery hole to be quickly rescued. As it turned out, with a very experienced driver, 'Dad' Etchells, all went according to plan, and by the end of that first work session both cabooses had been towed safely up to the station a couple of miles inland.

The first major milestone had been achieved without mishap, but immediately we were confronted with another potential show-stopper. The AIS used a very special log-periodic transmitting antenna which was both very large and very complex. Supporting it required two 45-metre vertical masts placed precisely 134 metres apart, the installation of which was in itself a major engineering challenge never attempted before. The antenna consisted of a series of horizontal dipoles steadily increasing in length as the height increased from the ground, and precisely spaced in height. These were tensioned between two catenary wires which stretched from near the top of the masts to two anchor points close to each other midway between the masts. A further

69 International Harvesters

pair of catenaries were attached to the top of the masts to support the highest and longest dipole. So, we could see that once installed it would look like the outline of a pair of giant stripy knickers hanging out to dry. We had a lovely big crate containing thousands of fixings, anchors, bottle-screws and rolls of antenna wire – everything to build our Y-fronts – but with one major missing item: no instruction manual, and not even a picture of what the final article should really look like. Martin, back in the BAS office, quickly got the manufacturer to send him the missing manual – but how could he get it to us? The only means of communication was by radio telex from the UK via relay from Stanley, and it could only handle text typed on a teleprinter. But Martin rose to the challenge, making an accurate scale drawing of the antenna on graph paper and then identifying each junction point by its x–y coordinates. These he sent in a text message so we could replot the diagram and thus have an idea what the blooming thing was supposed to look like. He also described what all the different bits were and how they were supposed to be used. While he was engaged in this exacting task we commenced the erection of the masts.

We had put much thought into the type of mast to use, and settled on a triangular cross-section lattice construction which could be built from the bottom up using 2.5-metre sections. Raising the mast started by mounting the bottom section on a foundation plate and attaching a derrick pole to one side of it to raise the next section and bolt it in place. Then two installers would climb the first two sections to manoeuvre the next section in place – hauled up from the ground by a two-person ground team – and so on until all 18 sections were in place. At each three sections, stay wires were run to ground-anchor points to hold the mast upright. This was a job for professional riggers, even in the benign setting of a field in England, where base plate and guy anchor points could be built from concrete. But we were going to build on an ice shelf which both accumulated about 1 metre of snow a year and moved westwards at about 1 to 2 metres a day. We had chosen the particular design – an LTS[70] mast – because we planned to deal with the snow accumulation by adding a new section to the top and raising the whole antenna system up a couple of metres once every two years. To prepare, we had all gone on a training course with the manufacturers, when we built a mast under supervision on a nice sunny summer day. The reality at Halley was a somewhat different experience, but the training had been invaluable.

Foundations for the masts and their staying points required some careful thought. For the masts these were made by digging a 2-metre-deep trench into which was laid a platform of railway sleepers. Onto these a two-section mast was bolted, ensuring it was as close to vertical as possible. (These had been installed the previous summer to allow them to be firmly entrenched with a stub of mast proud of the ice ready for the following year.) For the anchoring points we dug further 2-metre trenches into which

---

70 Light Tower System manufactured by C&W Antenna

Digging one of the trenches for the anchors for the mast stays. Some of these had to be dug more than once, as bad weather (wind and blowing snow) would quickly fill them.

went several old 200-litre oil drums filled with water, strapped together with steel wire rope and with a wire rope attached leading to the surface. These, as it turned out, were over-engineered, and in subsequent rebuilds we relied on professionally made ice anchors.

Mike and Dick had surveyed the site and had started filling drums and digging trenches before the ship arrived. But there were a lot to be dug – 10 per mast, making 30 in total, and all to be dug by hand. So there were still sufficient holes to go round once I had got settled ashore. But working all hours and in some unpleasant weather (minus 5° C and 20 knots of wind on more than one occasion) we had the first 45-metre mast topped off by the end of 14 January. To celebrate we took the evening off and flew a Union Jack from the top of the mast. For the next two days the weather was horrid – high wind and blowing snow – making work outside impossible, and even moving around outside something to be done with care. Still, we managed to commission the generator caboose and so were able to power up the AIS caboose. Much to our satisfaction (and relief) the AIS and all of its computers powered up without problems – vindicating our choice of containerization. Sadly, some anchor trenches had not been completed before the blow began, so they had to be redug. The weather improved enough for outside work to be possible, though we were still working in 20 knots with no surface contrast as the sky was overcast, so conditions were hardly pleasant. By 21 January we had the two 45-metre masts erected, the cabooses properly installed and raised on legs 2 metres above the snow level, and a complex array of dipole receiving antennae set up. It was now time to try to build the massive Y-fronts. The third mast was to be 'only' 30 metres

The collection of cabooses which together made up the AIS village. From left to right: the office, the AIS, and the generator caboose.

high to support the low frequency antenna (a vertical Delta – basically an inverted V of wire), so it went up fairly quickly.

The Y-front antenna took a day to assemble on the ground – and when we raised it the blooming thing didn't fit! It took until 24 January with two lowerings, fiddlings and re-raisings before we had something which, though not quite as the manufacturer intended, was at least functional. And on 24 January the sun finally shone on our endeavours, so it was all in all a grand day, though fatigue and stress were now taking their toll on us all. The sunshine came just in time.

However, a couple of days earlier, it had been a case of 'there but for the grace of God go I'. The station was by 1981 well buried in the ice shelf with its floor level probably 10 metres below the surface. The latter was reached by a series of ladders, with heavy stores etc lowered and raised in a vertical shaft. In the evening I was involved in moving 200-litre drums of gash out of the base, and was stationed at the bottom of the shaft to hook full drums onto the winch rope and retrieve empty ones. I was called away for a radio conversation with the captain of *Bransfield* with an incoming metman, Mike Blandford, taking my place. While I was away an empty drum came loose and fell down the shaft, hitting him on the head. Luckily he was not killed, but he did sustain a fractured skull. Whether I would have been bold enough, with all my experience by then, to walk around under a hanging load is a moot point, but it probably counts as one of my nine lives.

By 26 January the *Bransfield* was back in Mobster Creek, but as the sea ice was in poor condition Stuart, the captain, was keen to be off northbound again as soon as I reported that the AIS was operational. The installation was essentially complete, but

The Y-fronts in the sky – the AIS main transmitting antennae picked out with hoar frost, with two of the cabooses in the foreground. (Credit Ian Jones)

now the instrument itself was playing up, with lots of niggling little faults. My diary tells the story: 'We've got one more day and then we must go – it's so frustrating! So near and yet so far!' Tempers were getting ragged, but late in the day the machine finally decided to work, as my diary records, 'So in the end, and against the odds, we made it. We have a working system.'

I returned to the ship on 27 January with the intention that we should sail the next day, but the weather then turned really nasty and it was finally decided that Blandford would have to be evacuated, along with another man who had contracted something nasty in Montevideo, from which he sadly subsequently died. The weather stopped the personnel transfers, and then things got a bit tense for the ship, as the ice to which it was moored started to break up, requiring a hasty retreat out to sea. So the 29th was spent stooging about at sea off the creek waiting for a break in the weather. We finally took the two wounded soldiers off the ice foot by launch the next day, and we were homeward bound. We arrived in Montevideo for a visit to the meat market for a cold beer and a steak on 18 February. One positive aspect to having to hang about to do the medevac was that we were able to take three more days of data from the AIS home with us.

7

CAREER UP AND DOWNS
PLUS A SMALL CONFLICT

My path up the greasy pole in BAS had stalled with the appointment of Michael Rycroft. This was a significant frustration, because I saw myself more as an inspirer, manager and enabler of science than as a personal researcher; I was full of grand plans and ideas, but found the detail of research somewhat tedious. But over the coming decade I found great opportunities for masterminding big projects, and to develop a strong national and international reputation. Piggott had encouraged me in the late 1970s to get involved in international work and to build up a network of international colleagues. He had got funding for the ISSTP meeting in Boulder in 1976, which the AIS had come from. He then involved me in a working group of URSI,[71] called the Ionosonde Network Advisory Group (INAG) of which he was chair, taking me with him to its meeting in Geneva in January 1978. He also took me to the URSI General Assembly in Helsinki in August 1978, where I was invited to chair a new group called the International Digital Ionosonde Group (IDIG), charged with developing the modus operandi for a network of sophisticated digital sounders like the AIS. This was my first taste of such work, which I found I enjoyed. Piggott also encouraged me, and obtained the funds for me, to attend a series of meetings in Innsbruck associated with the COSPAR[72] meeting in May and June 1978. One in particular, held in the mountain village of Alpbach, was focused on the Antarctic and southern hemisphere aeronomy. Here, I got to know Professor Jack Gledhill, who was based at Rhodes University in Grahamstown, South Africa. And it was Jack who arranged for me to be invited the following year on an extended visit to South Africa.

The South African Council for Scientific and Industrial Research (CSIR) had a programme under the auspices of its National Committee for Geomagnetism, Aeronomy

---

71 The International Union of Radio Science (abbreviated URSI, after its French name, Union Radio-Scientifique Internationale) is one of 26 international scientific unions affiliated to the International Council for Science (ICS).

72 The Committee on Space Research (COSPAR) was established by ICS in 1958.

and Space Sciences (SANCGASS), which involved inviting an overseas scientist to visit South Africa, give a keynote lecture at the annual national conference of the Institute of Physics (SAIP), and visit various research centres around the country. At the end the CSIR looked for feedback from the visitor on the strengths and weaknesses of the South African programmes. This was an all-expenses-paid invitation, which included an opportunity to see some of the country. It was a significant feather in my cap to have been invited. However, as at the time apartheid ruled in South Africa, there was both an ethical and a political dimension to be taken into account before I could accept. Dick Laws and Roy Piggott were very supportive, while I saw it both as a scientific opportunity and a way of seeing apartheid for myself. But to be sure the visit would not violate any government guidelines the FCO was consulted. Consequently, I attended a briefing there. This turned out to be a lecture on how to avoid a honey trap (shades of my earlier strange experiences in BA), given by a gentleman who didn't really identify who he was or quite what his job specification was.

I headed to Johannesburg in early July 1979 for a visit that extended until early August, including the SAIP conference in Bloemfontein; Cape Town (including a visit to the Antarctic research vessel *S.A. Agulhas*); Hermanus (the geomagnetic observatory); Rhodes University; the University of Durban; Pretoria (the National Physical Research Laboratory of the CSIR); the National Institute for Telecommunications in Johannesburg; and the University of Potchefstroom. I also got to visit a deep gold mine (in the Orange Free State goldfields), and the Kruger National Park. I learnt much about the vexed politics of the country, the complexity of the racial divides, and the absurdities and horrors of the apartheid regime. I saw the stark contrast in outlook and beliefs between the two white tribes – those of English origin and those of Afrikaans origin – the one hoping for change, the other obstinately steeped in apartheid, and both unable to see that change was coming whether they liked it or not. I also made connections with key science leaders in South Africa, in particular Jack and Professor David Walker from Durban University. My connection with Dave blossomed greatly in the 1990s as apartheid was brushed aside and it became appropriate to develop major collaborations with South Africa (of which more anon). There were also some odd moments. The SAIP conference was at the beginning of the visit, and Bloemfontein – the capital of the Orange Free State, the heartland of Afrikaanerdom and, at an altitude of about 5,000 feet – is not a very welcoming place in winter. It was very cold, and the university student accommodation in which we were housed had no heating. I was nursing a nasty cold which quickly became worse. I managed to get through my presentations in good order, and then flew to Cape Town. I had been asked what I liked to do in my leisure time and had said playing squash and hill walking. So straight off the plane, still suffering from the cold (in both senses) I was taken on an arduous hike in the hills and then in the evening invited to take on the local squash champion. The outcome was never in doubt, but he was kind enough to let me win a few games.

There were two other notable moments in the trip. The first was a visit organized by Jack to the University of Fort Hare, which since 1916 had been the major academic centre for black Africans. It was then not actually in South Africa, but in the 'independent' state of Ciskei – another of the absurdities of apartheid, now thankfully long gone. It had a long and proud tradition of academic excellence,[73] but by then very little in the way of equipment or funding. The second was being taken by Dave Walker to a black African protest meeting in Durban where we all sang the freedom movement anthem 'Nkosi Sikelel' iAfrika' (Lord Bless Africa) with great gusto. I don't know to what extent my activities were being monitored by the security service, but they can't have been happy with that little episode.

In the autumn of 1979 I made an extended visit to Australia, visiting La Trobe University and the Australian Antarctic Division before participating in the IUGG[74] General Assembly, held that year in Canberra in December, where I gave an invited presentation. The Canberra meeting turned out to be seminal for the future of BAS ionospheric research, much as that in Boulder in 1976 had been. It was there that I was introduced to a new NASA proposal with the acronym of OPEN, Origins of Plasmas in Earth's Neighborhood. This was envisaged as a four-spacecraft project with a polar orbiter, an equatorial orbiter, a spacecraft aimed at the magnetospheric tail region,[75] and a fourth spacecraft sampling the solar wind streaming towards Earth. But the really exciting thing for me was that, uniquely for NASA projects up to that time, proposals from groups doing research from the ground and from theoretical space physics groups around the world would be invited to link with the space observations. I had a long talk to Don Williams (then head of the SEL in Boulder), who was a prime mover in the project, when I suggested that BAS might form one of the ground-based teams, and in particular we could investigate funding a transponder on the polar satellite which could be used to collect Antarctic data and feed it directly into the planned integrated OPEN scientific database. Don seemed much taken by the idea, so I wrote a long letter to Piggott describing not only what the BAS response should be to the OPEN proposal but what I thought the Antarctic community's response via SCAR[76] should be in terms of an integrated ground-based network of observatories, ideally delivering data to the OPEN database via the transponder. The letter also discussed what other ground-based facilities might be put forward, highlighting discussions I had held with Dave Walker and a new contact – Dr Ray Greenwald –

---

73 It played a very key role in creating a Black elite, many of whom went on to shape Africa one way or another: Mandela, Tutu, Mugabe, Kaunda, Nkomo and Tambo to name but a few.

74 International Union of Geodesy and Geophysics

75 The extended region of the Earth's magnetic field on the night side, which is created by the solar wind streaming past the magnetized Earth.

76 The Scientific Committee for Antarctic Research is another of 26 international scientific unions affiliated to the International Council for Science. Its remit is to initiate and coordinate international science programmes in Antarctica.

over the possibility of a joint project to put a VHF radar experiment in Antarctica. This was possibly my first meeting with Ray, but he was subsequently to play a very important part in my story. He was then at the Max Planck Institute for Aeronomy in Lindau, West Germany, from where he moved to the Applied Physics Laboratory (APL) of John Hopkins University in the USA.

Piggott would have got my letter just as he handed over to Michael Rycroft at the end of December 1979. Whether he shared its contents with Michael I do not know, but the fact that I wrote it is pertinent to what happened next regarding OPEN. Within the Atmospheric Sciences Division (ASD) we prepared a two-page summary proposal which we sent to NASA to indicate interest in OPEN. Preparation of this involved three ASD group leaders – myself, Dyfrig Jones and Andy Smith – plus Michael Rycroft. Importantly, our names were listed in that order on the proposal. Andy was a long-term BAS man like myself, whilst Dyfrig was a talented space plasma theorist who had recently joined BAS from ESA[77] (very sadly, however, he succumbed to a brain tumour within a decade). Dyfrig had invented a brilliantly catchy acronym (a very important part of any proposal, a good one carrying much more weight than perhaps it should): OPEN SESAME – OPEN Satellite Exploration Simultaneous with Antarctic Measurements. This outline contained the idea for a transponder, and offered the whole suite of BAS instrumentation from Halley Station, but did not dwell on the broader issue of international coordination of Antarctic measurements. We then put OPEN to one side, expecting to be invited to make a much more complete scientific proposal in due course. But instead in December 1981 I received a telegram from NASA informing me that OPEN SESAME had been selected as one of four ground-based proposals to participate in OPEN, with me as principal investigator (PI). I was also invited to the first team meeting, scheduled to take place at NASA GSFC[78] in mid-January.

I attended that meeting, giving a presentation on the BAS plans and making contact with the other ground-based PIs, who included Ray Greenwald. But when I got home I ran into a major controversy: Michael felt that as HoD[79] he should be PI, and took the view that NASA had only named me because I happened to be at the top of the list of proposers (though the list was not alphabetical). Dick Laws decided that Michael should be nominated, so contacted NASA to make the change. Interestingly, NASA was at first very reluctant to accept this.[80] I decided I should unilaterally withdraw from the project, but Dick would not accept that. It took the intervention of NERC and the British Embassy in Washington to shift NASA's viewpoint; I then became a co-investigator, with Michael as PI. But OPEN never really got off the ground as originally envisaged, and finally metamorphosed into a less grand mission called Global Geospace Science

77 European Space Agency

78 Goddard Space Flight Centre, Greenbelt, Maryland, USA

79 head of department

80 Telegram for the OPEN project scientist (J.K. Alexander) dated 18 February 1982 to Dick Laws

(GGS), still with ground-based and theoretical involvement. Ultimately I became the PI of the BAS contribution to GGS.

In the early 1980s my activities were many and various. I was staff side chair of the Whitley Council[81] and was chairing the BAS Computing and Electronics Working Group (and later the Computing Policy Committee), where I began shaping BAS computing strategy with Grahame Hughes. On the Whitley Council I became involved in health and safety policy and practice, and also in introducing a flexible working hours scheme – which made the lives of working couples with children much easier as well as giving all the chance to have a better work/life balance. My international commitments were expanding, plus there was a variety of UK external responsibilities, as well as managing the group and doing personal research. I wrote a popular article for *New Scientist* describing the AIS programme in 1981,[82] and a research paper on first results for *Nature* in 1982.[83]

Dick Laws encouraged me to take a sabbatical break overseas – possibly to give Michael a chance to get his feet under the table without my disruptive presence around. We organized a year at SEL in Boulder for me, and a position at the HAO[84] there for Helen. For a while this plan was a strong possibility, which could have led to us developing our careers away from BAS (that was at the back of our minds at the time), but it ultimately fell through, partly because of funding issues at SEL, and partly because our second daughter, Clare Helen, was born in November 1981. But we did get four months overseas in 1982, when I was hosted by Ted Rosenberg at the University of Maryland while Helen had a temporary position at GSFC. We took Helen's sister, Joanna, with us to help with the children. This was a very productive time for us both, which led on to greater things. I made strong links with the US network of ground-based Antarctic researchers, and the team at the National Science Foundation (NSF) that funded them, so in the years to come was often invited to attend their annual meeting in the USA. I also joined the American Geophysical Union (AGU) and regularly attended either its spring or its fall meeting until I retired. But perhaps most importantly this was the time when the seeds were sown for two more big ideas – coherent HF backscatter radars and automatic geophysical observatories (AGOs).

Ray Greenwald is a very talented engineer/scientist and a very likeable man. We hit it off very quickly. He had been using VHF coherent radars to study the E-region of the ionosphere, but realized that technology developments were making the combination of radio pulse coding married with digital signal processing applied to coherent backscatter at HF a very powerful approach for studying the dynamics of

---

81 The Whitley Council was the consultative body between management and staff side unions.

82 Dudeney, J.R. (1981) The ionosphere – a view from the pole. *New Scientist*, 91, 714–717

83 Dudeney, J.R., M.J. Jarvis, R.I. Kressman, M. Pinnock, A.S. Rodger and K.H. Wright (1982) Ionospheric troughs in Antarctica. *Nature*, 295, 307–308

84 High Altitude Observatory

the polar F-region. It had long been known that plasma irregularities in the F-region would backscatter HF radio signals, and that the irregularities themselves moved with the horizontal bulk motion of the plasma. Mapping these irregularities therefore gave a means to study the electric fields in the high atmosphere of the polar regions – themselves a key part of the coupling between the solar wind and the magnetized Earth. Ray had embarked on developing an HF radar to do this; key to its success was a very sophisticated antenna system he had designed, consisting of 16 horizontal log-periodic antenna very cunningly connected together to form a very narrow pencil beam, which could be swept over a wide azimuth to create a two-dimensional picture of the backscatter. In 1982, Ray was developing the radar to be sited at Goose Bay, Labrador, to look north into the polar cap.

I quickly realized that a unique experiment would be possible by installing a similar radar at Halley looking south, because the two fields of view would be conjugate[85] to each other over a very large area of the auroral oval and polar cap. There was then much interest in trying to understand the global coupling between the solar wind, the magnetosphere and the polar ionosphere (energy flow through geospace), and such an experiment would be very powerful, particularly if coupled with *in situ* spacecraft measurements. Ray and I immediately brainstormed the practicalities and planned how we might get funding. The US community was embarking on a new project – to develop a viable AGO which could operate year-round in Antarctica, running a variety of simple instruments. These would allow spatially coordinated ground-based observations under the field of view of the proposed radar. It turned out that the US programme was not suited to BAS logistics. Instead, with Dick Kressman's superb engineering skills we developed our own AGO, but not without controversy at BAS. So my time in Maryland proved a major stepping stone in my career. But of course for BAS the big event in early 1982 was the Falklands Conflict and its consequences for the long-term future of the organization, and hence for me and my grand plans.

Serious economic problems and industrial turbulence bedevilled the United Kingdom in the 1970s, and BAS was certainly not immune from the fallout. Our budget was under pressure as NERC tried to balance its books, faced with high inflation and falling government funding for science. The election of a radical reforming prime minister in 1979 determined to get the government finances under control and deal with the deep-rooted industrial unrest made this harder; BAS had to retrench to preserve the core mission. We also had the looming requirement to rebuild Halley Station (or withdraw from the southern Weddell Sea) because the station was deeply buried in the ice shelf, consequently becoming unsafe. BAS decided that the South Georgia research station, which also provided the government presence, would be closed. However, the

---

85 'Conjugate' here means that geomagnetic field lines originating in one field of view threaded the other.

FCO, for whom the political presence was crucial, would not agree to this. Finally, it agreed to fund a small permanent operation at Grytviken. This new arrangement was to commence on 1 April 1982.

On the broader stage, the British government had continued to attempt to convince the Falkland Islanders that their future lay with Argentina, though this policy had come somewhat unstuck because of the strong cross-party lobby in support of the islanders and the emergence of a nasty military junta in Argentina. Coupled with this was the retrenchment of British global military commitments, where defence of the Falklands was not seen as a priority. Consequent on this was the planned withdrawal of HMS *Endurance*, the ice patrol vessel and guard ship for the Falklands. The junta, with its own domestic problems to deal with, was thus emboldened to invade the Falkland Islands on Friday 2 April and South Georgia on 3 April, bringing the very short-lived FCO contract to a very abrupt end.

It is not my purpose to recount the story of the conflict – there are many books that do that – so I will limit myself to the impact on BAS, both short-term and long-term, and the consequences for me. For a short while on Friday 2 April, BAS probably knew more about what was actually happening on the ground in Stanley than anybody else. The *Bransfield* had just left there with its radio officer – Hugh O'Gorman – monitoring the FIBS (Falkland Islands Broadcasting Service) which continued broadcasting until it was overrun. He then relayed the story via Portishead Radio Station to BAS. So it was Dick Laws who was providing the government with a blow-by-blow account of the initial stages of the invasion. The ship ran for the safety of the Antarctic before being ordered to sail home, maintaining radio silence, without visiting any South

HMS *Endurance*, the Royal Navy ice patrol vessel. Its planned withdrawal from service was one factor that encouraged the Argentine junta to invade the Falklands.

American ports. In the afternoon Dick called all Cambridge-based staff together in the conference room to brief us on events, and what was likely to happen the next day in South Georgia. He rather dramatically announced that we would shortly be at war with Argentina. In retrospect this suggests that from an early stage he was privy to secret government planning.

On 3 April the BAS station at Grytviken was overrun after a brief firefight between a small detachment of marines landed there by HMS *Endurance* and the Argentine forces. The marines gave a very good account of themselves, shooting down a helicopter and severely damaging a corvette, before surrendering. They and the BAS personnel under Steve Martin's leadership were then taken prisoner before being repatriated to the UK, arriving home on 20 April. There were four field parties operating in South Georgia at the time, and they took to the hills, so were able to provide the military with valuable intelligence in the lead-up to the recapture of the island on 26 April.

April was a somewhat curious month at BAS. First there were lots of unusual visitors seeking detailed information ahead of the retaking of South Georgia. They got detailed briefings but sometimes appeared to ignore advice, consequently making life somewhat difficult for themselves in the early stages of Operation Paraquat.[86] We also immediately lost all direct communication with the BAS bases, since all traffic was then routed through Stanley. Dick Kressman, a keen radio amateur, very quickly set up his equipment at the BAS headquarters, and with remarkable alacrity we got permission from the Post Office to use it to contact our bases. It turned out this was not actually needed, as a relay via the US station at McMurdo was soon established. But it did demonstrate just how quickly red tape could be cut away in times of national emergency.

We also quickly got approval from high up to invest in satellite communications. This was just at the beginning of commercially available satellite systems for use on ships, and the system was provided by an organization called Inmarsat, based in London. It was relatively easy to install the system on the BAS ships, but we wanted the same for the bases. Here we ran into an administrative problem: Inmarsat was at the time supposed to limit its activities to provision of mobile systems. We managed to convince Inmarsat that Halley was like a ship, in that it was floating and moving, and we were thus allowed to install a sledge-mounted system there. Inmarsat was also prepared to accept a sledge-mounted system (nominally moveable) at Signy Island. So by the end of the 1982/83 Antarctic summer season we had voice communications via satellite to the ships and to Halley and Signy. The following year the other stations (Faraday and Rothera) were equipped likewise; by then the mobile restriction had been relaxed. Dick Kressman played a leading role in installing the systems – and was, I believe, the first person to suggest using fax as a means of communication over Inmarsat; this quickly

---

86 The British operation to retake South Georgia

became the normal means for passing messages, both official and personal, for BAS. He also was probably the first person to use the Inmarsat system to transfer digital data. From the beginning of 1983 he had a simple commercial software package in use to transfer AIS data, but the following year had written and installed his own bespoke system which he rather appropriately called Parrot. This allowed a magnetic tape of data to be copied directly from Halley to Cambridge very efficiently, hence removing the need to wait more than a year for the bulk delivery of tapes.

The main outcome from the conflict for BAS, however, was much more far-reaching. Mrs Thatcher decided that Britain should never be blindsided in the South Atlantic again, and that the way to do this was through a much-expanded BAS, with a much more robust scientific programme. She wanted Britain to be pre-eminent in Antarctic affairs, leading in the diplomatic forum (Antarctic Treaty) through world-beating science, with leadership also in SCAR. Our budget was thus effectively doubled overnight, and we were given a very large capital sum to revolutionize our infrastructure. This largesse came at a time of retrenchment elsewhere in government funding for science, so was not universally popular, not the least with the NERC.

In fact, from then on tension and enmity developed between BAS and NERC, which persisted for two decades thereafter over what became known as the BAS ring fence. It was never a satisfactory situation for BAS or NERC. NERC held the BAS purse strings, but found it had much less influence over BAS than it had over its other institutes. In any big strategic decision with a political dimension there was always the FCO (which provided no money to BAS) in the background, whose wishes would carry the day. For BAS it was very difficult to work for two masters – NERC and FCO – whose aims and priorities often differed fundamentally. So running BAS became much more complicated, as I was to discover during the last decade of my career.

The Antarctic Treaty parties had just successfully negotiated a major new convention – the Convention for the Conservation of Antarctic Marine Living Resources (CCAM-LR), which in spite of its name, is a very specialized fisheries management scheme as well as a conservation convention. Flushed with this success the parties moved on to attempt to negotiate a similar convention to cover Antarctic mineral resources. Consequently, the major thrust of the new funding went initially into marine biological science and economic geology. But such was the financial largesse that atmospheric sciences, meteorology and glaciology also saw significant benefits. Then there was the infrastructure programme. Over the next decade BAS had a major expansion of its home base in Cambridge – unofficially known as Galtieri Towers – accompanied by a new custom-built research vessel, the RRS *James Clark Ross* (*JCR*) to replace the *John Biscoe*; an expanded fleet of aircraft including a four-engined de Havilland Dash 7; and a major development programme at Rothera, providing a 900-metre gravel runway, a wharf, fuel storage facilities, a hangar for the aircraft and a state-of-the-art marine science and diving facility. Also along the way came money to replace Halley III.

There is an odd postscript to this story, an event which occurred on Saturday 18 July 1992, by which time I was a division head. Margaret Thatcher, now out of office, was keen to see what BAS had achieved with all the largesse she had bestowed. She and Denis made a private visit for afternoon tea, hosted by the members of the Directors' Committee. My diary records:

> It went very well, about 1 hr of presentations and another 45 minutes of informal tea and biscuits. Nothing like their stereotypes. Sharp and well read, but with prejudices showing. Very keen on the Americans (ie not on the Europeans), not keen on particle physics or CERN, couldn't get on with Hawking's book!

Her key interest was in our current research addressing climate change. There are many views on Mrs T, but one thing is certain: she saw the importance of science and the need to base policy upon it.

8

HALLEY AGAIN

By the early 1980s Halley was no longer fit for purpose. Its floor level was about 15 metres below ground, and the Armco tubes containing the buildings were becoming seriously distorted by the pressure and movement of the surrounding ice. Access was becoming difficult and unsafe. It was also slowly approaching the edge of the ice shelf, where it would ultimately depart to sea in an iceberg. It was time to build a new station. That work began in the 1982/83 season at a new site some 18 km from the old one. The new structure had been made weatherproof by the end of that summer, but the move of all the science facilities and commissioning of the station was to be carried out the following year. My task was to plan and oversee the move of the science on behalf of the division as well as carry out the very significant task of moving the AIS with all its cabooses, ancillary equipment and antennae. To do this I took my trusty team of Dick Kressman and Mike Pinnock.

The new station would be buried, but a new concept had been employed. Instead of Armco tubing, the outer shell – still a horizontal tube – was made from wooden panels joined together with flexible seals. This allowed a much larger diameter tube to be built at realistic cost, into which two-storey buildings could be inserted. The resulting structure was therefore much more spacious than any previous (or indeed later) Halley Station, although its plumbing was still rudimentary, with no flush toilets. It was expected that once the structure was buried and under pressure from all sides, the flexible panel joints would allow minor distortions to be taken up without impacting on the buildings inside whilst adopting a sound circular cross-section. That was the theory – but there was a fatal flaw which manifested itself almost as soon as the station became operational.

I had been invited to visit the Brazilian Institute for Space Research (Instituto de Pesquisas Espaciais, INPE) in São Paulo in November 1983 on my way south as a consequence of the Brazilian government deciding to develop an Antarctic atmospheric sciences programme. Dick accompanied me to spend two days in São Paulo in discussions on possible collaborations. I also gave a scientific seminar plus a general talk on BAS science. We were very well treated, with all local expenses covered, including two nights in Rio while we waited for the *Bransfield* to collect us for our onward voyage. We had time to do what tourists do in Rio – take the cable car to the top of Sugarloaf Mountain, visit the Corcovado, and take a stroll along the Copacabana admiring the scantily clad young ladies. Two such beauties approached us, smiling enticingly. One reached out and grabbed my private parts – but I grabbed my wallet before the other one relieved me of it, we smiled at each other, and we went on our separate ways. Dick and I joined the ship for a spectacular departure from Rio – surely one of the most stunning natural harbours in the world.

Arrival in Stanley at the beginning of December brought me back to a place I knew well, but one that had suffered the upheaval of invasion, war and liberation. No longer could one freely roam the countryside. Large areas were still suspect because of unexploded ordnance, and there were many carefully delineated minefields to be aware of. So the first port of call was the minefield information office, to get a minefield map. It turned out that some of the finest local beaches were now too dangerous to visit, including my favourite fishing spot, Black Point on the Murrell River. But now there was a new dimension to any hike – the local battlefield sites. Stanley was still a bustling military enclave (this was before the Mount Pleasant military complex was completed), but the military tried to make their presence as unobtrusive as possible, and there was a wonderful new vibrancy to the town.

Next, we visited South Georgia southbound, spending a long and tedious time on the relief of the biological station at Bird Island. Long and tedious because there is no protected anchorage, meaning the ship has to anchor in Bird Sound where there is normally a swell, making make cargo operations lively to say the least. Then on to Grytviken, now a military encampment with obvious signs of the firefight – the crashed helicopter, a landing craft on the beach, and more areas where it was unsafe to go. Our main purpose was to recover as much BAS equipment as possible. We then headed to Signy Island to carry out the annual relief before turning south into the pack ice. Christmas was celebrated on the ship, hove to for the day in the ice. So it was certainly a white Christmas. And I had my goodies box from Helen and my girls to enjoy. Over the years my family have provided me with some pretty splendid Christmas boxes, containing taped messages (and songs) from the girls, drawings, books and various sweetmeats. They were always a source of admiration and envy when I sat down to open them – and sometimes to share some of the edible contents.

Although the redeployment of all the science programmes was a substantial under-taking, overall it was a more relaxed project than had been the AIS deployment, mainly because we had more time, arriving off Halley on 27 December and not leaving until 14 February. However, 'relaxed' is a relative term, since the relief period required 24-hour working (in two 12-hour shifts), then 10- or 12-hour working days without a break. But with that level of effort we were able to declare the new base operational, and close the old one, over the weekend of 11/12 February. During the period of 24-hour working we were hot-bunking. I shared a bunk in Halley III with a chap who had a craving for chocolate

– as I found out one night when I awoke to the feel of something sticky in my hand; it turned out to be a slowly melting bar of chocolate secreted down the side of the mattress. Sleeping at Halley III was an unusual experience, the floors now sloped sufficiently towards the bedhead (where shelf and reading light resided) that it was necessary to have that as the foot end – unless one could cope with the rush of blood to the head. Also, as the ice slowly pressured the Armco tubing, the fastening bolts would occasionally shear with an alarming bang. None of this helped that much to get a good night's sleep.

The journey home involved calls again at Signy, Bird Island and Grytviken. At the latter we had an opportunity to take a day of R&R, go for a hike etc. But this went a bit awry when two men set off on an over-ambitious walk and became lost in fog. They had not returned by nightfall, so a SAR[87] was mounted at first light, organized by the ship's first officer, in which I participated. It all turned out well, with only self-esteem seriously injured, but both men were very lucky to have survived, having broken most of the rules for successful mountain walking – including getting separated. Our final landfall was at Montevideo, where the meat market provided a very welcome change from the ship's diet, which by then was rather boring.

While at Halley we took the first steps on a long road which led to the installation of an HF backscatter radar there. One uncertainty with such a development was whether the complex antenna system could be built and operated successfully on a floating, moving ice shelf. So we brought one of the antennae to Halley, erected it and left it for the radio operator to test over the winter.

Halley IV started falling apart under its own weight as soon as it was erected. The first manifestation was a sagging of the panels at the tops of the tubes. This continued until the panels had fallen down to press on the roofs of the internal buildings. They had thus to be dug out of the surrounding ice, cut up and removed, after which the void had to be maintained by a constant programme of ice mining. It was very quickly apparent that a new base would be needed – and needed soon. And thus another chapter in my career unfolded.

The first half of the 1980s was a fruitful time for me. Several lines of personal research resulted in published papers, and I also contributed to a major coffee table-style book, *Antarctic Science*.[88] I continued to work with Ray Greenwald on the plans of an HF radar at Halley associated with his new installation at Goose Bay. There was also computer policy for me to deal with, and my national and international committee work to do. Then in March 1986 I was sent south at very short notice (10 days), and in strict secrecy, by Dick Laws, to close Base F, to save money. But it turned out that NERC had not got final approval from the FCO, which the FCO was not inclined to give, so just as the ship approached the station the mission was aborted. I ended up having

---

87 Search and rescue operation

88 Dudeney, J.R. (1987) The Antarctic Atmosphere. In *Antarctic Science*. Ed. D.W.H. Walton, Cambridge: Cambridge University Press, pp 192–247

a pleasant visit to the station, with everyone but me having no idea why I had come south. Still, it provided an opportunity to see the huge infrastructure developments in the Falklands and to use the newly established airbridge between the UK at RAF Brize Norton and the Falklands via Ascension Island, as well as indulge in a nostalgia trip.

But now a new and unexpected responsibility came my way. By 1985 it was clear that a replacement for Halley IV was needed urgently, along with new thinking to provide a viable long-term solution. Though surface cabooses had been used in a small way at Halley in the past, the AIS deployment was a really major demonstration of their value. We had built a self-contained village, fully fit for purpose and had successfully kept it free from burial by incorporating simple jackable legs to keep the cabooses above the snow surface. We had also demonstrated that the whole village could be moved and re-established during the 1983/84 summer period. My group reliably came up with innovative solutions and delivered them on time and cost, particularly through the skills of Dick and Mike. Halley was then solely the purview of the ASD, making it appropriate that the division be engaged in planning the new station from the outset. I was the natural person to lead that engagement, but I believe that Dick Laws was looking to release my broader talents, so I was quickly expected (by him at least) to be involved in the research and planning for the whole rebuild, not just to represent ASD's needs. This did not find favour necessarily with the head of the Administration Division, but a small, initially informal, group made up of the head of logistics (Paul Whiteman), the head of building services (Big Al Smith) and I came together in spring 1986 to explore alternative building options.

At first little credence was given to the idea of a surface base; instead another buried tube was envisaged. But by early June 1986 Paul and I were talking about the possibility of a surface base and whether he, Big Al and I should investigate what other folks' experience had been. At the time the German Antarctic Programme had built a small surface base on the Filchner-Ronne Ice Shelf. It was built on a platform which itself was jacked around 2 metres above the surface (much like our science village but on a bigger scale), and had been designed by Christiani & Nielsen (C&N), a German company. At the other end of the spectrum the US military had built gigantic jackable radar stations – part of the Cold War early warning system – on the Greenland icecap, weighing in at 3,000 tons or more. Their technical support came from a US Army research laboratory – the Cold Regions Research & Engineering Laboratory (CRREL) in Hanover, New Hampshire – and an American civil engineering company, Metcalf & Eddy. We agreed there was merit in the surface option, and by chance I had a meeting with Dick Laws later that day so could sound him out, and I was encouraged to develop a plan. It probably was not the most tactful thing to have done, since I was cutting across the command structure of the Administration Division – in retrospect I recognize that I was a bit like a bull in a china shop those days; impatient and focused on doing the best job possible and expecting everybody else to be completely onside (which they sometimes were not). I suppose I was somewhat arrogant and did not suffer fools gladly, but I could at least be relied on to produce the goods on time.

Over the next few weeks Paul and I drafted a plan for visits to Germany, the USA and the Greenland icecap. Our memo, entitled *New Halley – Survey of Surface Building Possibilities*, dated 8 July, was the subject of a meeting on 15 July attended by the director, Michael Rycroft, Charles Swithinbank (head of the Geoscience Division), John Bawden (head of Administration), Paul, Big Al and me. My diary records that at this meeting 'an interesting change in attitudes – from there being no possibility of building a surface base a few months ago, to a real consideration of the possibility of a surface base'. Our proposed fact-finding mission was approved. The visit to C&N was relatively easy to arrange, and took place at the end of July. There we met Detrick Enns, the general manager. Detrick turned out to be a very able and charming man with a very good grasp of our engineering needs and of the English language; after a day with him, I was starting to believe that a jacked station could be a real possibility. The visits to CRREL and to the radar station on the Greenland icecap took longer to organize because of the issues of security clearance, not finally taking place until the autumn. We went first to CRREL, where we met Malcolm Mellor, a senior scientist, an ex-Yorkshireman, and a very pleasant and capable man; and Wayne Tobiason, an impossibly tall American engineer, who gave us a very informative overview of the various building techniques the US Army had developed for use in the polar regions. Mellor introduced us to his experimental wind tunnel, which used electrically activated clay particles to simulate snow and so allowed simulation of snow drifting around structures. We also visited the contractors who had done the heavy work at the radar sites in Greenland, Metcalf & Eddy, located in Boston. It was clear that M&E took its technical guidance from CRREL, so it was CRREL that we should concentrate upon.

The trip to the icecap followed, with only a day back at home before setting off again. Getting there involved flying to Copenhagen, then a commercial flight to the US military base at Søndre Strømfjord (now Kangerlussuaq) on the western side of Greenland and 60 miles north of the Arctic Circle. Given the lengthy hassle we had suffered getting clearance, we found that security was essentially non-existent – nobody required us to show any ID, and we had the freedom to roam where we liked. We spent a comfortable night in the officers' mess before being flown by a Greenlandair ski-wheel Twin Otter up onto the icecap, to DYE-3.

'A remarkable day!' This is how my diary entry for Saturday 4 October begins, and a remarkable day it certainly was. My diary continues:

> Here I sit at DYE 3 at an altitude of 8250 ft on the Greenland Icecap. It is just magic! The feel and the crunch of the snow under my feet and the glisten of the sun on the sastrugi is such a pleasure to me – there is no doubt but that the polar regions own my soul.

The station itself was breath-taking, engineering on a majestic scale, weighing in at 3,000 tons, multi-storey, topped by a 60-foot-diameter geodesic dome housing the radar; the whole structure was jacked 45 feet above the snow surface and all supported on ice foundations. Photographs did not do it justice, particularly because it sat on a featureless snow plain with nothing to give a sense of scale. But its environment was in many respects similar to conditions at Halley: about 1.5 metres of snow accumulation annually, and when we were there a temperature of around minus 20° C. We were welcomed by station supervisor Jay Klick, who was an old polar hand, having wintered in the Antarctic at the American stations of Palmer and Siple. He gave us a tour inside and outside, and I was amazed how crude and outdated the radar displays were – though maybe I shouldn't have been, since the facility was by then upward of 30 years old. We descended about 80 feet below the surface inside one of the legs to inspect the footings in the ice on which the station stood. A remarkable place – but on a scale of size and cost way outside our needs and budget. An ancillary building which particularly interested us was a pontoon-mounted garage, which was regularly re-sited, and subsurface fuel storage in bladders housed under Armco arches. Both these concepts were used at the new station – a garage and a two-storey accommodation building (for use in the summer months) both pontoon-mounted, as well as underground arches for bulk fuel storage.

The US radar station (DYE-3) on the Greenland icecap as it looked during our visit in October 1985. There were four DYE radar stations in Greenland, part of the Distant Early Warning (DEW) line. With the collapse of the Soviet Union, and given the expense of maintaining the stations, DYEs 1 to 3 closed in 1988, and DYE-4 in 1991. The figure leaning on the left-hand foundation block gives a sense of the incredible size of the structure. (Credit Al Smith)

We stayed the night on the station – it turned out to be a special party night (a Danish evening) with lots of good food and lots of toasts. We three caused a bit of a stir by doing the gash after the meal. Then next morning we were flown back to Søndre Strømfjord by Twin Otter. The flight lasted about 90 minutes and since it was a lovely day and we were the only passengers, the pilot took us muskox spotting in the valleys on the edge of the icecap. It was very exciting zooming down between the peaks at no more than 200 feet above the valley floor, and we found the muskoxen.

Back home it fell to me to write a detailed report and set of recommendations[89] for the next meeting of the group considering the next steps (by now referred to as Halley V group). There were actually two meetings, one on 21 October, which just involved BAS staff – Dick Laws, John Bawden, Big Al and me – and another, two days later, involving people from NERC as well. At the first, I led on presenting our findings and recommendations. My diary for that day says 'we agreed that we should go for a surface base and that we should follow up with wind tunnel tests at CRREL'. At the more official meeting two days later, my diary records that I gave the main presentation and that it seemed 'as though the case for a surface base has been accepted by NERC'. The pace now picked up quickly, with C&N invited to carry out a design study with sufficient detail to set a budget, and Malcolm Mellor at CRREL asked to start carrying out snowdrift testing on representative models of the buildings proposed by C&N. So in early December I was back for a very short visit to CRREL to agree the guidelines for the wind tunnel studies. Then back to visit C&N in early February 1987 (this time with John Bawden) to assess progress, and to CRREL again in late February with Big Al Smith to participate in the wind tunnel tests on representative models of the new base. I found these studies intellectually fascinating, and believe I contributed significantly to the design of the tests and their interpretation. A pretty clear story emerged: the building should be long and thin, single-storey, and oriented with its long axis at right angles to the wind. For the size of structure that we had in mind the base of the building needed to stay approximately 5 metres above the surface.

The finale to all this was a series of meetings at BAS in March 1987, which involved Enns and Mellor and at which the final decision was taken to go for a surface-jacked station. Having played a significant part in swinging BAS in the direction of a jacked station, and made a strong contribution to its design and layout, I then stepped back somewhat to concentrate on other projects, though I continued to lead on planning for the science facilities and for the overall layout of the station.

---

89 This was entitled 'Survey of Design Options for the Rebuild of Halley', dated 13 October 1986.

9

A HOLE IN THE SKY

The appearance of the hole in the stratospheric ozone layer over Antarctica in the 1980s had a profound impact on humanity and the way many of us viewed our place in the ecosystem of Planet Earth. It wasn't just an interesting piece of environmental chemistry to raise the excitement level for scientists, otherwise out of sight and mind over the frigid continent. It wasn't just a topic that got environmentalists a bit hot under the collar, or caught the attention of politicians. No, it hit just about all of us smack between the eyes, making it clear that the world was not infinite, and humanity could wreak serious havoc by accident or design. It was a moment when we all started to get the message that humanity could not just continue to consume the planet's riches – we had to learn to conserve and protect our home.

Why did it have such an impact? Well, first it was not a small perturbation; for a short period in the Antarctic springtime effectively all the stratospheric ozone over the Antarctic disappears, allowing very harmful fluxes of solar ultraviolet radiation to reach the ground. Second, it didn't occur over industrialized regions, but rather over an isolated, pristine and protected continent. Third, it was almost immediately obvious that it was entirely human-made, arising from our reliance on halocarbons as refrigerants, fire retardants and aerosol propellants. It generated international action, and agreement to ban the use of halocarbons, at a pace not seen before. From the publication of the first paper in May 1985 it was just four years before the Montreal Protocol[90] came into force.

So why did such a large perturbation in O_3 occur, and why over the Antarctic? Halocarbons had been seen as wonder chemicals because they seemed to be stable and inert. However, with time the gas released migrated up into the stratosphere, where solar UV light degraded it, releasing chlorine. Chlorine acts as a catalyst to facilitate the breakdown of two O_3 molecules into three O_2 molecules. This was already recognized as a potential threat to the ozone layer, which absorbed harmful solar UV radiation,

---

90 The Montreal Protocol is an international treaty designed to protect the ozone layer by phasing out the production of numerous halocarbons responsible for ozone depletion. It was agreed on 16 September 1987, and entered into force on 1 January 1989.

allowing life to flourish. However, the effect was at first thought to be at the few per cent level. Even so, the USA invested in a global monitoring programme from 1978 using a satellite, Nimbus 7, carrying an instrument to monitor ozone – the total ozone mapping spectrometer (TOMS).

But it was not TOMS that discovered the hole. It was discovered by an obscure trio of physicists led by a real eccentric working at BAS in my division! Joe Farman was one of a kind, a throwback to the Victorian era when observatory physicists made measurements of all sort of things without really feeling the need to publish much, concentrating instead on making the most accurate and internally consistent measurements they could. He did not suffer fools gladly, and, as mentioned earlier, was normally to be found surrounded by a cloud of evil-smelling smoke from his pipe, the density of which was directly proportional to his distaste for the person to whom he was talking. He could be an exasperating colleague, but I quickly learnt to listen to what he had to say, and had a deep respect for him. The second member of the team was Brian Gardiner, a man with a very sharp mind and a wicked sense of humour, who had wintered with me when I was base commander. Brian was also somebody it was wise not to dismiss. Jon Shanklin was the third member – he was then a junior staff member tasked with curation and analysis of the datasets that Joe's group generated. And the instrument that they used? – a Dobson ozone spectrophotometer, invented in 1924 by physicist Gordon Dobson. Very simple in concept – it measures the ratio of the intensities of two wavelengths of UV light falling on the Earth, one (UVA) which is not absorbed by O_3, and another (UVB) which is absorbed, and which is more harmful to humans. The ratio measures the total column content of O_3 above the instrument. Simple in concept, but more challenging in practice to make an internally consistent data set over a long period of time. Here Joe and his team excelled. They meticulously calibrated and cross-calibrated the Dobsons in use at Halley and Base F to give very robust long-term trends in ozone. A Dobson had been at Halley since 1957, so by the early 1980s there was a quarter of a century of high-quality data available. But there was almost no output of research papers using those data, and there was a question mark over whether the cost of maintaining the Dobson was justified.

In, I think, early 1984, Jon had done some time series of the monthly average ozone concentration over Halley for those 25 years, and had noticed a startling effect, sufficiently extreme to be suspicious. Joe had at first sent him away rather dismissively, so he came to see what I thought of it. What it showed was an accelerating decline in ozone in the Antarctic spring starting in the 1960s – but not a *few* per cent. This was massive! I was stunned, and told him that if correct, it could be the most important result that BAS had ever produced. He persevered with Joe and Brian, finally convincing them that they should take note. They did, but to their credit said nothing and published nothing until they saw what happened in the next Antarctic spring. After which, their paper[91]

91 Farman, J.C., B.G. Gardiner and J.D. Shanklin (1985) Large losses of total ozone in Antarctica reveal seasonal ClOx/NOx interaction, *Nature* V 315, pp. 207–210

Mean October ozone at Halley

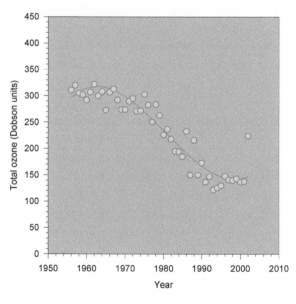

Above: The discoverers of the ozone hole: (from left) Joe Farman, Brian Gardiner and Jon Shanklin with a Dobson ozone spectrophotometer, used to determine stratospheric ozone concentrations. (Credit Chris Gilbert, UKRI/BAS)

Left: The monthly mean total columnar content of ozone for October above Halley Station plotted for a period of nearly 50 years, as measured by a Dobson ozone spectrophotometer, showing the dramatic decline of ozone from the 1960s onwards. (Credit Jonathon Shanklin, UKRI/BAS)

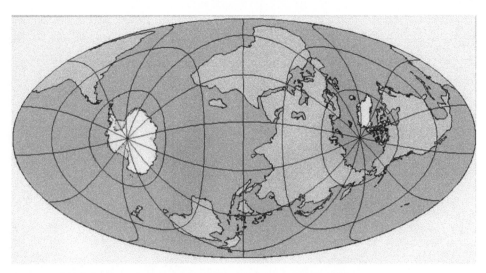

An unusual global map projection which highlights the geographical differences between the Arctic and Antarctic regions that underlie the reason for the ozone hole being so prominent over Antarctica. (Credit UKRI/BAS)

in *Nature* describing the result burst on the world like a nuclear blast, and changed it for ever. Joe was very bright, so that first paper, even though it didn't get the chemistry right in detail, pointed the finger firmly at chlorine from halocarbons as the culprit.

So why did it take three obscure guys at BAS to make the discovery when Nimbus-7/ TOMS had been making measurements for the previous seven years? Well now, nobody had been expecting ever to see such low values for the total column content as were happening over the Antarctic, so the data validation algorithm for the TOMS data had a lower threshold – below which the data had been discarded as bad data! As soon as the Farman et al paper hit the streets, some very embarrassed scientists in the USA recovered the discarded TOMS data and very quickly generated beautiful maps of the spatial extent of the hole.

Now is a good time for a digression to explain why this dramatic phenomenon appeared over Antarctica and not elsewhere. Fundamentally, it comes down to geography. The Arctic is a pole-centred ocean surrounded by continental land masses, whereas the Antarctic is a pole-centred continent surrounded by ocean. As a consequence the surface albedo of the Arctic is quite variable in space and time, while that of the Antarctic – highly energy-absorbent ocean surrounding a highly reflective continent – is not. Over both poles there is a strong pole-centred stratospheric circulation from west to east, forming a vortex. In the Antarctic autumn, winter and spring this vortex becomes very stable, because there are no major variations in topography and albedo to disturb it. In the Arctic, however, both topography and albedo variations cause the vortex to be weaker and more unstable. Effectively, the Antarctic vortex seals the stratosphere

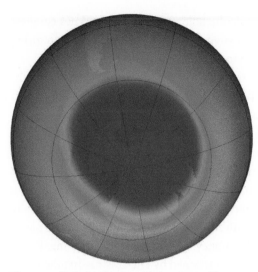

The ozone hole for October 1989 as imaged by NASA from space. (Credit NASA Ozone Watch)

off from lower latitudes in winter; when the sun sets for winter the temperature plummets to such low values that ice particles form onto which the chlorine attaches providing a platform for the chemistry to occur – but energy is needed to set off the reaction:

$$2O_3 + Cl + h\upsilon \rightarrow 3O_2 + Cl$$

That energy is provided by the sun rising in the springtime, driving a photochemical reaction, and effectively all the stratospheric ozone within the vortex is consumed. As summer approaches the vortex weakens then breaks down, allowing an influx of ozone-rich air from lower latitudes to replenish most of the lost ozone. There is a similar effect in the Arctic, but much less pronounced.

BAS has dined out on the ozone hole discovery ever since, but the subsequent story of BAS research did not really add to the glory, or indeed push the science on. Instead, the focus shifted very quickly to the US Antarctic Program. There were two reasons for this. The first was structural; to be successful, Antarctic science requires a lot of support infrastructure and planning. But over the years the BAS approach had settled into carrying out mostly in-house, long-term programmes with relatively little scope for making sudden major shifts in response to startling new developments. Ours was a top-down, command-driven programme highly optimized to get the most efficient use of the logistic capability available. We were very good at operating long-term environmental studies, and hence maintained daily measurements of ozone for 30 years.

Conversely the US programme was entirely reactive, driven bottom-up by the peer reviewed grant applications which came through the door in rather broadly defined science areas. Each general science area had a program director at the NSF Office of Polar Programs, who organized the allocation of funds. The resulting portfolio was generally short term and less coherent. John Lynch was then responsible for their programme of polar aeronomy and astrophysics. He had sufficient autonomy to give ozone research priority in the next annual grant round and so engineered for 1986/87 a major multi-institute study – the first National Ozone Experiment (NOZE-1). This was followed the next year by NOZE-2, a multi-million-dollar undertaking which deployed the NASA

ER-2 high-altitude research aircraft to sample the hole *in situ*. BAS could not compete with this. But the US funding model was not good at supporting long-term monitoring studies such as the one that had enabled BAS to find the hole in the first place.

The second reason that BAS did not respond more comprehensively was, sadly, down to personalities. The chemistry between Michael and Joe was even worse than that of either of them with me. So the sort of relationship in which Dick Laws might be persuaded to allow risks to have been taken or radical approaches adopted did not exist. Moreover, Joe always found it easier to see the deficiencies in a plan rather than its strengths. There was initial reluctance to recognize the importance of the BAS data – it took practically a divisional strike for the ozone result to be included in the paperwork for an external review in 1985 of the division's work. Even Dick Laws was not initially seized by its importance. I had a meeting with him to discuss my group's future plans, in which I said I was expecting much of the money in the division to be immediately diverted into ozone research, and was somewhat stunned by Dick dismissing the result as just a bit of serendipity. He soon changed that view.

Many years later, in April 2004, I was invited to Penang, Malaysia, to give a presentation on developing a sustainable scientific strategy for Antarctica.[92] In this paper I made the comment:

> Of course there is also the serendipity factor to be allowed for. Nobody could have guessed Antarctica would turn out to be the most important natural laboratory for observing and understanding the impacts of humankind's releases into the atmosphere of halocarbons. But it was there that the ozone hole appeared in such dramatic fashion. It is arguable that all the money spent on Antarctic work would be fully justified if that were the only result that ever came from it. This is because of the paradigm shift it caused, not just amongst scientists, or amongst politicians, but in the awareness it gave to the person in the street of our potential as a species to wreck our environment.

Even though there have been other discoveries from Antarctica equally important for the benefit of humankind, I stand by this statement.

Meanwhile I was concentrating on Halley matters, computing policy and staff side issues, plus as much science as I could shoehorn in. But big changes were afoot in BAS management and organization. Dick Laws was about to retire, marking a big change in itself. On top of that, a NERC science and management audit[93] had concluded that the

---

92 Dudeney, J.R., (2005) Developing Sustainable Scientific Strategy for Antarctica, In: *Antarctica, Global Laboratory for Scientific and International Collaboration*, A. Tan Shau-Hwai, Z. Yasin & M. Mansor (Eds), Pub: Academy of Sciences Malaysia ISBN: 983-9445-13-8, pp. 15–16

93 Science and management audits were the NERC's way of checking on the performance of its institutes – the audits involved a group of independent, often international, experts giving the organization the once-over for science quality, output and management practices.

current management structure was unwieldy and provided insufficient opportunities for advancement for middle management staff – such as myself. It was therefore decreed that the three science divisions (Atmospheric, Geological and Life Sciences) should be split to create six new ones, and there would also be a new Administration Division, all of them led by a division head at senior principal level (one grade above my grade). Also, along with Dick, the deputy director (Ray Adie) would be retiring. In principle this seemed good news for me – but as it turned out, it was not.

The Geological Sciences, led by Charles Swithinbank (about to retire) was split, to create a Geology Division and a Geophysics Division. Glaciology was combined with Meteorology and Ozone Research to create a new Ice & Climate Division (an interesting and powerful regrouping), while what was left of my division became briefly known as the Space Science Division, which described it well, and then Upper Atmospheric Sciences Division (UASD), which did not. The enforced name change was because NERC did not like the idea of its remit so obviously containing space sciences. Ironically, some years later as a result of a shake-up of the research council remits, NERC did end up funding all ground-based near-Earth space sciences.

Life Sciences was split into two, creating a Marine Life Sciences Division and a Terrestrial and Fresh Water Life Sciences Division. Several of my peer group were able to compete for these new jobs, but there was little for me, as Michael remained in charge of the rump of ASD. I was encouraged strongly by Dick to go for the new head of administration, but it went to the incumbent, to see him out until his retirement at the end of the decade. Dick also encouraged me to bid for the Ice & Climate job, but I quickly learnt that I was blocked from the shortlist by somebody very senior in NERC because I (along with Grahame Hughes) had been such a thorn in the side of the NERC Computing Service in its battle with Dick over representation at BAS; Dick had put us in the firing line, where we had made the mistake of being right in front of some very senior NERC staff. There was one memorable meeting in which one side consisted of the senior folk from NERC concerned with Computing, IT Services and Engineering, and the other was Grahame, Dick and me, with the meeting chaired by the chief executive, John Bowman. He declared at the start that there would be no record kept. Just as well I suppose, because Grahame in particular relentlessly and logically destroyed the other side's arguments, and the meeting was notable for the only occasion that I ever saw Dick lose his temper. Little wonder that I was sidelined (if only temporarily) whilst it was made clear to Grahame (deniably of course), that he would never get further promotion unless he toed the party line – and he never did, so never did – which for a man so able was inexcusable.

However, I was able to protect my position and group within the new division by getting a new group structure approved by Dick Laws before he left. So UASD ended up with two groups – Geospace Research Group led by me, and Space Plasmas Group led by Dyfrig Jones.

Dick Laws retired at the end of April 1987, and was replaced by David Drewry, who had been director of the Scott Polar Research Institute (SPRI). He was a glaciologist with a particular interest in radio echosounding to determine the thickness of ice sheets. I was feeling somewhat exposed; I had been protected by Dick in my relationship with Michael, and so needed to form a strong relationship quickly with David. This did not appear easy at first, as my relationship with Dick had been forged through necessity and a strong sense of mutual respect. But thankfully David soon got the measure of the situation. Dick meanwhile began a new career as master of St Edmund's College, Cambridge, and one of his first acts was to invite Helen to join the fellowship, so I continued to meet Dick regularly through that connection. Helen remains a fellow to this day. She first became a tutor, then deputy to the senior tutor, followed by five years as senior tutor. In 2017, when she retired, she was honoured, as mentioned earlier, to be elected a life fellow in recognition of her outstanding service to the college

There was another opportunity for promotion, the post of deputy director, as Nigel Bonner was about to retire. Even though it would have meant a grade skip for me I thought I had a good chance, and David Drewry assured me that I would be shortlisted. It was not to be, though – not while I was in such bad odour with the NERC chief executive. The job went instead to a contemporary, a marine biologist, Barry Heywood. So, seeing no promotion prospects within BAS for the foreseeable future, I decided to make a bid for Drewry's old job, director of SPRI, which was now up for grabs. I was shortlisted and interviewed, but the job went along the predictable path of being offered to the internal candidate – something I became heartily grateful for as my career developed in the 1990s.

Even though I was frustrated at the time not to have got the advancement I sought, I had very challenging and exciting projects afoot. The HF radar project with Ray Greenwald was really cutting-edge stuff; the science was really important and the engineering of the system was new and innovative, and if that was not sufficient there was the whole issue of whether we could engineer such a sophisticated system to make it viable on a floating ice shelf. Along with this I foresaw the need for a network of ground-based observatories with magnetometers (amongst other things) laid out under the vast field of view of the radar. This could only be done by developing automatic geophysical observatories. So now it is time to tell the remarkable story of the HF radar and the AGOs.

10

EXCITING NEW PROJECTS AND A NEW OPPORTUNITY

The HF radar project was unique in its time because it allowed the interactions between the magnetosphere and polar ionosphere to be studied simultaneously in both polar regions over a very large spatial area at high time resolution. It did this by measuring the drift of disturbances in the ionosphere to estimate electric fields generated through the magnetosphere/ionosphere interactions. Crucially, we could do this at the opposite ends of the same geomagnetic field lines as they came down to the ionosphere in the Arctic and the Antarctic. This is important, because a disturbance on the sun rattles the whole of the Earth's magnetosphere, in turn rattling both polar regions of the ionosphere. But the effects in each hemisphere are subtly different depending on the exact nature of the solar disturbance. Our experiment could study those differences directly. The acronym PACE (Polar Anglo-American Conjugate Experiment) was therefore both catchy and fully descriptive of the purpose. Both it and a very artistic logo were dreamt up in a splendid rural establishment in Maryland, the Olney Ale House, with Ray Greenwald and his team over some beer in 1986. Coupling the PACE measurements with those from spacecraft making simultaneous observation created an incredibly powerful experiment. To start with, there were just two radars, one at Goose Bay, Labrador, and the other at Halley, but ultimately PACE spawned a truly outstanding network of radars in both hemispheres with overlapping fields of view, known as SuperDARN[94] (of which more anon).

The logo for the Polar Anglo-American Conjugate Experiment, invented over some beers in the Olney alehouse. In a completely irrelevant coincidence, my mother was born in the small Bedfordshire village of Olney. (Credit for original artwork APL/JHU)

94 Super Dual Auroral Radar Network

PACE was jointly funded by NERC and the National Science Foundation, which funded APL. The proposal was peer reviewed by NSF, receiving outstanding results, making the funders minded to approve it. The official start day was Tuesday 27 May 1986, when Ray and I met in Washington with the head of the NSF Department of Polar Programs (DPP), Dr Peter E. Wilkniss, to formally sign the deal. We expected to sign a Memorandum of Understanding (MoU), drafted by me and Ray, but the DPP, on advice from the State Department, went shy on that, so the MoU became a more informal agreement between us two PIs. I did not warm to Wilkniss, but the objective was achieved, and we could steam ahead. Luckily for me Mike Pinnock had already agreed to lead on the engineering and installation. He had already assisted to install and commission the Goose Bay radar, and several years later helped the South Africans to build a radar at their SANAE[95] Antarctic station, with a field of view overlapping that of Halley.

My first introduction to the radar came through a week-long visit to Goose Bay in Labrador. Goose Bay is a tiny community in the middle of nowhere, which a large number of the world's travelling population fly over without realizing it. It is home to a Canadian military base used by several NATO air forces, and is a key navigational landfall for transatlantic airlines. In June 1987 there were fast jets from the Luftwaffe, the RAF, the USAF and the Dutch air force there, with surprisingly little security. As I was being hosted by the USAF I had the run of the station, and access to USAF vehicles to access the radar site in the forest nearby. We even got to climb all over a USAF F-16. So I got my first opportunity for hands-on operation, which proved very useful for framing my thoughts on how the two radars might operate together effectively. It also allowed me to spend time with a key member of Ray's team, Kile Baker. Kile was Ray's software engineer as well as being a pretty good scientist himself. We had agreed that he should be part of the installation team at Halley in the coming (1987/88) summer season. Kile and I found we both had a taste for dim sum, so we would often contrive thereafter at the fall AGU conference in San Francisco to meet in Chinatown to indulge our shared pleasure.

Deployment of PACE at Halley was as big an engineering and logistical undertaking as the AIS had been, with a similarly constrained timeframe set by the relief period (nominally about four weeks by then). PACE had a very large antenna array, consisting of 16 large log-periodic antennae mounted horizontally on 15-metre towers, arranged in a line 250 metres long, precisely aligned and spaced to millimetre accuracy, to create an integrated array. By cunning phasing of the feeds to each antenna, a narrow beam 4 degrees wide was formed, and swept through 16 positions covering about 52 degrees of azimuth to create the field of view. Building such a system on flat solid ground was a relatively easy undertaking. Doing it on a floating ice shelf was something else. We

---

95 South African National Antarctic Expedition

decided that the only practical way to accurately align the towers was to mount each one on a small sledge. We would first level and groom a 250-metre patch of the snow surface using a snowplough/blower. Then, as each tower was erected, it could be brought into alignment using small nudges with a big hammer and a couple of theodolites. As with the AIS, we housed the electronics and computers in a jacked caboose. There was one serious uncertainty: the test antenna had performed well – but just how well would the beam form when sitting on an ice shelf floating in a salty ocean? The only way to determine this was to try it.

My group also had to reinstall the AIS, which had been shipped home in its container the previous season for renovation and a computer upgrade. So we were in for a very busy season, with a big team required. Under my direction, Mike would mastermind the PACE deployment while Dick oversaw the return of the AIS.

So there was much preparation during 1987 to be ready in time. But I was still heavily involved in computing policy, health and safety, and staff/management relations, along with group management and personal research. The planning and design of the AGOs was also under way. The latter began to cause some serious disagreements over who should lead this project. Michael wanted to have titular control, with the title of principal investigator. This was not, however, something I could accept, as all the intellectual input lay in my group. The argument rumbled on for several months, brought to a surprising end towards the end of 1989, as we shall see.

The PACE deployment took me away from home for three months over the winter of 1987/88. This was hard on my family; I departed on 26 November and was not home until 24 February, so was away for Christmas and New Year, and my older girl's ninth birthday. It was now possible to phone home occasionally via a satellite phone, but it was outrageously expensive, so calls were perforce kept short and infrequent. It was very hard to be separated from Helen and my girls, but it was much harder for them; at least I was very busy and in my element.

The trip started with the airbridge to Stanley via Ascension Island with Mike, Grahame Hughes and Dick. Grahame came to install a general-purpose computer at Halley. We had two days in Stanley eating superb food in Sparrowhawk House – fresh wild sea-trout and fresh local mutton – before boarding *Bransfield* and sailing for South Georgia. Then on to Signy Island for a couple of days, where my diary contains the following observation:

> My abiding impression of Signy Island – which has been reinforced for every visit except my first in 1966 – is of crouching in a heaving launch or scow with cold wet hands in cold wet gloves, with an icy wind beating snow in my face, waiting to take my turn at jumping for the pilot ladder to get back on the ship. Today was NO exception!

From there we headed eastwards for the South Sandwich Islands, to skirt the Weddell Sea pack ice before turning southward and into the ice, finally arriving off the Brunt Ice Shelf after some ice-bashing on 21 December. The voyage was long but not tedious, as there was much planning to be done to coordinate all the summer activities – and that was my role, to be in overall control with my old colleague Big Al, who was leading the building and maintenance work (including the preparations for Halley V). I had also brought my guitar to amuse myself, if not others, with my attempts at Bach and Villa-Lobos.

I moved up to the base the next day, and was shocked at how badly it had deteriorated. My diary says it all:

> What a change in four years! The floor slopes alarmingly – there is the continual background sound of water dripping on the roof, and the occasional drip of water into bowls and buckets placed strategically around the building. Basically the wall has been forced down all along one side of the building as the tube panels pressed down on the roof. The base excavated the snow and roofing panels during the winter to create a cavern over the building which has arrested the damage – but that is all. If ever a justification for the jacked station was needed, one evening in the lounge of the current one did the job!

Work started immediately with two 12-hour shifts per day, and no stop for Christmas. Christmas dinner (Christmas breakfast for the other shift) consisted of what were quickly named carpet burgers (because of their interesting texture) and beans, but I was able late on Christmas Eve to open my Xmas box. This was a delight, with all sorts of tasty treats, homemade cards and pictures from the girls; there was even a tape of messages and music from them. A lovely yet heart-rending moment. I treated myself to a truffle a day until 8 January, when I treated myself to the last two, because that was the day we finished the outside work for PACE and became independent of the weather.

Such was the pace of work that by the evening of Christmas Day Dick was able to report that the AIS was powered up. Boxing Day was particularly trying for the PACE team. Kile Baker had his first baptism of fire (actually ice) that day. We were assembling antenna towers in the underground garage, but had run out of supplies – all neatly stacked outside in wooden crates. Our problem was that there was a full gale with heavy blowing snow. The first job was to get a hand-line rigged for safety because visibility was just a few feet and it was too easy to become disorientated in those conditions. I was out opening boxes – snow goggles icing up and being in constant danger of being tumbled by the wind – while it drifted the boxes in as fast as I could dig them out. But we stuck at it, and as a result got four of the sixteen towers assembled that day. I do not think poor Kile had ever experienced such a day before. New Year's Eve was declared a holiday for ship and base, but we kept working. My diary notes 'This is my seventh

Erecting one of the 16 antennae for the PACE radar. I am the figure with the red helmet.

The completed PACE array at Halley sitting on a floating ice shelf.

New Year's Eve in Antarctica and my third at Halley. How many more will there be, I wonder?' (A lot more as things turned out.)

By 6 January we had completed the erection and alignment of the antennae and by 10 January we switched the system on for the first time. It worked! The beam formed as required, giving some nice initial data. We officially opened the radar on the next day with Kile and I cutting a tape across the steps to the caboose while champagne was served to all and sundry – nicely iced at the air temperature of a balmy minus

13° C. There was still much to do, but I was now able to leave the teams to complete commissioning PACE and the AIS while I concentrated on broader management issues. A diesel mechanic had suffered injuries requiring a medevac, with a replacement needed for the next winter. There had been a seriously disruptive individual during the previous winter, requiring me to convene a disciplinary hearing which had ultimately resulted in his resignation. As an aside, the medevac was the first conducted by the UK entirely by air, with the help of an RAF C130 from Stanley, so the patient was in RAF Ely Hospital just five days after the accident. I was also pretty busy coordinating with the BC, Big Al and the captain of the *Bransfield* to get the rest of the programme done and the ship northbound. We made our first coordinated measurements with the Goose Bay radar before I boarded the ship on 21 January – worn out, as were the rest of the team after four weeks of continuous work. Boarding the ship brought its own interesting moment; the fast ice had vanished, so the ship just stuck its bow against what was left of the snow ramp and I had to climb up a free-hanging rope ladder over the bow. It was a lovely calm sunny day, but looking down at the icy blue/black water beneath me gave me a real shudder. Still, we had achieved what we set out to. It was a stupendous moment to stand on a floating ice shelf and admire what we had built.

We headed northbound on 23 January for Montevideo via Signy and South Georgia. There was just one less-good thing; Grahame had been diagnosed early in the month with high blood pressure and angina. He was subdued for a while but soon back to his larger-than-life style – a style that, as mentioned earlier, sadly saw his heart explode in a peaceful Welsh pub garden 12 years later. But his summer was very successful, with the installation of the micro-Vax computer networked around the base, and even networked back to Cambridge via the Inmarsat link when required. This was key to the success of PACE, giving field staff the opportunity to analyse data and return promising material to Cambridge in near real time (instead of once every 12 months).

The journey back was uneventful except that another one of my nine lives got spent. We were unloading oil drums at Bird Island – a notoriously difficult place, because the ship rolls and pitches at anchor in Bird Sound. On returning to the ship the launch got tangled up between the anchor chain and the bow, with the swell sucking us hard up against the hull under the bow. Only full power and lots of pushing against the hull as the launch started to list dangerously popped us out between chain and bow into safe water before the launch was swamped. By then I had taken a green one[96] down my front and removed skin from my palms on the hull, so I was not in the best of moods when we finally got on board.

There was a lovely moment when we arrived at Montevideo. Pat Lurcock, who was travelling home to be married after spending two years at Halley as a beastieman, saw his wife-to-be, Sarah, waiting on the quayside. He was quickly put over the side before

---

96 big wet wave

Kile Baker and me cutting the ribbon on the stairs of the PACE caboose to officially declare the radar operational.

we were cleared by customs to be cheered as they ran towards each other along the dock, just like a scene from a romantic movie. There were three days in Montevideo, enough time to enjoy the meat market again and visit some more upmarket restaurants as well. On the first evening I was invited to a buffet dinner at the house of the British defence attaché, Roger Garnett, in the company of the ambassador, E.V. Vines, and his wife. There I spent time explaining the ozone hole to Mrs Vines while grazing on the excellent food. I had to sing for my supper, though, the next day because Mrs Vines needed a brief on ozone for a talk she was giving, and actually visited the ship to acquire it. Then it was northbound – but not homewards. Instead I headed to Goose Bay, via Rio, Toronto, Montreal and St John's, Newfoundland, where I had an overnight stop. I arrived in Goose on 16 February to step out into a temperature of minus 29° C and 20 knots of wind. The purpose was to make coordinated observations using the two radars with Ray. We had a week there in temperatures mostly around minus 30° C. It was a magic time, with superb data to enthuse about, cross-country skiing in the forests around the radar, and fabulous auroral shows to be overwhelmed by. A quote from my diary for 16 February:

> After dinner back to the radar. Temperatures well below minus 30° C but with less wind. Saw a fabulous aurora. Started as a quiet arc, but then became very bright and active, an awe-inspiring sight with the snow squeaky cold under one's feet. Put me in mind of Robert Service poetry. Once seen never forgotten!

What my diary does not record but is burnt into my memory is that Ray and I stopped worrying about the radar and just lay in a snowdrift with a beer, each living the event unfolding above us.

Then finally it was time to head home to my family via a short stop in Toronto, to be collected from the airport on 24 February at Heathrow, 13 weeks after I had left them.

As the 1980s drew to a close I had a very fulfilling, exciting and diverse professional life even if I hadn't managed to progress further up the greasy pole. The PACE radar was a world-class research tool, with other teams/nations keen to participate. But there was now the AGO project starting to take shape. There were two separate but linked threads, acquisition of AGOs tailored to our needs, and taking a leading part in developing plans for an international AGO network in Antarctica. The US AGO programme was led by Lockheed for the NSF. I visited San Francisco in September 1988 on my way to Tasmania for a SCAR meeting for general discussions and to see how the US system under development by Lockheed was progressing. At the SCAR meeting I was heavily involved in discussions about AGO technology and various national plans. This resulted in me proposing that SCAR should establish an international programme to coordinate the siting of AGOs to best address the scientific questions, to coordinate the baseline set of instruments to use, and to establish a central database to hold the data. Having stuck my head above the parapet I was, of course, tasked with drafting a proposal to be considered at the next SCAR meeting in 1990 – this proposal I named Agonet.

Having seen what other nations had planned, I decided we should design our own AGO matched to our science needs and logistical capabilities. Working with me, Alan Rodger played a key role in making a detailed scientific case. Meanwhile Dick Kressman turned his prodigious skills to designing the overall system. I took an oversight and coordinating role, whilst also helping Dick through brainstorming sessions and dealing with the logistical requirements, which had to fit within BAS capabilities. A particular limitation was that our AGO had to be deployable by Twin Otter, which constrained both size and weight. Besides all that, I was continuing developing the broader case for Agonet.

Collectively we had much experience of what could be made to work in Antarctica and what could not. We also started from the principle of working with the environment as far as possible. The high plateau of Antarctica is a very hostile place, where the mean annual temperature is around minus 55° C with a minimum of minus 70° C or below. But there was one aspect that we could potentially tap – the wind. The behaviour of the surface wind on the polar plateau is unique in that it is controlled not by large-scale atmospheric pressure systems but by the slope of the terrain. Basically the cold surface inversion layer of air slides down the slope under gravity at a speed set by the slope and in a direction set by the combination of slope direction and Coriolis force. The resultant wind is called a fall line, or inversion, wind. A slope of just 3 metres in a kilometre produces a constant wind of around 12 metres per second in a constant direction. Just ideal for running a wind generator. Also in the summer, solar panels will provide energy for several months. So our AGO power system utilized wind generators and solar panels to charge lead-acid batteries. We chose cheap off-the-shelf electronic components housed in a small caboose to be kept jacked above the surface. Since this meant the electronics would need to be kept warmer than freezing, the caboose was highly insulated, and any spare energy was used to provide heating for it. We decided to provide a thermal lock consisting of half a ton of water in 24 plastic containers (two-thirds full to allow for expansion on freezing). When there was insufficient power to run the system it would close down in an orderly fashion, but as the water slowly froze it would hold the temperature at around freezing for quite a long period, so that when power became available the system quickly became operational. This approach worked amazingly well. We also knew from our experience with surface cabooses at Halley that, perhaps paradoxically, heat sometimes needed to be dumped out of the caboose even at very low outside temperatures. So power from the wind generators was switched to external heat dumping as necessary, which proved vital for successful operation. Once operational it was not unusual in the depth of winter for there to be a temperature differential between the inside of the caboose and its outside of upwards of 100° C, with the internal temperature a balmy plus 30° C. The caboose was designed in prefabricated panels sized to fit through the cargo door of the Twin Otter.

It took two years to develop the first prototype, partly because we made meteorological measurements at the first field site for a whole year using a simple well-tested automatic weather station (AWS). These data allowed Dick to optimize the thermal insulation needed, the size of wind generators, the size and pointing direction of the solar panels, the amount of water and the details of the controlling software using a bespoke computer simulation. Consequently, we had a lot of confidence in how the first prototype would perform before it was deployed. Two prototypes were deployed in January 1992 – one as an accessible testbed at Halley, and the other on the Recovery Glacier at approximately 77°S (given the designations A76 and A77 respectively). Three more operational stations were deployed: one each in January 1995 (A80), January 1996 (A81) and December 1997 (A84). They proved highly reliable, with the higher-latitude stations (A81 and A84) running continuously without any data gaps though a complete year. A real *tour de force* for Dick.

But the AGO programme was not only highly successful technically; it also ushered in a big change in my circumstances in BAS. Throughout 1989 Michael and I had been at loggerheads over leadership of the AGO programme. I was unhappy because the amount of intellectual effort and innovation I and my team were putting into the project meant that we should retain leadership. I dug my heels in – perhaps I should not have done so, but I did. The matter was taken up by the deputy director, Barry Heywood. A key characteristic of Barry was his direct manner. He didn't let matters fester. In fairly short order a new position was identified for Michael by mutual agreement in the university – and on 9 January 1990 I became the acting division head. I worked as 'actor' until 27 September, when I was interviewed for the post and awarded it. And thus my career took a new path, as I became a full member of the BAS management team.

11

THE EARLY 1990S, CAREER ON THE UP

The 1990s started really quite well for me – promotion to head of division – with an exciting and challenging job that I had waited a decade for. Also, super data was flowing from the PACE radars, AGOs were under way, and the new surface station for Halley was taking shape. At home Helen, whilst still on 'soft money' at her department, had found a new sense of place and belonging at St Edmunds College, whilst both our girls were seemingly happy and doing very well at school. I had joined the senior management team: Director David Drewry, Deputy Director Barry Heywood, Head of Marine Life Sciences Andy Clarke, Head of Terrestrial Life Sciences David Walton, Head of Ice and Climate Sciences Liz Morris, Head of Geophysical Sciences Peter Barker and Head of Geology Mike Thomson. I therefore became a full member of what was then called the Directors' Committee (or DC for short).

The early 1990s were a time of great development in BAS. The construction of the new Halley Station had commenced in the 1989/90 summer season with a small team left to occupy it during the 1990 winter to carry out the internal fitting out. The keel of the new ship, the RRS *James Clark Ross*, was laid in April, and it was launched in December that year. The BAS headquarters was undergoing major development, and at Rothera (Base R) we had embarked on a very large expansion of capability – a 900-metre gravel runway, a large hangar, a fuel storage facility and a wharf big enough to take our ships. The purchase of a modified four-engine Dash 7 aircraft was in hand, plus plans to redevelop the biological station at Signy Island. All of this was part of the Falklands Conflict dividend. Only Base F (now known as Faraday) was not in line for redevelopment. Once again its whole future was in question: it was highly valuable as a monitor of natural and anthropogenic changes (it was already showing a possible signature of global warming), but otherwise it was not a platform for the exciting new projects that both my division and the Ice & Climate Division wanted to pursue. So closure was under discussion – but so too was the possibility of offering it to another nation. Change was afoot in the administration with John Bawden retiring, to be replaced by Frank Curry who joined us from the Ministry of Defence. I quickly developed a great respect for, and friendship with, Frank.

On the international stage I became vice chair and then chair of the SCAR working group on Solar Terrestrial and Astrophysical Research (STAR), whilst continuing as chair of the Interdivisional Working Group on Antarctica in the International Association for Geophysics and Aeronomy (IAGA). I had also become (finally) the BAS PI in the NASA OPEN mission, now re-scoped and renamed the Global Geospace Science (GGS) Mission. So life was very full and rewarding.

The new Halley Station was scheduled for its first operational winter in 1991, though the old station would stay open until the following summer when the bulk of the science programmes would be moved. But I planned to get PACE moved in 1990/91, so Mike Pinnock joined the *Bransfield* southbound from Stanley in November, charged with masterminding that effort. I planned to visit the station in my new capacity with David Drewry, Frank Curry, John Bawden and John Hall (BAS field operations manager). We were expecting to join the *Bransfield* in Stanley in early January, after it had made one voyage into Halley to get the summer season started. But early in December half of its main electric motor burnt out, leaving it reduced to half-power and stuck in heavy ice, having not yet reached Halley. By some strange irony, we had all been celebrating the launch of the splendid *JCR* in Newcastle just two days before. But now all plans for going south were thrown into doubt. Three days later, however, the trip looked likely to be back on; we would join HMS *Endurance* in Stanley to be taken to Rothera, and from there be flown to Halley, to arrive after the *Bransfield* had got there on 22 December, to commence the annual relief. So I found myself flying via the RAF airbridge from Brize Norton to the Falklands on 31 December, my daughter Lizzie's 12th birthday. Not the best choice of days, but at least I was at home for Christmas. For me, New Year arrived somewhere over the Atlantic Ocean at 41,000 feet travelling at 510 mph.

We had three days kicking our heels in Stanley before departing on *Endurance*. Here I had the first of many encounters with Mrs Burgle. Alexandra Burgle, née Shackleton, is Sir Ernest's grand-daughter, known to all and sundry as Zaz. She was travelling as a guest of the captain. Our plan was to visit Base F on our way to Rothera to continue our deliberations on its future. The Navy has a way of doing things, and on this occasion rather than take the ship there it was decided that we would all be flown in from 50 miles or so north in Lynx helicopters. Thus we had a splendid trip, launching from the north end of the Neumayer Channel, flying down it and then through the Lemaire Channel – 'we' being David, Frank, John Bawden, John Hall and me – getting there in time for lunch. We had two and half days ashore, which I found very pleasant and relaxing, even though we were there to assess whether or not to close the station. The Navy way brought the visit to an abrupt end, with the weather deteriorating. The ship

Boarding the Twin Otter for the flight to
Halley; Brian Newham in the foreground.

was leaving, and it was up to us to get out to it a couple of miles off the station. This made for a very bumpy ride to the ship and another cold and slippery pilot ladder to negotiate. Poor David Drewry mistimed his attempt and so got soaked to the waist. I was very grateful that the BAS boatman (Russ Manning) who took us out was ex-Special Boat Squadron – he needed all his skill that night in the swell that we encountered. I worked with him subsequently in the Antarctic tourism industry, after I retired.

We arrived at Rothera on 12 January – and what a huge transformation since my last visit, in 1977. Then it had been just a small traditional fids base where the BAS aeroplanes operated from a snow skiway some miles away on the ice piedmont.[97] Now it was a major complex with a 900-metre runway under construction, a hangar that could take all the BAS planes at the same time, and a fuel farm. We were to be flown to Halley in the Twin Otters, along with some essential cargo. The flight to Halley was, however, 910 nm (1,686 km) by the shortest route. So the aircraft carried an extra 'ferry' tank in the fuselage and consequently had a reduced cargo capacity – and even then it would be taking off at an overall weight of 14,500 lbs. Your normal airline operation this was not. I was rostered on the first flight with the ingoing Halley Base commander, Brian Newham. There would just be the two of us plus 800 lbs (360 kg) of essential cargo.

We set off in overcast conditions on Sunday 13 January and were quickly in cloud. The long slow climb-out was somewhat unpleasant as we crested the Antarctic Peninsula in icing conditions with big lumps of ice breaking off the propellers and the wing leading edges, to bang into the fuselage beside us. Later we were forced to descend through the cloud out over the ice-choked Weddell Sea to escape the icing. The contrast between that and the 'normal' world is summed up by my diary entry written at the time;

> What a scene of desolation! Back in icing conditions. The contrast between this and the thought of Helen and the kids tucked up cosy in bed is stark. What the hell am I doing here!?

This was before GPS was readily available to navigate us safely there, so we came down to 500 feet for the last 60 nm or so, flew on until we encountered the cliffs of

97 an ice-covered strip of coast

the ice shelf, and then turned left. Luckily, left was the right way to go, and finally what little there was to see of Halley IV above the surface hove into sight. We landed in the small hours of Monday in white-out conditions. Definitely a flight that counts as 'marginal' in my book.

I spent a week at Halley IV, but now in a very different capacity. No more getting my hands dirty on project work; now my role was much more managerial and strategic. The station was in a very poor state structurally, but also there had been serious personnel issues through the winter. The winter BC had been unable to assert his authority over a small group of

WHITE-OUT CONDITIONS

A white-out is a very peculiar meteorological condition. It is not, as many people think, a blizzard. It occurs when there is an even and complete overcast above a snow surface. Light then bounces back and forth between the snow and the cloud to completely remove any shadows. The visibility can be perfect, and any non-snow feature – a mountain or a matchbox – will be visible as if floating in a featureless white world. With no colour or contrast, a white-out is extremely dangerous – it would be possible to walk over a snow cliff edge without even knowing it was there. Landing a plane in such conditions is a challenge to say the least.

strong-minded and disruptive individuals. One team member, in the thrall of the disruptive folk, was being subjected to emotional and possibly physical abuse, with alcohol playing a very big part. His mental condition gave considerable cause for concern. We decided on medical repatriation and offered any support he might need when home, but sadly a few years later he died in a traffic accident. This was possibly the worst individual case I had to deal with in my entire career with BAS. My diary for 21 January 1991 sums up the winter at Halley IV as 'really terrible – nasty and demeaning'. And the atmosphere persisted, with an untidy and slovenly attitude, with little inclination by base members to carry out necessary communal tasks. The incoming winter base commander – Les Whittamore – had a formidable task ahead of him to get the station back on track for its final year. (He managed this handsomely, and went on to have a successful career in BAS logistics.) It was therefore a great joy for me to head 11 km or so across the shelf ice to the brand spanking new Halley V, to see my dream come true: the external work on the station had been completed the previous summer with a small wintering team left to carry out the internal fitting out. The whole atmosphere was different on the station, with morale high and folk much more motivated.

On what turned out to be the last day at Halley V, I had a grand day out with a flight south to service the AWS deployed the previous year at the first planned AGO site (77.5°S 23.9°W, 1,500 metres altitude) to provide weather data to hone Dick's AGO simulator. The AWS was quickly sorted out, and we enjoyed a picnic lunch in glorious

My dream come true! The main living platform of the new surface station, Halley V.

weather at minus 12° C. But this trip was notable for two other reasons. It marked my first steps (but not my last) onto the great East Antarctic Icecap. It was also the first (but also not the last) time I got my hands on the controls of a BAS Twin Otter. I was sitting in the right-hand seat and suddenly found I had control to fly us back to Halley, a flight of about an hour and a half, of which 30 minutes was in cloud so I got to practise my instrument flying skills. I was allowed by the real pilot to position the aircraft on the downwind leg before the landing, and then follow through with him on a zero-contrast landing. 'Magic!' is how my diary describes the experience. Quite what the director, who was sitting in the back, thought when he saw my hand going up to adjust the throttles for our approach is another story!

Then suddenly it was rush, rush, rush to get the ship on its way to Cape Town. So the senior team boarded it and we sailed on 27 January – but with only half engine power and bad sea ice we went nowhere much. We were south-west of the Stancomb-Wills glacier tongue, a barrier across the shore lead[98] and one against which the pack ice got pressured. Rounding the Stinky Wills, as we called it, was a challenge at the best of times, and this was certainly *not* the best of times. To cap it all we had only 25 days' fuel endurance, having graciously given some to the German ship *Polar Stern* (we got it back, though, a few days later). After a few days of going nowhere, it was time to start thinking about the unthinkable – the ship stuck here for the winter – and what we might do about it. Plans and counter-plans were voiced while we swanned around in a small lead of open water, joined strangely enough by a large school of whales, also presumably waiting for a break in the ice to be on their way. Finally, after nine days, the director decided that he, John Bawden, and I should leave the ship and fly back to Rothera, leaving Frank on board with the crew. This felt a bit like the rats deserting the sinking ship to me, but in truth we didn't have anything to contribute on board; our

---

98 a narrow passage of clear water through the frozen ocean between the shore and the pack ice often created by an off-shore breeze

The *Bransfield* stuck in pack ice off the Stancomb-Wills Ice Stream (seen in the background), otherwise known as the Stinky-Wills because of its habit of disrupting operations.

place was back home, getting on with our jobs. My diary shows that I agonized about whether to insist that I stay, but the entry concludes 'if I stayed what use could I be? Only another mouth to feed and a body to wash – I have no really relevant skills to aid this ship out of the ice'. So the ship stuck its nose against the ice and on 5 February we were unceremoniously lowered by ship's crane onto the ice to be whisked off by Otter, back to Halley IV. At my retirement do 15 years later, Frank presented me with a picture he had taken of the 'rats departing'.

But then on leaving Halley IV we had a problem getting airborne, as the plane was well over normal max take-off weight and the snow surface was very sticky with fresh wet snow. After several attempts, the only way to get the nose ski unstuck was for the three of us to climb into the tail compartment to make the plane tail-heavy, then zip back to our seats once airborne. Towards the end of the flight over the southern end of the peninsula we got into good weather. Again my diary, written as we flew the last 90 miles, says it all: 'Clear, low sun angle, a majestic awe-inspiring sight. A rare privilege – and to think I am being paid for this!' There was another flight from Halley the next day bringing three more rats. The following morning we travelled by Twin Otter to the Chilean station on King George Island, to be hosted by the Chilean Air Force for a night and then flown in a C130 to Punta Arenas, and from there home via Santiago and Paris.

A magic moment. The view from the right-hand seat of the Twin Otter as we fly northwards towards Adelaide Island (the island in the far distance) with the magnificent vista of the Southern Antarctic Peninsula laid out before us.

Thankfully the ice finally allowed the ship to escape into the open sea around 17 February, but there followed a difficult few hours in heavy seas when the other half of its main motor stopped working. But finally it made port safely in the Falklands on 21 February.

In 1991/92 season much of the new infrastructure was coming online: the *JCR* made its maiden voyage, and the gravel runway at Rothera, together with the hangar, the fuel storage facilities and the wharf there were all commissioned. Also the science facilities were re-sited at Halley V. For the first time I was not there to oversee this move. Instead I had entrusted this to Alan Rodger, assisted by Dick Kressman. Not only was the main living accommodation a jacked structure, but the two science divisions operating at the site each had their own laboratories on jacked platforms. The UASD one was called the Space Sciences Building (SSB for short – we didn't advertise its full name to NERC!). It was subsequently formally named the Piggott Building. It was completely self-contained with its own diesel generators, water melter, offices and labs, so it was the emergency shelter in the event that the main building became uninhabitable for any reason. Dick also deployed the two prototype AGOs, one as a development test bed at Halley, and the other at the first field site named A77 (since there was no discernible feature there to provide a name we used its latitude, and also for subsequent AGO sites).

The science move went exceedingly well, Halley IV was closed on 19 February, and the new station began its first fully operational winter on the 23rd. BAS also proceeded with the purchase of the Dash 7 aircraft, with grand plans to have a ski/ wheel conversion designed for this aircraft. A large amount of money was expended on this, but it became clear that the plane would have to operate with a fixed rather than retractable undercarriage; the former would so degrade the aircraft's performance that it made no sense. But we did have an extra-large cargo door designed and fitted, plus long-range fuel tanks. BAS had suddenly gone from a band of happy but under-resourced amateurs to a very major, if not pre-eminent, player internationally.

In the early 1990s science funding in the UK was not particularly bright. The BAS budget was, however, protected in cash terms at least by the afore-mentioned ring fence. This meant that none of the BAS budget could be cut by NERC, or indeed redeployed by it to shore up other parts of its operation. Sadly, the other parts of NERC were taking real financial cutbacks – including redundancies – which caused resentment because of the lack of freedom for NERC to move BAS money to what it saw as higher priorities. The FCO always had the final say on BAS funding, and its priorities were often quite different from those of pure blue skies research as espoused by the research councils. An interdepartmental committee, the BAS review group – whose members came from the OST (Office for Science and Technology, the government agency in charge of the science budget at the time), FCO, NERC, BAS and Treasury – oversaw the long-term strategy and financing of BAS, and the group was chaired by a senior official at the OST.

But even though our budget was protected, there were two serious factors that were starting to cause significant financial tension for us. The first was the costs of completion and operation of all the major new infrastructure, which were, predictably, significantly higher than planned. The second was driven by the need to account for the emerging new governance regime in Antarctica. The Environmental Protocol to the Antarctic Treaty (also known as the Madrid Protocol) had been signed in 1991, requiring wide-ranging environmental protection, and banning mineral prospecting and extraction. It did not come into force until 1998, but Britain moved quickly to enact its requirements in UK law as the Antarctic Act 1994. I will discuss the treaty and protocol in more detail in Chapter 15; suffice to say here that the impacts were many and various. The impact on the BAS geology and geophysics programmes was immediate. Part of the Falklands dividend had been to bolster research into the economic geology and the opportunities that mineral extraction might offer the UK. The Geology and Geophysics Divisions had consequently grown quite significantly. Economic geology ceased overnight, and not only that, but every geology/geophysics project had to be individually permitted by the FCO to ensure that it did not stray anywhere near 'prospecting'. This made the work of the scientists much more onerous than it would otherwise have been. So the two divisions entered a period of retrenchment, ultimately leading to them being merged in late 1992 under the leadership of Mike Thomson.

The protocol contained strong environmental protection measures, one of which required that parties remediate any sites that they had abandoned. For the UK this became a major potential cost driver, because of the large number of stations that had been built since 1944 when Britain had first occupied the continent. Also, stations that were currently in operation or planned would have to meet much higher environmental standards than hitherto. Consequently, we faced a significant retrenchment to cover the extra costs of both the infrastructure and the requirements of the protocol, as well as providing some headroom for new projects. The strong preference of BAS was to close Signy (Base H) and Argentine Islands (Base F), then concentrate our resources around the new infrastructure, Halley and Rothera. There were real advantages in consolidating the biological work hitherto done at Signy in new custom-built facilities at Rothera, whilst at Base F much of the work was routine monitoring – very important, particularly so for the long-term climate record – but something that might well be automated.

Even closing these sites would not be easy, firstly because the protocol required a complete clean-up and removal of the structures if a station was closed, although there was a short-term option of mothballing. The only other alternative was to declare a site a Historical Monument – but that would require maintenance and curation of the monument. Secondly there was the political dimension: BAS was expected to maintain a specific size of footprint in Antarctica to preserve the UK's standing in the Antarctic Treaty, CCAMLR and SCAR – that was, after all, why we had been given the ring-fenced funding. Moreover, there was an added historical dimension to the closure of Signy, resulting from the original handing over of a station on Laurie Island to Argentina in 1904 by William Speirs Bruce,[99] whence the Argentine territorial claim developed. This made the FCO very resistant to losing a British presence in the South Orkney Islands. We had no real scientific imperative for keeping Signy open, but in the end reached a compromise to operate a small summer-only station whose research facilities would be offered to external scientists both national and international. This clearly demonstrated how the FCO held all the power, even though it did not provide funds itself.

As for my old base, we considered either: closing and removing it; keeping it open but with significant investment to bring it up to the new environmental standard, and automating the key long-term data sets; or passing the station on to another nation to operate. There seemed interest from the Dutch. The Netherlands had become a

---

99 William Speirs Bruce led the Scottish National Antarctic Expedition of 1902–1904. SNAE wintered in 1903 at Laurie Island and then Bruce gave his observatory to the Argentine Meteorological Service. Argentina has maintained the station since then, making it the longest-running Antarctic research station by far. See:

Dudeney, J.R. and Walton D.W.H. (2011) From 'Scotia' to 'Operation Tabarin' – Developing British Policy for Antarctica, *Polar Record*, DOI: 10.1017/S0032247411000520, printed as 2012, No 4, 48, pp. 342–360

Williams, I.P. and J.R. Dudeney (2018) *William Speirs Bruce, Forgotten Polar Hero*, Stroud: Amberley Publishing, ISBN 978-1-4456-8081-1

Dudeney, J.R. and J. Sheail (2019) *Claiming the Ice: Britain and the Antarctic 1900–1950*, Cambridge Scholars Publishing, ISBN 978-1-5275-3048-5

consultative party in 1990, but the Dutch uniquely had decided that their interpretation of a 'substantial programme of research', did not mean building their own station. But they backed out. The South Koreans also showed some interest, but that did not develop. However, a new player finally appeared – the newly independent country of Ukraine. It turned out that Ukrainian scientists had played a major role in the Soviet Antarctic programme, but after the Soviet Union had dissolved in 1991 the newly emerging Russian Federation retained ownership of all the old Soviet Antarctic stations, leaving the Ukrainians out in the cold. There was thus the potential for a deal which would benefit both the UK and Ukraine. Negotiations were soon under way which led to the sale of the station for £1 providing that Ukraine undertook to maintain all the basic monitoring programmes BAS required, and delivered the data to BAS once per year. The station was handed over in 1996; we will return later on to my part in that.

So with these changes in place, and our powerful new infrastructure, it was possible to develop new programmes to project BAS presence and science much further into the vast continent of Antarctica, including funding for four AGOs under the field of view of the PACE radar. I was also negotiating with both the Japanese and the South Africans to have a joint programme to build two more HF radars in Antarctica: one at the Japanese station, Syowa, and the other at the South African station, SANAE. The fields of view of the two new radars would overlap with PACE, allowing the vector flow of the plasma in the ionosphere to be determined uniquely. It resulted in a new acronym – SHARE, Southern Hemisphere Auroral Radar Experiment.[100] Ultimately, the three radars became part of SuperDARN, mentioned earlier; it had been the brainchild of Ray Greenwald, and generated an amazingly successful international collaboration which brought together networks of radars in both polar regions. I worked closely with Ray in developing the concept and the details of how the collaboration would work, and was one of the seven founding principal investigators. SuperDARN continues today, and now has a total of 35 radars.

The problem of strategic funding was not the only issue vexing our senior management in the early 1990s. Since its inception in the dying days of World War II, BAS had resolutely refused to employ women in any operational role, and certainly not in a wintering party. Both Sir Vivian Fuchs and Dick Laws had firmly turned their faces away from any discussion of the matter. BAS was even given an exception from the provisions of the Sex Discrimination Act of 1975 to ensure we were not troubled by a continuous barrage of court cases trying to force a change in our policy. But by the early 1990s the whole of the management team was from a younger generation, who did not see the issue quite the same way. Our primary concern was that we were throwing away around half our potential workforce arbitrarily, and so we began tentatively to change our policy, first by allowing women scientists to join science cruises, then to carry out

100 Dudeney, J.R., K.B. Baker, P.H. Stoker and A.D.M. Walker (1994) The Southern Hemisphere Auroral Radar Experiment (SHARE), *Ant. Sci.*, 6, 123–124

The historic signing ceremony for the SuperDARN Principal Investigators' agreement on 4 May 1995 at Madingley Hall, Cambridge. The founding signatories, left to right: Prof N. Sato, Prof A.D.M. Walker, Dr J.R. Dudeney, Dr R.A. Greenwald, Prof T.B. Jones, Prof G. Sofko and Prof J-P. Villain. (Credit UKRI/BAS)

summer research programmes at our stations. By the mid-1990s we started introducing women into our wintering teams. By the turn of the century BAS was completely gender-blind, with women having the opportunity to compete for all jobs from pilots to steel erectors, although scientist and medical officer posts were the most popular. We made little attempt to dictate how the mixed societies should organize themselves, deciding that the members of each wintering party would have to work through the social relationship issues themselves and that each group would be different. The only restriction imposed was that pregnancy would be treated as requiring a medevac.

I must now relate a somewhat unusual tale. In 1992 I was chief officer for the STAR working group in SCAR. I was therefore in charge of organizing and running the activities of STAR at the International SCAR meeting to be held that June in Bariloche, Argentina. In preparation, I had put together a programme of three workshops, a half-day symposium on Antarctic Astronomy and a business session to discuss future plans etc. What I was not prepared for was the very strange occurrence which confronted me at this meeting. Some background is necessary. Arrival Heights is a small area of high ground extending along the west side of Hut Point Peninsula, just north of Hut Point in Ross Island. A strange little teacup, then, to be the focus of a significant international storm involving New Zealand and the USA over an apparent violation of the rules of the Antarctic Treaty!

Even odder, perhaps, that I ended up playing a central role in defusing the conflict. 'How so?' I hear you ask. Like this. First, a little background. A fundamental cornerstone of Antarctic governance was the creation of a system for the protection of SSSIs (Special Sites of Scientific Interest). Almost exclusively the regions so designated protected flora, fauna or areas of great geological importance. Each had an agreed management plan which included seriously restricting access through a system of 'permitting'. Once the Madrid Protocol was agreed, these SSSIs became SPAs (Specially Protected Areas), although that did not formally come into force until 1998.

Arrival Heights was designated as SSSI No. 2. But this was not for its intrinsic local biological or geological importance; uniquely, it was so designated in order for it to be a radio quiet area. It was an area which naturally would have a very low background level of human-made electromagnetic noise, so was a good place for sensitive instruments designed to study naturally generated noise such as whistlers, as far as possible free from interference. So its management plan was somewhat different from those of other SSSIs, in that it required the careful siting of potential sources of interference outside its boundaries to limit the noise level inside it. This was particularly an issue because it was very near to the huge US McMurdo base and the much smaller New Zealand Scott bas. Both the USA and New Zealand had several long-running experiments in the SSSI, studying natural radio emissions.

The cause of the dispute was the installation in late 1991 of a Satellite Earth Station (SES) on the margin of the boundary of the SSSI by NZ Telecom to provide communications for Scott Base with the outside world. It appears that this had been done without prior consultation with the USA, and because the boundary of the SSSI was not particularly well defined whether the SES actually physically infringed it was disputed. What was not in dispute, however, was that its beam was radiated across the SSSI at low elevation. Enraged US scientists with experiments at the site were reported as likening what had been done to siting a nuclear power plant in a penguin rookery. So tempers were running very high. The issue made the press through news items in journals such as *New Scientist*, *Science* and *Eos*.[101] I was aware through the press articles that there was an issue to discuss, and made space for this in the business session. What I had not allowed for was the heat and anger emanating from my US colleagues, one of whom (Ted Rosenberg) was also a close friend. The passion became clear on the second morning, when I convened the first session of the business meeting. Both Ted (for the USA) and David Geddes (for NZ) had come with formal prepared statements, which they read. It was immediately clear that given the passion and entrenched positions there could be no sensible or rational debate. So I called a halt for coffee and got the two sides together in the margin of the meeting to see whether there was a way forward.

---

101 Anderson I., Antarctic Satellite Station 'Violates Treaty' *New Scientist*, p. 8, 2 May 1992
     Fraser-Smith et al, Antarctic Environmental Concerns, *Science*, 256, pp. 949–950, 1992
     Simarski L.T., Antarctic Science Preserve Polluted, *Eos, Trans. AGU*, 73, pp. 104–195 April 28, 1992

This quickly descended into a shouting match, but I finally got them to agree to a private meeting under the good offices of the president of SCAR (at that time Dick Laws), then I closed the topic and moved on to other matters.

The meeting with Dick took place a couple of days later over lunch and behind closed doors; although it started with the previous antagonism, finally Dick and I brought both sides round to focusing on how to take the matter forward in a sensible way. The solution reached was to convene a meeting of scientists from the two sides on neutral ground with a neutral chair/convenor, with the aim of determining whether there was a real problem with radio interference in the SSSI. If there was, then the group would identify what the sources were and how they could be mitigated, then make recommendations to the SCAR executive on the way forward, with the aim that these would be endorsed by SCAR and presented to the next Antarctic Treaty meeting. And the proposed independent chair? Me. That nearly put the matter to bed, except that Ted was determined to put forward a resolution that required the SES to be removed immediately. But finally we got agreement on a composite resolution that effectively recommended the plan agreed at the meeting with Dick. This was passed by vote of the SCAR national delegates at the end of the meeting, so becoming the official stated position of SCAR. My main reaction at the end of it all was – phew!

The summit meeting took some while to get organized because both sides needed to independently get measurements made of the noise environment at Arrival Heights, to track down the various sources of radio noise, and to determine to what extent experiments there were adversely impacted by it. Finally, I convened the meeting for 10 and 11 March 1994, and asked Dick Kressman to be an independent technical advisor. There were three delegates from each country: Dr Davey, Dr Keys and Professor Axford representing New Zealand, and Dr Lanzerotti, Professor Rosenberg and Dr Fraser-Smith representing the USA. All three of the US delegates were well known to me; the New Zealanders I was less familiar with, but had met them all before. My diary records for the end of the first day:

> Lots of talking round in circles. Not sure we are getting anywhere practical. But everybody is still talking to everybody else by the end of day one – that must be a good outcome!

The next day was a bit fraught, but I managed to get the outline of a draft report agreed, and more importantly obliged the two sides to agree conclusions and recommendations before the end of the day.

The six participants produced a final report for SCAR, dated 26 August 1994, which contained these without any change. The report was released to coincide with the SCAR meeting in Rome, running from 28 August to 5 September. The findings were that the site was impacted by a variety of sources of local interference and had been for some years, but that there was no evidence that the SES had added to that. Mitigation measures were discussed, and it was recommended that the site be embedded within a circular Antarctic Specially Managed Area (ASMA) with a radius of 100 km, whose management plan would be aimed at limiting the level of noise by careful siting, installation and maintenance of equipment. I had organized a half-day session of talks on the topic, and had to make a presentation to the SCAR executive of the report's findings and recommendations. Finally, I got agreement by the national delegates to SCAR of the report's recommendations. SCAR then reported the outcome to the next Antarctic Treaty meeting the following May. I was not present at the latter, but SCAR put forward a paper laying out the recommendations.[102] New Zealand and the USA also put forward a joint paper[103] thanking SCAR for its work – and particularly thanking the chairman of the STAR working group. It seems that there the matter rested, with little action of implementing the recommendations, particularly not the plan for an ASMA. But Arrival Heights is still a protected area – now designated as ASPA[104] 122 – and its management plan was updated in the early years of this century.

But in the midst of all this controversy it was time for me to head south once more at the end of 1993 – into an emotional firestorm at Halley.

---

102 ATCMXIX INF 57 Concerning the situation at Arrival Heights (SSSI No. 2), submitted by SCAR

103 ATCMXIX INF 86 Concerning the situation at Arrival Heights (SSSI No. 2), submitted by USA and NZ

104 Antarctic Specially Protected Area

12

THE UPS AND DOWNS
OF THE MID-1990S

In the early 1990s the management of BAS stations in Antarctica was reorganized. We instituted a new position, permanent base commander (PBC). This individual would be a staff member based in the UK who would oversee the operation of the station but would go to the station each Antarctic summer to manage it directly. During the winter period a winter base commander (WBC) would be appointed from the wintering team to provide day-to-day leadership and management, as well as being the interface between the PBC and the wintering team. The PBC was generally somebody who had wintered at the station in question, often as WBC, and so could be expected to be well aware of the particular issues encountered there. This system was generally working out well, particularly at Rothera, which was now a very complex operation in the summer. But at Halley the short length of the summer season, hitherto delineated by the arrival of the ship in late December at the earliest and its departure in late February at the latest, meant that the PBC was less connected to the station than desirable. Also the station required a great amount of technical maintenance each year – raising the platforms, grooming the snow around them etc – which fell under the management of the logistics/technical department in Cambridge. In 1993 a combination of poor communication internally at Cambridge and a number of not very well-suited folk wintering at Halley led to what was a perfect storm of personnel difficulties. Difficulties in which I found myself immersed up to the neck in January 1994.

I accompanied the director, David Drewry, on a visit to Halley to assess how my division's work was going there in the new facilities we occupied. We joined the *Bransfield* in Cape Town in early January after it had returned from its first visit, in which it had taken in the PBC, amongst other folk, to carry out the annual relief. We had been aware for some time that the atmosphere was not good on station and that relations had broken down between the staff there and Cambridge, but it was only in late December that the full extent of the issues became clear. When *Bransfield* had arrived on 13 December, the relief operation could not get under way because there was a real threat of physical violence from some of the winterers, directed at the PBC. A stand-off developed between ship and shore, and the base members started trying to dictate the terms under which they would cooperate. Initially they would allow only a personnel representative and the captain ashore. It became clear to us from afar that during the winter a seemingly irrational hatred had developed for the PBC, and that the WBC had not countered this; rather, it was the lowest common denominator that seemed to have set the standards. It appeared to us, too, that the station had been run more like a commune than a professional wintering station. We learnt it had taken two days before the situation had calmed enough, and the PBC had asserted enough control, for the relief to commence. But the situation was clearly unsustainable in the long term. So it was against this backdrop that on 12 January the director and I joined the ship in Cape Town and sailed south.

We had required the outgoing WBC to come back up to Cape Town to be debriefed by us there (and to get him off the station, to allow the PBC a fair chance of imposing order). As we sailed south we had the outgoing wintering doctor on board to debrief, as well as briefing the ingoing WBC. As the voyage south took 10 days we had ample time to get a fair picture of what had gone wrong, and what we would do about it, before we arrived in the poisonous atmosphere of the station. It was obvious that there had been little coordination between the PBC and Logistics/Technical at home, the latter not briefing the PBC on what they were saying to their team on station. It also became clear that the WBC had compounded things by not bringing this to light and by not supporting the PBC. Finally, amongst the wintering team there were several characters who had been very disruptive.

As there were very few people on board, the voyage otherwise passed quietly, except for one very sharp moment for me. On 21 January the ship was off Cap Norwegia, working its way through ice on a gloriously sunny day when I got one of those messages from the radio room – 'Phone home immediately!' I launched like a rocket up the several decks to the radio room, my head swimming with all sorts of disaster scenarios. Turned out to be the least worst of all the things that go through your mind: my younger daughter's cat had been killed on the road outside our house. But Clare was a pragmatic little girl, and when she had decided she wanted a kitten she had also chosen to have two just in case of this eventuality. I talked to her about it, but my diary has the poignant entry 'I wish I could give Clare a cuddle now and tell her it is all right!'

On 22 January we arrived at the creek – Maggie's Ditch[105] – that was then providing access onto the shelf and the station, and after a brief pow-wow with the PBC and Mike Rose, who was down for the summer to mastermind the UASD summer programme, we headed up to the station early the next morning. Our general plan was to interview

---

105 So named, rather irreverently, because it became usable just as Maggie Thatcher was ditched by the Conservative Party.

all members of the wintering team, and send whose who were outbound straight to the ship. Then to interview each of the difficult individuals, with a view to either inviting them to resign honourably or, if necessary, sack them, aiming to get them all off base to the ship before the end of the day. We were taking a risk that at some point in the future an employment tribunal might question our actions, but we knew that speed was of the essence. As it happened, nobody felt the need to take any action against BAS as a result of our actions.

Sadly, the weather got in the way before we were able to deal with the most difficult cases, so we had a very uncomfortable night on station. In the middle of the night the fire alarms sounded – set off deliberately so that we all had to go outside in very bad weather – obviously to make a point. There were also rather unpleasant graffiti on the noticeboards, aimed at us. But the following day we went through the very difficult process, and I saw a new side to David. I had hitherto seen him as somewhat of a showman, but now, when faced with some very unpleasant folk and situations, he demonstrated great courage and calmness. We had taken over the base library for the interviews, and after one particularly stressful session I turned to a bookshelf and pulled out a book at random, letting it fall open. It was one of those magic moments that cannot be predicted. It was a volume of Robert Service poetry (my favourite poet) which had opened at the poem entitled 'Cheer'. I read it out loud and it immediately lifted our spirits.

Once we had dispatched all the likely bad influences back to the ship the atmosphere on base lifted immediately. But the place was very scruffy; there had been a pretty complete breakdown in discipline, one manifestation of which was that the weekly scrub-outs had not been done, so there was deeply ingrained grime everywhere. I took it on myself to set an example by giving the dining room and bathroom a good clean-out, whilst the PBC and the incoming WBC got down to rebuilding an effective team spirit. We had banned any of the folk we had dispatched to the ship from coming ashore, so were not particularly pleased that the captain took to referring to his ship on the radio as the Prison Ship *Bransfield*.

At Halley there were actually two almost independent bases in operation – the permanent wintering base, and a temporary camp (in a Weatherhaven tent) located about 500 metres away, where the large team of summer maintenance staff and contractors were living. The atmosphere there was completely different – very can-do, happy and hard-working. It was a pleasure for David and me to walk there and soak up that atmosphere. Also visiting and living at the Weatherhaven was Detrick Enss, mastermind of the design of Halley V. He was now acting as a consultant, helping to develop the most effective procedures for raising the platforms and for managing the drift of snow around them. It was very enjoyable to spend time with him discussing how our brainchild was performing in practice.

I spent just over two weeks at Halley, and once the horrible situation had been dealt with I was able to focus on how my division's operation was working out and what new

CHEER, BY ROBERT SERVICE

It's a mighty good world, so it is, dear lass,
When even the worst is said.
There's a smile and a tear, a sigh and a cheer,
But better be living than dead;
A joy and a pain, a loss and a gain;
There's honey and maybe some gall:
Yet still I declare, foul weather or fair,
It's a mighty good world after all.

For look, lass! at night when I break from the fight,
My Kingdom's awaiting for me;
There's comfort and rest, and the warmth of your breast,
And little ones climbing my knee.
There's fire-light and song – Oh, the world may be wrong!
Its empires may topple and fall:
My home is my care – if gladness be there,
It's a mighty good world after all.

O heart of pure gold! I have made you a fold,
It's sheltered, sun-fondled and warm.
O little ones, rest! I have fashioned a nest;
Sleep on! you are safe from the storm.
For there's no foe like fear, and there's no friend like cheer,
And sunshine will flash at our call;
So crown Love as King, and let us all sing –
"It's a mighty good world after all."

This poem is in the public domain

opportunities the much-upgraded facilities offered. Hitherto the limited communications and computing on station had meant that there was little scope for more than equipment operation and data collection. But now, with digital networking between Halley and Cambridge plus powerful onsite computing facilities, it was possible to envisage a much more integrated operation, with analysis and research being carried out on base rather than waiting until data were returned home. So much of my time was spent planning this new approach. One outcome was a rationalization of wintering staff, with an integrated engineering support team plus post-doctoral science staff carrying out their own research.

By now the first AGO had been operating for a year at A77 near the Theron Mountains. I was able to take a flight out there to check the station over. It had survived very well indeed, and was operating exactly as intended. And finally I departed Halley in style – in an RN Lynx helicopter to the new HMS *Endurance*.[106] It was assisting BAS in laying some fuel depots at the head of the Weddell Sea, and provided both Detrick Enss and me with a ride to the Falklands on our way home. Landing on *Endurance* in the Lynx was a much more civilized method of boarding than climbing over the bow on a rope ladder. As a Navy ship it was very heavily crewed, so Detrick and I shared the sick bay for the fortnight we were on board, but we had free use of the observation lounge (now the wardroom), a splendidly appointed room with floor-to-ceiling windows looking out on the world. So we travelled in some style. I was struck again, however, by the Navy way of doing things. In civilian life *Endurance* had been designed to pretty well sail itself, with just a single watch officer and crew member on duty on the bridge. But now there was a whole marching army of officers and crew up there passing messages and orders one to another. When they weren't doing that, there were almost continuous drills – fire, man overboard, flood etc etc – to be enjoyed. Still, it was overall a pleasant interlude in which I could catch my breath and do some strategic thinking whilst enjoying a cruise to the Falklands via the South Orkneys.

There was a nostalgic moment in the Falklands, as I was there for a few days during which the last of the BAS huskies were flown out of Rothera Station en route to a new life in the Arctic. Their removal from Antarctica was a consequence of the Environmental Protocol. But to mark the 50 years of continuous service that dogs had given to Britain in Antarctica, BAS decided on giving this team one last real working field trip, codenamed Lost Heritage. This was an eight-week, two-man trip to carry out a GPS survey and do some shallow ice coring on the Uranus Glacier. Once this had been completed the dogs were flown via the UK to Boston, USA. From there they were trucked to Chisasibe on the eastern shore of James Bay, Quebec, from where they were driven as a team to their new home at an Inuit village, Inukjuak, on the eastern shore of Hudson Bay. Sadly, however, their retirement was short, as they succumbed to diseases against which they had no immunity.

My involvement was to be a talking head for the press when the dogs arrived via our Dash 7 in the Falklands. There was one more bit of excitement for the press to get their teeth into, and for which I was the talking head for the Falklands at least. On 20 February Prison Ship *Bransfield*, having just sailed from Halley, suffered a serious engine room fire which destroyed one half of its propulsion motor and left the other half too severely damaged to be operational. The ship was thus adrift in the pack ice.

---

106 The *Endurance* of Falklands fame had been decommissioned in 1991. This *Endurance* was a relatively new-build general-purpose ice-class utility ship, previously MV *Polar Circle*, recently purchased from Rieber Shipping by MoD. It had both science equipment/lab space and accommodation, making it suitable for Antarctic tourism.

The *JCR* was dispatched to take it in tow, and for several days the situation was quite tense. However, the chief engineer (with sterling help from some of the folk we had dispatched from Halley, it has to be said) managed to strip the damaged motor down, working in awful conditions, and repair it sufficiently to get the ship under way at half-power just as the *JCR* arrived. The two ships then sailed in close company to Stanley. After an inspection, the repair was deemed sufficiently robust for *Bransfield* to head home in safety. For me, after those bits of excitement and a few days to catch my breath, it was the RAF airbridge to Brize Norton, and home to my family.

Back in the office in the spring of 1994, life was busy. There were big changes in the way science was being organized in the UK. The OST had been created in 1992 under the direction of the chief scientific advisor to government, with the remit to oversee the research councils and distribute funds between them. Sir William Waldegrave (later Baron Waldegrave), the minister responsible for science, had decreed that government-funded science should be judged by two criteria: Wealth Creation and/or Quality of Life, with the real priority on Wealth Creation. But more broadly the changes in strategic approach drove the way the research councils were run, so they were more like businesses. A new post of director general of the research councils (DGRC) was created in 1994, with Sir John Cadogan, lately head of research at BP, its first post holder. Answerable to him were the heads of the research councils, who were now titled chief executive officers. They in turn were advised by boards chaired by non-executive chairs. The board membership was drawn from universities and other organizations with an interest in the work of the council and industry. The chair was appointed for a fixed term from outside the council, providing a link to industry, whilst the CEO would also normally come from outside on a fixed-term contract. Our new CEO was Sir John Krebs (later Lord Krebs). He came from an illustrious scientific career as an academic at Oxford University. Sir Robert Malpas was the NERC chair; he had come from a broad engineering background in industry, particularly ICI and BP.

For us, managing BAS, much time and effort was devoted to interpreting what these changes meant. BAS was not really able to contribute to Wealth Creation, not the least because of the restrictions placed upon us by the Antarctic Treaty, so our work only matched the Quality of Life banner. But our new CEO was much exercised in re-evaluating, rationalizing and restructuring the way in which NERC was organized and the manner in which the directors of the institutes operated within it. Our dual role as the instrument of British Antarctic Policy as well as a remit to do world-class science, combined with our ring-fenced funding, meant that we were somewhat immune to the more extreme possibilities – but still we had to fight our corner in this somewhat fluid new science policy world.

One of the changes introduce by Krebs which had a real effect on BAS – and on me – was the creation of what was effectively a deputy CEO role. For this role he chose David Drewry on a four-year secondment. This was announced to the HoDs at the

Directors' Committee meeting on 4 July 1994. Krebs also decided that Barry Heywood would step into Drewry's shoes as director, and his post of deputy director would be advertised! We HoDs quickly convened a Mouse Lunch[107] to consider the implications. It was obvious straight away that none of the HoDs wanted the post; rather, they saw me as the natural person to throw my hat into the ring – so there was just one internal candidate.

David Drewry left in September, and I was asked by Barry to step up as acting deputy director from 12 September, pending the interviews. I handed UASD over to Alan Rodger, as acting HoD, and moved up to the deputy director's office adjacent to Barry's office. Interviews were set for 10 November, for just me and one external candidate. I had my interview, which was held in Barry's office, and it seemed to go very well. I then expected to hear one way or another straight away. But no; Barry studiously ignored me, as did the rest of the panel, and so started one of the most humiliating periods of my life. It wasn't until 15 November that Barry gave me any feedback; they had offered the job to Dougal Goodman, an executive from BP, but he hadn't accepted yet so nothing could be said, and if he did accept he would not be joining for three months. Barry also told me, perhaps as a sop, that Krebs had put a specific charge on him to bring new senior staff in from industry, so actually I had stood very little chance. But Barry was heading south on 17 November, so in all conscience I could not step back from the acting job to leave BAS rudderless, because I would be now deputizing for him as well. No public announcement occurred until 1 December, and one way or another I had to keep up on the acting job until the end of April 1995. I was however very heartened by the outpouring of sympathy and support I received from staff at all levels, and from colleagues outside the organization. And as things turned out I only had to wait another three years for the wheel to turn again in a surprising way – but that is for later.

I was soon thrust into dealing with another crisis down south. Our air facility at Rothera was now fully operational and available for use by the Antarctic programmes of other nations (known as national operators). Rothera was proving popular with them as a transit/refuelling stop for aircraft flying into the Antarctic in support of other national programmes. A private Canadian company – Borek Air – was often chartered to provide Twin Otters, and it would fly them from its Canadian base via Punta Arenas to Rothera and then on to wherever they were needed. On 23 November in the evening a Borek twin arrived at Rothera after the long flight from Punta. It was en route to the Italian station in Terra Nova Bay via fuelling stops at a summer camp called Patriot

---

107 Early in my tenure as HoD I had suggested the HoDs should meet regularly for lunch to coordinate activities and endeavour, not to compete against each other. We called ourselves the mice in a nod to the phrase 'while the cat's away the mice will play'. The venue was a local pub – the Blue Lion – which did an excellent chicken curry lunch. The lunches allowed us to informally cover areas of concern without the presence of the director and deputy director.

Hills and the US McMurdo station in the Ross Sea sector. To make such long ferry flights the aircraft had to operate considerably above their normal maximum take-off weight of 12,500 lbs, and there was a special dispensation to do this with ferry tanks fitted in the fuselage. Normally such flights were supposed to be carried out with a flight crew of just two, but this plane had four people on board, plus their gear and survival equipment. The flight from Punta had taken a little over 7 hours, so ideally the pilot should have taken up the offer of a night's rest at Rothera, but he did not. Instead, after a meal and refuelling he opted to continue. Unfortunately, there was a large iceberg sitting just 10 metres off the southern end of the runway. It was roughly square with sides of about 50 metres, and had two peaks, one behind the other, each about 30 metres high, with a deep valley and melt pool between them. After two hours on the ground the aircraft headed off down the runway, the pilot having been advised by the resident BAS pilots not to attempt to go over the top of the berg, but rather to bank gently to pass alongside it, as there was then a clear over-water route to gently gain altitude. The pilot opted instead to clear the peaks, but the aircraft entered a stall, hitting the furthermost peak near its top with very little forward motion, then sliding back down the slope, exploding into flames as it did so, to end up in the melt pool. There were no survivors. The PBC, Paul Rose, had rescue boats in the water immediately but ruled very wisely that it was too unsafe to land on the berg while the fire was burning. The following morning, he advised me that he thought the berg was too unstable for it to be safe to recover bodies, and I backed him up on that. The maximum permitted take-off weight in ferry configuration is 17,500 lbs. The subsequent Air Accident Investigation Branch report on the crash determined that the likely weight on take-off was around 18,500 lbs[108] – at least 1,000 lbs over the maximum allowable. As far as I am aware no further action was taken in apportioning liability. For BAS, however, there was much toing and froing between the FCO, NERC, the Canadian media etc in the ensuing days, with John Hall (operations manager) and Frank Curry dealing with the detail, and me dealing with media requests and the big picture. We resisted any suggestion of putting people onto the berg to recover anything, and over the course of the next few days it drifted off and slowly broke up. I ensured that the BAS medical unit made every effort to provide counselling for any base member who needed it. Overall a very sad tale.

So the run-up to Christmas 1994 was not an easy or comfortable one. I was able to get away for a few days at the beginning of December to attend the Fall AGU meeting in San Francisco, where I had a chance to reflect on what had happened while soaking up the kindnesses of my colleagues, as well as playing a full part in presenting the results from our PACE radar research. Of course the office kept me busy remotely – the technology existed by then to log on to the BAS computing system to collect the many emails. And then when I got home I found a significant consolation prize – I had

---

108 AAIB Bulletin No 2/95

A visit to Buckingham Palace to receive a second clasp to my Polar Medal from Her Majesty, accompanied by my three lovely ladies.

been awarded a second clasp to my Polar Medal. One never gets to see the citation, but I like to think that it was in honour of the incredible technical achievements of my team in successfully delivering the impossible – the AIS, the PACE Radar and AGOs – and for my innovative involvement in the Halley V project, plus my leadership in computing policy, staff relations, and health and safety. Whatever the reason, on 25 July 1995 I presented myself in a rented morning suit at the palace for the investiture, along with my girls dressed in their best frocks. They were much taken by our drive in through the gates of the palace in our reasonably presentable Ford Sierra, goggled at by the crowd looking for celebs. The palace does these events with very great professionalism, but also with a real effort to make the experience personal. An equerry took me aside to tell me I was 'special' today because I was the only person getting a clasp (or bar) to an existing honour that day, so when it was my turn I would have to hold out my hand to the Queen – apparently one of the very few times that protocol allows this. Her Majesty is a consummate performer at investitures, and in my experience of two with her, she has always had some special questions or comments, making the event very personal.

Dougal Goodman took up his post on a five-year fixed-term appointment at the beginning of May. It would have been a very hard ask for anybody to step into that job from outside without any previous experience of the BAS operation, or indeed of the Antarctic, though Dougal had got a lot of experience working with BP in the Arctic. This was not the best of times, either, because there was a great deal of sympathy for me and therefore rather little sympathy for the newcomer. The role needed somebody with excellent interpersonal skills as well as high latent intelligence and ability to pull it off. Dougal has an impressive intellect and is a man bubbling with ideas, a very hard worker and a good strategist – but sadly, in my judgement, interpersonal skills were not his strongest point. I believe that this was an Achilles heel that he never fully got over. I doubt that I helped much, although I did start out, I like to believe, by trying to work with him.

However, our first encounter set the tone. He asked to visit me in my office on 9 May. That, I thought, was a very good sign, and I assumed that we would at least nod to the situation in which we found ourselves, carry out some sort of handover, and discuss how to establish an effective *modus operandi*. But no; he made no reference whatever to the need for us to forge a working relationship. He just wanted to talk about an idea he had for starting a project on environmental risk. It was actually a very good idea, one outcome of which was that Richard Horne (from my division) began a project to examine risk to commercial spacecraft from solar storms using data provided to him by the spacecraft operators. His code enabled him to model energetic particle and wave fluxes in the near-Earth environment, the environment in which geostationary communications satellites operated. This is a project that has proved highly effective, and continues at the time of writing.

While I was still coming to terms with the new reality of BAS management and trying to get enthusiastic about leading my division, I got involved in trying to encourage the UK solar terrestrial physics community to come to terms with the new landscape for science funding. The government, through the DGRC, was now looking for science to support the community more directly. I had been consciously pushing my division's programme in the general direction of what was becoming known as space weather. The UASD programme was now oriented to the strapline 'Energy Flow and Dissipation in Geospace'. As I have already pointed out, the upper atmosphere of the Earth, ranging from about 70 km out to several million kilometres, often called geospace, is the outermost region of humankind's environmental envelope. It is where the tenuous atmosphere – mostly ionized – and the terrestrial magnetic field interact with the sun's atmosphere – the heliosphere – and its embedded magnetic field (known as the interplanetary magnetic field, or IMF for short). Geospace is highly dynamic, driven by solar activity with storms that can disrupt modern society through damage to orbiting satellites (hence loss of communications and disruption to GPS) and, amongst other things, interference to terrestrial electrical power systems.

The BAS programme was funded by NERC, whilst the rest of the academic solar terrestrial physics (STP) community competed for its grant funding from what was then known as the Particle Physics and Astronomy Research Council (PPARC). I wanted to get the UK STP community engaged in space weather research because I saw it as a way of sustaining their funding, by showing that there was a real national requirement for understanding how that research could impact society. I thought that my division was uniquely placed to make an initiative, because we did not then compete for PPARC funding. So I proposed to host a UK-wide meeting 'to discuss the opportunities and challenges for the UK STP community' offered by space weather. The meeting was a two-day event: 'Space Weather Forecasting – is it practical, is it useful, is there a role for the UK community?' The format was to have some formal presentations by leaders of the community, a wide-ranging discussion, and then two break-out groups – one to focus and report back on why the answer was yes, and the other on why the answer was no – followed by a final debate.

My diary indicates that the meeting was very interesting, with folk being fully engaged. A series of next steps were identified. But as it turned out a few key leaders of the PPARC community decided that working on space weather was too 'applied' for them and for the ethos of PPARC. So the initiative was stillborn; with the benefit of hindsight I was over a decade premature. Ironically there are now major efforts involving the UK academic community and the UK Met Office to develop a practical space weather forecasting scheme to provide early warning of damaging space weather events. But I gave up trying to energize the PPARC community and instead focused on how BAS could contribute to much more enlightened efforts in the USA to develop a practical forecasting system through our involvement in GGS and SuperDARN. And anyway it was time to head home again, to the great white wilderness.

13

DEEP FIELD, AND GOODBYE BASE F

I set off again for Antarctica on 20 November 1995. This trip lasted just under 14 weeks, a long time to be away from my family, and taking me away from both my daughters' birthdays, Christmas, New Year and Valentine's Day – pretty well a clean sweep! Although I have travelled south many times since then, this was the last long summer working season that I did, and at its heart was a deep field trip to help construct an AGO, as well as a lengthy period at Halley and the formal handover of Base F to the Republic of Ukraine.

The trip went from the sublime to the ridiculous in terms of comfort. I was treated as a VIP by the RAF for the airbridge flight from the UK to the Falklands – though that didn't improve the quality of their food. I also had the stateroom allocated for my exclusive use on the *Bransfield* – but then I ended up living in a tent 8,500 feet up on the Antarctic Plateau for two weeks. The VIP treatment had also meant that for the Ascension Island refuelling stop, rather than being stuck in the cage (a fenced-off area on the apron serving as the departure/transit lounge and into which travellers were locked) with everybody else, I had been given a tour of the main features of the island, including a visit to the eerie plague cemetery – the Bonetta cemetery – set in a lava field on the coast in Comfortless Cove. The cemetery is named after HMS *Bonetta*, which had brought its fever victims ashore here in 1838; fever-ridden 19th-century ships were required to drop anchor for quarantine in what was originally known as Comfort Bay, but unsurprisingly the bay was renamed Comfortless. I found the cove was aptly named; the place had an unpleasant brooding atmosphere even in the bright tropical sunshine. Then after landing in Stanley the same day, I joined the ship sailing for Halley via South Georgia and Signy Island that night. But this time I travelled in state, with my own suite of cabins: a day room, a bedroom and an ensuite bathroom. I also had the service of the captain's steward. A very different style of travelling than my first trip south on the *John Biscoe*! It had its downside, however; being high up in the ship's superstructure, just one deck below the bridge, its motion in heavy weather was sometimes quite startling. But it was very luxurious and spacious discomfort.

Our first landfall was Bird Island. As normal, there was a swell running in Bird Sound, so boarding the launch to get the station was not the most pleasant of exercises. I got a tour of the station and climbed up through the tussac grass to have a close-up encounter with wandering albatross chicks, before turning to in the afternoon for a strenuous session of cargo work. By the time that was finished the wind had risen to gale force, so the return to the ship was equally exciting (and wet). However, the next day we anchored off the old whaling station at Husvik on South Georgia, and with no particular duties to carry out, I packed myself a cheese and pickle sandwich and took to the hills for a hike amongst the wildlife on a splendid sunny day. One highlight was witnessing the birth of twin reindeer calves. South Georgia on a sunny day is a paradise like no other on Earth, and I defy anybody not to fall in love with the place after such a day.

The next day we were at Grytviken to deliver stores to the whaling museum which had been established there four years before by Nigel Bonner.[109] After helping with that I paid a courtesy call on the commander of military garrison at King Edward Point. I also had some lunch with Pat Lurcock, now harbourmaster for the government of South Georgia and the South Sandwich Islands. Then it was off to Signy Island.

We spent six frustrating days at Signy because of very variable weather which hampered the relief operation. For me it was important to get involved with the cargo work because firstly it is good exercise, but secondly and more importantly it is very good for team morale for the senior chap (as I was on the ship) to be seen to be getting stuck in – particularly given the elevated status of my accommodation on board. But we finally got most of the job done and were off via the South Sandwich Islands to Halley on 6 December. And for once my diary records that both Saunders Island and Montague Island were visible. This was one of the few times I have ever actually seen any of the South Sandwich Islands – normally they are hidden in fog and cloud – so I managed to get my one photograph of Saunders, taken from about 10 miles away. The journey into Halley took around 11 days – busy days on the ship, with training, briefings and planning meetings covering the summer programme of science and maintenance work. We also had the Weddell pack ice to contend with for several days; a quote from my diary for 10 December sums that up for me:

> The sun also shone so it was magic. That delicious reverberating crunch as the ship drives into a floe, followed by the hissing swish as the blocks of ice boil up around the ship's side! Never fails to excite me!

---

109 The museum had been the brainchild of Nigel Bonner, but by then it was under the charge of Tim and Pauline Carr. They had arrived at South Georgia on a small yacht and just stayed, living on their yacht to begin with, and becoming Mr and Mrs South Georgia over many years thereafter. Pauline could always be relied on for a cup of tea and some homemade cake whenever I visited, and once the Carrs had retired Sarah Lurcock, married to Pat, the new harbourmaster, took on that essential duty.

But we broke into a large shore lead after a few days, and this was big enough for the wind to build quite a sea – bad news for us, as by the time we arrived off the Brunt Ice Shelf there was no sea ice left from which to access the shelf. It wasn't just us it was bad for. There is a sizeable emperor penguin colony in one of the creeks close to Halley. My diary speaks for itself:

> The Emperor Penguin colony in Windy Creek has been devastated. A tragic disaster, with unfledged chicks clinging on for grim death (which is what it will be!) to any bit of ice foot or bit of brash they could find. All looking cold and sodden. Some feebly trying to paddle through the porridge and climb onto floes. Nature is cruel sometimes!

Effectively a whole year's production of chicks was lost. Everybody on the ship was very subdued watching the event unfold without any ability to help. We spent three days in weather varying from indifferent to downright horrible before finding a small bay with sea ice about 40 miles north-east providing access to the shelf and a skiway from which to operate a Twin Otter. We were then able to ferry mail, priority equipment and people (including me) to Halley Station, with me arriving on 20 December. And there I found a base completely different from two years ago. It was clean, tidy and full of happy enthusiastic folk. I gave a briefing and Q&A session in the evening, and was

The *Bransfield* arrives off Halley to witness the devastation of the emperor penguin colony. The black dots on the ice are unfledged chicks who are all condemned to a watery grave by the break-up of the ice. Nature can be cruel.

surprised to receive a hearty round of applause at the end of it. The relief/resupply of the station was disrupted by bad weather and the poor state of the landing sites, but was ultimately achieved after a fortnight or so.

My time at Halley was busy straight away – there was the usual debriefing and participating in the programming of the summer work, but my main role was to be part of the four-man team to erect the AGO at 81.5°S 3°E (and 8,500 feet altitude) on the icecap in Dronning Maud Land (the site to be known as A81). On top of that there was the need to do my fair share of cargo work and filling the melter for water, plus entertaining Dougal Goodman on station for four days.

My preparation for the AGO field work had started well before I arrived on station, with the annual field training course held in Derbyshire the previous September, plus a week-long mini-paramedic course with the BAS medical provider (then housed at Aberdeen University) which included two days in the local A&E department and two days with an ambulance crew. Then on station there was a field refresher, including pitching camp and spending the night under canvas. But the main effort was getting all the gear together, sorting it into Twin Otter-sized loads (around 1,000 kg), and getting a refuelling dump established halfway to the site. Luckily on 4 January 1996 a weather window allowed me to be on my way (for most of the rest of the month the weather was pretty ropey). For the second part of the flight, from the refuelling stop, Andy Allsop, the pilot, let me fly the plane for about 90 minutes. My diary says it all:

> Quite pleased with myself cos I managed to stay within 100ft of the chosen altitude and 0.5 nm of track all the way! Andy was even moved to compliment me on my skills!

A81 is about as desolate spot as can be imagined. Just a flat featureless snow field in all directions, sitting on an ice field a mile and a half thick and with nothing to catch the eye. No discernible slope, though there was in fact one of about 4 metres per kilometre, which produced a continuous fall line wind of 10–15 knots. The temperature varied from about minus 15° C to minus 30° C during our stay there, so at its worst twice as cold as inside your domestic freezer. A brutal place, but with its own stark grandeur when the sun shone and the air was glittering with diamond dust, or with solar parhelia. A lonely place, with not a living creature, animal or vegetable for hundreds of miles in any direction. The high altitude was an issue, so that part of our contingency equipment was a portable hyperbaric chamber known as a Gamow bag in case any of us got altitude sickness (thankfully it wasn't needed in anger).

Our camp consisted of two two-man tents, a toilet tent and a larger Weatherhaven work tent. The toilet just consisted of a tent outer covering a hole in the snow.[110] In BAS

---

110 Nowadays all waste is removed, but back then the Protocol had not yet been fully implemented for BAS field camps.

Making the morning porridge.
The BAS camping system is very
traditional – note the primus – but
very comfortable, safe and effective.

parlance, for the purposes of communications we were known to the outside world as Sledge Sierra. We nicknamed the camp High Sierra, and ultimately it became A81, but it was best described as the middle of nowhere. My tent companion was John 'Diggers' Digby, while Mike Rose was sharing with Dudley Knott. My diary describes our morning routine:

> Awake at 7 am, start the primus and get the tent warm – heat some water, make porridge for breakfast with honey and raisins, plus a mug of tea. Whilst eating that melt some more water for washing up. Clean teeth with a little water in a tumbler. Then get outside clothes on for a visit to the toilet tent. Have crap, clean bum with some snow (and toilet paper!), then stick head back into tent for a quick wash of hands and face in a small pannier of water. Then off to work!

What my diary does not reveal is that the real trick was to pretend to be asleep in the hope that your tentmate would be first to stick his nose out of the nice warm sleeping bag into the nasty cold tent to get the primus started and the brew going!

The work occupied us for 12 days, full on except when the weather was too horrid. There was always the wind to contend with, sometimes brilliant sunshine and sometimes a white-out. The sunshine days were special, with brilliant deep blue sky and an opportunity to take in the scale of the location. A description from my diary:

> It is a fascinating place here. The distinguishing feature of the snow surface is quite large low sastrugi,[111] but just dotted about. For all the world it looks like a view of an ocean! Also there is a definite rise to the South West, otherwise the ocean feel is amplified by a flat circular horizon all round. It is very difficult to gauge the scale, so the rise could be a few km away or it could be the continuation of the general rise of the continent into the far distance. There is no way of knowing.

The white-out days were very trying because with no colour, shadow or contrast it was impossible to distinguish any features on the surface whatsoever, which meant walking about became stumbling about, tripping over previous footholes in the snow

---

111 long wind-blown snow ridges

and feeling as though everything – tents, people, boxes – were floating inside a ping-pong ball. Very disorientating and tiring. On one particularly hard day we found ourselves building a 50-foot mast for an antenna in a 15-knot wind with an air temperature of minus 28° C; not good for the fingers. But when finally, we had a working system I broke out the Christmas cake from my goodies box, and we celebrated with that and a bottle of wine I had brought along for the occasion. My diary notes: 'Well, we have been a good and effective team – very impressed with all three of the others, both for their humour and their commitment.' My goodies box also provided interesting spices with which to invigorate the otherwise rather bland dehydrated sledging rations.

I had been asked by the BBC to take a small digital voice recorder on the trip to record a 'fly on the wall' account of my doings. This was to be presented in a 30-minute broadcast, contrasted with the activities of a tourist on an Antarctic tour ship; the Christmas cake moment made a fine counterpoint to the tourist enjoying the casino as his ship steamed through the grandeur of the fjords of the Antarctic Peninsula. And there was one surreal moment for me, lying in my sleeping bag at the end of the day listening to BBC World Service on a little portable short-wave radio. What was I listening to? The panel game 'I'm sorry, I haven't a clue'. There, on an icecap thousands of feet thick, with just two layers of canvas between me and a windy freezer, must be the silliest place that that silly radio programme has ever been enjoyed. I was back at Halley Station again on 15 January – ready for a delicious shower and some 'proper' food.

The completed AGO with the team (from left to right): me, Dudley, Mike and Diggers.

There were two weeks at Halley, before I was whisked off by Twin Otter to Rothera. My time was split in several directions, coaching the incoming UASD staff, (including Dr Kate Charles, our first woman scientist to winter at Halley), analysing data from the AGOs, participating in the management of the summer programme, and of course taking my turn on base jobs. I also took a turn at jacking the main building; each leg had to be jacked a small amount simultaneously by a team using manual jacks. It was hard slow work, but good exercise. After a few years we moved to electric jacks. I took a trip out to AGO A80, on the Recovery Glacier in the Shackleton Mountains, with Dudley and Mike, to retrieve data and establish a camp for Mike and Dudley to spend a few days servicing it. Paul Robertson was the pilot and he gave me the controls for an hour or so outbound, including a period of real instrument flying, which I greatly enjoyed. We left Mike and Dudley and headed home in steadily deteriorating weather with me doing another 30 minutes or so in control. By the time we got close to Halley we had a wind gusting 40 knots, no contrast, no definition, 200 metres visibility in heavy blowing snow. So rather than try to locate the skiway we just turned into wind some way from the station and used the boundless flat shelf to do an instrument landing. Once on the ground we used the GPS to taxi the 3 miles to the station.

My flight to Rothera gave me one of those magic moments when one has to pinch oneself to realise that one is being paid for the experience:

> The flight over the Peninsula was absolutely magnificent! Clear sunny weather with unlimited visibility and me flying the plane – what a way to spend a Monday! We could see Adelaide Island from over 100 nm away, and by 70 nm the island was mirrored in a flat calm sea – superb!

The time at Rothera was really just a week-long waiting game, waiting for the *Endurance* to come to collect me to take me to Base F to formally hand the station over to Ukraine. So I spent my time getting to grips with the operations there and generally lending a hand where needed. I also got to act as copilot for a flight with Andy Allsop down to the BAS summer field station at Fossil Bluff in King George VI Sound. So I got more instrument flying time on the Twin Otter there and back, including an instrument descent to break cloud, followed by a flight at 500 feet over Marguerite Bay back to Rothera.

I joined *Endurance* on 4 February and had the Amundsen suite to myself, ostensibly much more comfortable than the usual accommodation on board. But I soon found it was not to be a comfortable trip. The ship's passive stability tanks seemed wrongly adjusted so that rather than damping out the rolling of the ship they appeared to have enhanced it. This was bad enough, but also it caused the loss of another one of my lives. The ship was rolling so uncomfortably that I wedged myself into my bunk. At one point I got up to get some food. When I came back there was a very large trunk on the bunk just where my head had been. I found it to be full (of what I know not) and very heavy. It had been stored by the previous occupant on top of a cupboard next to the bunk.

The plan was to fly me into Argentine Islands early in the morning by helicopter so I could have a full day with the outgoing BAS team, meet the new Ukrainian wintering team, carry out a formal handover and then depart with the BAS team back to the ship by helicopter. The captain, Barry Bryant, also planned to come ashore with his personal piper to provide gravitas to the occasion. Sadly, the best-laid plans ... I lost yet another of my nine lives in the process. It had all started well enough; I was fully kitted up and briefed, and in the Lynx helicopter ready to go, when it suffered an electrical fault. No problem; it took an hour to prep the second Lynx, so there I was yet again strapped in ready to go, with joshing from the flight observer that we might not go because his pen was unserviceable – when the chopper developed a hydraulic fault. That brought ops to an end, and we sailed instead for Port Lockroy to make a personnel pick-up whilst attempts were made to fix the chopper. That did not go well, so the new plan was to return and anchor at Argentine Islands then put me ashore by boat. But the anchorage was choked with bergs, and Captain Bryant was not happy to anchor or commit a boat. However, somewhat to my surprise there was now a helicopter available, so off I went at 5 pm for a much-reduced visit with no piper and, quite reasonably, no captain. And now fate decided to use up yet another of my lives. As we approached the base the pilots were unsure quite where to land. I tried to guide them but my intercom was not working. So I watched with horror as we flew towards an antenna wire stretched between two masts. The wire very luckily passed under the main rotor, to wrap around the cockpit and be cut by one of the antennae on the roof of the plane. Had we flown a foot or two lower, that wire would have wrapped round the rotor. And that would have been that. Neither pilot nor observer mentioned the incident once we had landed; I am not sure to this day whether they even saw it.

Anyway, I was ashore for a quick tour of the station with the BAS BC (Duncan Haigh) and the new Ukrainian leader, Dr Gennadi Milinevsky, and a quick private chat with Duncan. Then we did the formal lowering of the Union Jack and raising of the Ukrainian flag. Base F was no more – arise Vernadsky![112]

Captain Bryant was very keen to get on his way out of the berg-infested anchorage, but whilst the BAS personnel were being ferried aboard by Lynx he gave Duncan and me leave to take a boat round to the old historic Wordie Hut, where we raised the Union Jack we had just taken down. A fitting final touch – and then it was back to the ship by chopper for dinner.

Looking back at my diary I find that it was rather negative about the handover:

---

112 The base was named for the eminent 19th/20th-century Russian/Ukrainian scientist, Vladimir Ivanovich Vernadsky/Volodymyr Ivanovych Vernadsky.

Lowering the Union Jack at Base F and raising the Ukrainian flag over Vernadsky Base.

Having talked to various people now and from my own very brief visit, do not have a very optimistic view of how things are likely to go. All rather sad and distasteful. If I am completely honest with myself, I feel ashamed for Britain, for BAS and for myself that we could knowingly have handed the place over to such an unlikely bunch in the name of expediency!

How wrong I was! I have revisited Vernadsky regularly since, and can attest that the Ukrainians have made a great success of the station. They have always supplied the long-term data sets that they were required to do, as well as keeping the station immaculate and making a cult of maintaining all the best BAS social traditions.

The voyage back to Stanley was uncomfortable not only because of the ship's lack of stability but also because with over 30 BAS and contractor folk packed into it there were tensions that I, as senior BAS person, had to deal with. I also had some interviews with the UK press concerning the handover. But we got to the Falklands safely and were lodged ashore in a strange hostel accommodation at FIPASS[113] by Saturday 10 February to await our airbridge flight back to the UK on 14 February 1996. In the interim I managed to wind down by doing some hiking and report writing. I was also invited, along with Captain Bryant, to lunch at Government House as guests of the governor, Richard Ralf, and his wife. And finally I went home.

---

113 FIPASS: Falkland Islands Interim Port and Storage System. A 'temporary' dock system set up in Stanley Harbour in the aftermath of the Falklands conflict in 1982. It remains the main port, and has wharves and office accommodation all built from steel panels. Back in the 1980s and 1990s the office space was used as hostel accommodation for people in transit.

14

THE WHEEL TURNS, WITH A SURPRISING OUTCOME

1996 was a busy time for BAS and a busy time for me. I had several overseas trips – two to the USA, two to Japan, one to Austria and one to Tasmania. BAS hosted the XXIV meeting of SCAR in Cambridge in August, in which I was deeply involved through both the STAR working group and the local organizing committee. On the wider front the programme of infrastructure developments at Rothera Station and Signy was well under way. But the relationship with NERC was starting to turn quite sour. As previously mentioned, BAS had ring-fenced funding and we expected NERC to put up with that. And now, although NERC was facing serious funding issues, it still couldn't touch our funding in any real sense. BAS had two masters – FCO and NERC. FCO put in no funding, but as long as the UK wanted to maintain a strong presence in the South Atlantic the views of the FCO outweighed those of NERC. So we knew that we could rely on support from FCO if there was too much pressure/interference from NERC. BAS management settled down behind the ring fence whilst NERC management circled it like a lion prowling around a boma at night. In retrospect, it didn't help that the BAS director and his deputy had somewhat combative styles, which rather got in the way of a smooth relationship. As for the HoDs, we lined up behind our directing team as far as the outside world was concerned whilst privately bitching about them at our mouse lunches. This was not a healthy state of affairs.

The next summer season saw Barry head south leaving Dougal in charge. And now the wheel began to turn. On his way home Barry had an accident in the Falklands, which seriously damaged an ankle. He was anyway due to retire in September 1997, so he took early retirement. Dougal was asked to become acting director, and surprise, surprise, I was invited to be the acting deputy (again). For a while during the summer of 1997 it looked as though David Drewry would just step back into the director's job. But the senior team at BAS was not keen on that – and neither, I believe, was David. Luckily he was offered the job of director general of the British Council (and subsequently

155

became vice-chancellor of Hull University), so now the post of director was going to be advertised. Dougal and I managed to keep BAS running – marking time, really – through the summer and autumn of that year, though it was clear to all that we would be rivals for the top job when the time came.

Then a very curious thing happened, for which I have no documentary evidence, but it is burnt into my memory. NERC let it be known that I was required to apply for the director's job. I was also informed that I would not get it unless there was no credible external candidate. My diary for 1 October notes that I was told by somebody who shall remain nameless that:

> John Krebs' one worry about me was that I would have a strong anti-NERC attitude because of my failure to get promotions in the past that in retrospect I was the best person for.

The interviews were set for 10 November, and on the day beforehand I got a lot of support from many folk from within and outside NERC. One external contact asked me to phone him in the evening. He had been phoned by Krebs to discuss me. He let me know that there were three candidates: Dougal, me and Professor Chris Rapley. And that Krebs' dream ticket for BAS was Rapley as director and me as deputy director. It was with these views in my mind that I turned up in Swindon, where NERC was based, for my interview.

After it, I thought I had performed well, and subsequent feedback from various sources revealed that I had done all that was expected of me, and that I was appointable. However, it took a week until it was finally revealed that Chris Rapley had been given the job and had accepted it. I found the next few weeks very unpleasant and stressful, and I am sure that it was very humiliating for Dougal (and about to get even worse). Not only did we have the uncertainty of what the future held for us personally, but also there were serious issues afoot over the science and management audit (SMA) of BAS that had been undertaken over the past months. The fact that this had even been contemplated while BAS was without a substantive leader was bad enough, but the tensions between NERC and BAS came really to the fore in handling the draft report and conclusions. I found myself, with Frank Curry (head of BAS Administration Division), trying to inject some calmness and reason into a very inflamed situation. Dougal headed off for a trip to South Georgia that occupied much of December, leaving me to deal with the SMA and other policy issues. But my own mood was one of deep despair – I just could not contemplate the idea of having to step back to being a HoD again, having been passed as fitted for the director's job, back to the *status quo* with Dougal as deputy director. All sorts of rumours were circulating and hints being dropped, but the only substantive news I'd had was a formal letter telling me that I would revert to HoD from 3 January 1998. The rumours and hints must have been very hurtful for Dougal. But this was the state of high uncertainty in which he returned to the UK, and I set off for a whistle-stop trip to Rothera and Halley on 2 January.

As I headed south I was in a quandary about my status and even whether I should go at all. Was I still in the role of deputy director? Or head of the Upper Atmospheric Sciences Division? I decided that I should adopt both roles for the purpose of the visit, as there was much that needed dealing with from a BAS-wide perspective – particularly in reviewing health and safety practices – as well as a need to reacquaint myself on key UASD issues, having been away from the division for much of the year. Also, I thought that it made good sense to be well out of the way when Chris took up the post (which he did on 7 January), to give him a chance to get his feet under the table and make up his mind about what he wanted to do with regard to me and Dougal without my presence complicating things.

There was a lot to deal with. On the UASD front, we had hosted an American Program at Rothera – an MF radar – to study the dynamics of the mesosphere. We had also come to an agreement with a German group (University of Bonn) to launch sounding rockets from Rothera to measure the wind and temperature profile as a function of height in the mesosphere in conjunction with the US programme. Martin Jarvis was leading on this for UASD and was travelling with me to host the rocket programme. Also I had instituted a new regime at Halley where we had changed the staffing to include two post-doctoral scientists (Kate Charles and Moray Grieve). I was keen to review how that had worked out for them and for BAS. On the more general front, Rothera had ceased to be a traditional BAS Antarctic station and was now a multifaceted complex requiring detailed management. It now had a significant management team, led by a permanent base commander, a field operations manager, a domestic manager and a facilities and engineering manager, who split their time between the HQ in the Antarctic winter and Rothera in the summer. They were supported by a junior administrative officer – chosen from the junior staff at HQ – to deal with all the paperwork. The latter post was much sought after. The station was the base for all air operations, the staging post for field operations, and the base for scientific diving. It was also home to a very sophisticated year-round biological sciences laboratory, the Bonner Laboratory. In the summer time the complement might rise to 120 or more people. So arriving there was now a very different experience than it had been hitherto, with a very formal induction process occupying several days to ensure folk were effective and safe, and including refresher training in fieldcraft. So there was much to review with the management team to ensure that all the appropriate protocols were being followed and to give them a chance to bring issues to the ear of the top team. Operations at Halley were not quite so complex, but were fast becoming so, with a similar need to review and learn.

At Stanley there was a weather delay of four days for our flight on the Dash 7 to Rothera, but I occupied this in reviewing the BAS operation in the Falklands, discussing mesospheric science and the forthcoming campaign with Martin and our German guest, Professor F-J Lübken, and doing some hiking (when my thoughts were often focused on what my future might be). The flight took about five hours with nothing to see except cloud, but this time there was no getting into the cockpit to have a go at flying the beast: this was an airliner operated by the crew of two in that mode.

Then straight into the wall-to-wall briefings. The atmosphere was very positive and very busy, with lots of excitement. As well as the rocket programme, Rothera was hosting a BBC news team, and a visit by the composer Sir Peter Maxwell Davies seeking inspiration for the composition of a new Antarctic symphony that BAS had commissioned, so life was hectic – yet late in the evening my diary records:

> I went out for a quiet walk on my own just to reacquaint myself with the sight, smell and sound of the place. One of those soft, calm mostly overcast evenings which I love so it was a very peaceful and tranquil welcome back.

I spent three very busy days at Rothera, mostly taken up by management meetings and reviews/inspections, particularly to assess the compliance with BAS health and safety guidelines. I was also able to witness two rocket launches. These were conducted by the German Aerospace Centre (DLR) from a containerized launch and tracking facility. The Viper rockets were designed to reach 110 km altitude, where a small inflatable metal-coated sphere was released to be tracked by radar as it fell under gravity. From the manner in which it moved as it fell, both the temperature of the atmosphere and the wind speed could be determined. Professor Dave Fritts (University of Colorado), for whom we were operating the MF radar, was also visiting, so there was a real international scientific buzz; these were the first combined mesospheric dynamics studies in Antarctica.

On 11 January I set off for Halley, and under the watchful gaze of the real pilot had the opportunity again to fly the plane for most of the journey, including a period of instrument flying, which was great fun. I had just over a week at Halley – a very busy week. The atmosphere was not as buoyant and positive as it had been at Rothera, and the PBC was obviously overloaded. But there had been a very productive winter, with Kate Charles doing some very nice research using the AIS adapted to make soundings of the mesosphere; these coupled with the work going on at Rothera, and linked into a global study programme on mesospheric behaviour. Dick Kressman had deployed the fourth operational AGO in December; and a brand-new experiment for studying the lower ionosphere – an imaging riometer[114] – was being constructed by Mike Rose while

---

114 A radio receiver which records the amplitude of cosmic noise (at 30 MHz). The strength of the signal is modified by the behaviour of the lower level of the ionosphere, so it provides a measure of ionospheric disturbance. An imaging riometer is a family of receivers designed to provide a two-dimensional image of the disturbances.

I was there. There were some personnel issues to deal with, and lots of more general management matters associated with the maintenance and development of the station infrastructure, but my overall assessment was that Halley V was a great success and would certainly last for its design life of 20 years. I had a trip out to the AGO A80 on the Recovery Glacier, again getting to do much of the hands-on flying.

Then came the rumours about what was going on back in Cambridge. Some were relayed to me directly by phone from the office and others more indirectly. It is not worth summarizing them now because I was not party to what was actually going on. Suffice it to say that Chris had confronted the issue of deputy director head-on as soon as he started work, taking soundings both internally and externally. But nothing concrete had emerged by 20 January, when the time came for me to head back to Rothera. The flight back went off quietly until about an hour out from Rothera, at which point there was a radio call from there telling me that Chris wanted me to phone him in Cambridge as soon as we landed. So, with some trepidation, I did. And the long and short of it was that he offered me, and I accepted, the post of deputy director from the beginning of February! This was before he and I had even met for the first time, so it was a real leap of faith on his part. But BAS had now got Krebs' dream team at the top.

It took a couple of days before the news broke at Rothera, but when it did I was overwhelmed by the positive atmosphere it engendered amongst everybody there, BAS staff and visitors alike. I suspect that there was the same response at Cambridge when the news broke there – that must have been very hard for Dougal. His contract was for a fixed term of five years, and I imagine that NERC might have offered to buy him out. But for whatever reason he chose to stay and was given the title of deputy director innovation. However, I made it plain that I considered there could only be one deputy director in an executive and operational sense, so Dougal's role for the remaining two years of his contract was essentially back-room support to Chris as far as I was concerned.

I got home on Thursday 29 January, and took up my new role on Monday 2 February. A small office adjacent to the directorate was very quickly created for Dougal, and I moved into the deputy director's office. John Krebs wanted my old job, as HoD put out for external competition, but Alan Rodger was doing very well in the role and already had the required grade on an individual merit basis, so I strongly counselled Chris to give him first refusal. This was accepted, so Alan didn't have to suffer the anxiety of competing for the job. Then very soon Chris himself set off for a whistle-stop trip to Rothera, leaving me to run the shop. And so the wheel had turned.

Chris had certainly taken a big risk by appointing me sight unseen, but I firmly believe we made an outstanding duo which together steered BAS to new heights of effectiveness and scientific excellence, making it an international exemplar and a national icon. Though we did not become close friends, we developed a strong mutual respect and a powerful working relationship in which we always presented a single unified face both to the staff and externally. But I always felt able, and considered that Chris expected it of me, to argue my corner and debate issues in private when I thought we were not heading quite in the right direction. In retrospect, the choice of Chris as director with me as deputy was inspired. Chris, coming from outside with new ideas and new contacts, was able to push for radical change, whilst the staff trusted me sufficiently to be more inclined to accept such radical moves if they saw that I was completely behind them. Chris proved himself not only to be an excellent broadly based scientist, but also a natural leader and somebody who knew how to manage a complex organization effectively. He is also an excellent communicator. I, of course, from my long experience knew in great detail what was required of senior management to run BAS and could therefore deliver BAS at an operational level to Chris as a finely honed tool for him to use. Though being director would have been a fine crown for me to wear at the end of my career, I am convinced that we were the right people in the right roles at the right time for BAS and for the UK's influence in Antarctic affairs. Thus the last eight years of my career were a golden period for me.

There was much to do in revitalizing the BAS science programme and in repairing our relationship with NERC. A fundamental strategic goal to which we both quickly committed was to cease any perception of hiding behind the ring-fenced funding, but rather work to make the outside world recognize that BAS science stood on its own two feet for quality and importance to humanity, so it should be supported on its own merits. My view was that much of the BAS portfolio had already passed that test, but it was necessary to demonstrate that by rigorous external scrutiny and competition with the HEI[115] sector. There were also structural impediments, both human and organizational, that needed to be dealt with – finding new ways to empower our key scientific movers and shakers, and breaking out of the silos that had inadvertently been created by the BAS divisional structure with its top-down (from the HoDs) control of the science programmes. BAS science programmes were set up, funded and operated in five-year (quinquennial) blocks. 1998 was the fourth year of what was known as the Second Quinquennial Programme, and through 1997 we had been starting to plan what programmes to propose for the Third Quinquennium (Q3), to begin in April 2000. Chris decided we should take a radical look at how we should define, approve and implement Q3. I was completely in agreement with him, and my notebooks from the time show that by March 1998 he and I were very deeply engaged in debating how we should do this.

In the two years leading up to Q3 we radically reorganized the whole of the BAS approach to science research and science delivery. First we defined what the Vision for BAS should be, and then developed a Mission Statement describing what our purpose was. Visions and Mission Statements are often derided, but actually if

---

115 higher education institution

time and effort is spent in carefully defining them, and they are not just stuck in a drawer thereafter but placed front and centre in strategic discussions, they can provide a powerful focus. Out went the old hierarchical divisional ownership of the science projects, to be replaced by science prime movers (the principal investigators – PIs) who were chosen by competition and who were outside the old divisional structure. They proposed science programmes which could be multidisciplinary in nature but then had to compete for the necessary resources though independent (of BAS) peer review. The science divisions became the providers of scientific resources (scientific personnel and well-found laboratory) with the HoDs becoming managers charged with delivering the services required to the PIs. The divisions themselves were reshaped and merged, to provide three science groupings: Physical Sciences, Geo-Sciences and Biological Sciences. A completely new division was created – the Environment and Information Division (EID) – which provided environmental expertise, mapping, imagery and public relations, whilst the administration was restructured and renamed the Administration and Logistics Division. It was tasked with delivering logistic support – particularly the Antarctic logistics required – to the PIs. By the time Q3 was up and running the original HoDs had moved on, either into different roles, or out of BAS entirely.

At the top of the shop, too, there were changes. Dougal moved on as his five-year contract came towards its end, becoming the director of the Foundation for Science and Technology. Frank decided he needed a change and was snapped up by our sister organization, the British Geological Survey, as its senior administrator. This brought a new face into our midst – Alan John Pye (or JP as he was almost universally known). He joined us from the RAF, where he had been a career logistician, rising to the rank of air commodore. JP was an excellent choice. He was a very able and disciplined logistician, clear, outspoken, direct in his approach and completely unflappable, who brought a whole new rigour to the way BAS operated. He drove his team hard, but was very loyal to them all. Woe betide any HoD who criticized one of JP's team in front of others! But woe betide the team member if there was any substance to the criticism! I never regretted our choice of JP, and learnt a lot from him, which improved my performance as deputy director. We occasionally had significant disagreements, but they never soured our relationship – JP was not that kind of man. I had great respect for his abilities and like to think that he reciprocated.

In 2001 we repurposed the Directors' Committee – making it much more like a company board – renaming it the BAS Board in recognition of that change, and appointing non-executive members from without BAS to provide us with new insights and experience. The first of these was Dr Bruce Smith, an engineering entrepreneur who had built up several high-tech companies, and who brought a challenging but welcome technical/business insight to our deliberations. We also employed an external coach to facilitate regular residential board meetings where we would develop the longer-term strategy for the organization as well as firmly building a working team. In this way we were able to draw on the best techniques to evolve the management of BAS, to reach a peak where our efficiency and effectiveness were the envy of all of our international peers.

Chris and I quickly sorted out how we would organize our roles within the directorate. To put it simply, he did the upwards and outwards (grand strategy), while I led on the downwards and inwards (day-to-day running of BAS). There was one exception to this: whilst Chris led on international scientific coordination primarily through SCAR (where he became president), I led on Antarctic logistics oversight and coordination, becoming the UK representative on the Council of Managers of National Antarctic Programmes (COMNAP) and an expert advisor to the UK delegation to the Antarctic Treaty. I no longer had any time to continue any personal research – not that I was doing much by then, anyway. It was also time to divest myself of various international scientific roles I still retained.

I now had a very rich and broad-based portfolio of challenging leadership roles, all of them fascinating. I had day-to-day management of the whole of the Q3 programme as line manager for the PIs. This meant that I had to get up to speed very quickly, at least at a first-order level with the key scientific goals and questions, and with the strengths/ weaknesses of the PIs themselves, to be able to provide them with effective career guidance and support. Whilst I would never claim to have a detailed understanding of many of the projects, I was able soon to judge what was good and worth supporting across the whole portfolio, and what was not. I was line manager for the HoDs, so I took a supervisory role in the delivery of resources to the PIs and in acting as a broker between them and the HoDs. The health and safety portfolio also landed on my desk, which in BAS was fascinating, complex and diverse – and of course hugely important. Along with that came oversight of the contract we had with Derriford Hospital to provide medical services (including doctors in the field) for our staff. On top of all that were the more ad hoc jobs, particularly chairing project boards for major projects. I was sad to lose regular contact with my international family of scientific colleagues, but the COMNAP and treaty work brought a whole new family of very interesting folk with whom I now worked.

An early decision that Chris and I took was that one of us should normally visit all the major field locations each summer season. This was to keep us grounded and to give the field staff an opportunity to have their say. For me it also involved onsite assessment of health and safety performance, issues and problems. Occasionally I had to conduct formal investigations of incidents, and there were nearly always staff issues to address. The field operation split broadly between the northerly stations – South Georgia and the South Orkneys – and the southerly operation – Rothera and Halley. I got into a routine of going south each year, visiting the northern and southern operation in alternate years, starting with Halley and Rothera in 1998/99.

The 1998/99 trip was my first as deputy director, and it was notable in several ways. Firstly, I had to investigate the circumstances surrounding two oil spills that had occurred at Rothera during the previous winter and an apparent attempt to cover up what had happened. Secondly, BAS had managed to convince a media team from ITV to invest the time to go to Halley Station to make a series of news reports, and thirdly, it was the last season of operation for the *Bransfield*. I headed south in mid-November using the RAF airbridge from Brize Norton to the Falklands. Then in Stanley I joined the *JCR* to sail to Rothera; a more leisurely trip than usual, with stops at various points down the peninsula to inspect old and disused British bases as part of an ongoing plan of clean-up and restoration. The trip was graced with both horrid weather, with winds exceeding 75 knots, and magic moments of calm and beauty. An entry from my diary from 25 November 1998 sums up one such moment:

> One of those rare heart stopping experiences late in the evening. The ship was driving into a strong wind down the Bransfield Strait into the setting sun. The sky was almost completely clear with just a few clouds to pick out the glow of the setting sun. Ahead was a silver and gunmetal sea, darting from wave top to wave top were squadrons of Cape Pigeons flying line astern riding the updrafts. On the southern horizon – majestic but sombre and only half seen were the mountains of the northern peninsula – and to cap it all the ship would stick her nose into a wave and send a golden rainbow threaded curtain of spray up over the foredeck to crash against the wheelhouse window before flying over the top of the ship. As she stuck in her nose so she would shudder and the wind whistled outside. I thought of a picture but no camera could have caught the experience – it was there to be lived and remembered for all its tactile and visual and aural glory!

The view astern as the RRS *James Clark Ross* steamed at speed through rotten sea ice in Penola Strait.

The rest of the trip to Rothera was equally pleasant, with fine weather and some extensive areas of first-year fast ice where Jerry Burgan (the captain of the *JCR*) was delighted to demonstrate the capabilities of the ship, steaming through it at speed.

For the first few days at Rothera things were difficult because I had to determine how the oil spills had occurred, why the oil spill recovery plan had not been immediately instituted, and whether there had been an intentional cover-up. This was not merely of internal significance. BAS was legally bound by the Antarctic Act 1994 to take immediate response action and to report all spills to the FCO, so the FCO was looking over my shoulder. The several individuals involved knew that disciplinary action might well be taken, making the atmosphere on base quite edgy. So I carried out a series of formal interviews, opting to do them on the ship rather than on the station. To cut a long story short, the standing instructions on oil tank filling had not been adhered to, and there had been a systemic failure in not ensuring that base members were aware of the oil spill recovery plan and trained to use the equipment. But there was no evidence of a concerted cover-up. Once reminded of the oil spill procedures, the BAS members concerned had made very good efforts at clean-up in very trying conditions, and although one individual had been negligent, I decided on only a minor financial sanction in that case. Once that was over, the whole team heaved a big sigh of relief and got on with what was otherwise a positive and successful summer season. And with that rather difficult job behind me, I put on my health and safety hat to review operations at Rothera and at our summer field camps further south. The most interesting one was Sky-Blu.

BAS had been expanding its reach into the interior of the continent using the fleet of four Twin Otters, and for this a forward refuelling station was needed during the summer season. It needed to be suitable for operations with the Dash 7 aircraft, which could deliver bulk fuel in drums. It was becoming possible to utilize areas of blue ice as natural runways for wheeled aircraft, and we found a suitable blue ice field near the Sky-Hi nunataks[116] at 74°51'S, 71°36'W, which provided a runway of about 1.2 km at an altitude of about 1,500 metres. After proving trials, to establish to the CAA's[117] satisfaction that the Dash could operate safely off the blue ice, the small summer camp, Sky-Blu, was established there to maintain the runway and provide weather reports etc for flight operations. The Dash could deliver a load of around 3,000 litres of fuel per rotation, which allowed a sizeable stock to be built up quickly. Operations had begun the previous season, so I was keen to review the setup for myself. I was able to make two visits in the run-up to Christmas, the first by Twin Otter, stopping at our other, more traditional, forward field site, Fossil Bluff, and the other by the Dash. It is certainly a surreal experience, landing for the first time on what is essentially a gigantic skating rink. Landing into wind normally means flying directly towards the nunatak – in this

---

116 A nunatak is an isolated mountain peak which protrudes from an otherwise unbroken ice field.

117 Civil Aviation Authority

Final approach to land at Ski-Blu blue ice runway with Mount Lanzerotti in the background. Blue ice is ice that has had most of the air bubbles squeezed out of it. Extensive fields of blue ice can occur in the vicinity of nunataks, where high local winds continually scour the covering of snow away, leaving a hard blue surface, which if extensive enough provides a safe runway for large wheeled aircraft.

case Mount Lanzerotti[118] – which is quite unnerving, and even more so when taking off towards it. But there is no real problem manoeuvring and stopping our planes on the ice, because they have two (or four) engines with reverse pitch. However, disembarking is another matter; over the years that I have been going to Sky-Blu my first action, more often than not, is to fall over.

I left Rothera for Halley late in the evening on Christmas Eve, flying via refuelling stops at Fossil Bluff and a new, unmanned, fuel depot on the Ronne Ice Shelf. We got to the latter early on a sunny morning and celebrated the arrival of Christmas Day with a mince pie and coffee while we refuelled with a manual pump. Another somewhat surreal moment. We arrived at Halley mid-morning, the ship had only recently arrived so relief was in full swing with round-the-clock shifts to get the station resupplied. Even so, the chefs provided a Christmas dinner, but also Christmas breakfast for the other shift. And as usual, I had a beautiful Xmas box to open, put together by Helen and the girls.

---

118 Mount Lanzerotti is named after an American space science colleague of mine – Lou Lanzerotti, from Bell Labs. I was able to send him a framed picture of his mountain, which he had never had the opportunity to visit.

Apart from a general review of operations and safety practices at Halley, the main highlight for me was taking the ITV crew out to the AGO in the Shackleton Mountains, where I gave one of the more unusual interviews of my career. The location must have made it mind-blowing for them. The interviewer was the well-known ITV News science editor, Lawrence McGinty, a pleasant and able man. We had a superb flight back – another one of those moments to pinch oneself and consider that one is being paid for it. From my diary for 27 December:

> We went low over the Shackletons to inspect the Bernacchi Heights and Mount Sheffield Depots. The blue ice at Mount Sheffield is vast! Makes Sky Blu look like a pin prick. The Slessor Glacier was also an incredible sight. But the real climax was the Therons – Not been there before. We approached from the South East where the mountains are largely hidden, then swooped over the edge of the cliff – just stunning, first the ice fall and then the 3000ft cliffs of the mountains. The sedimentary layers and huge basalt stripes are fantastic. Apparently the basalt flows are 100 MY old – the product of subterranean volcanic eruptions. One layer is over 200 m thick! The sediments are from 270 MY ago with alternating coal (thick vegetation) and sandstone (marsh & river bed). We landed there and strolled over to the scree. Collected some coal. The real finale was the vast cloud of Antarctic Petrels wheeling high over the ridge – there are thousands nesting there.

My stay at Halley was short. I joined the *Bransfield* on 3 January during its last season with BAS. It was a quiet ship, with very few passengers aboard: the ITV team and their BAS minders and one or two others. It was also a quiet ship because it was shortly to go out of service with BAS – something the crew, and Captain Laurence in particular, were not happy about. So my ear was bent quite significantly on the subject as we sailed via Signy Island to the Falklands and my flight home. Later in the year (1 October) I made a poignant journey with Chris, Dick Kressman and Mike Pinnock to Grimsby to say a final goodbye to the fine old tub as it passed out of BAS ownership to make its final voyage to the breaker's yard in India via a final cargo of cement to be delivered in Algiers. A very sad end for a fine ship – Dick and I were the only ones present to be able to claim that we were present on its very first voyage and its last one for BAS. We had both been on board when its sailed from the shipyard where it had been built in Leith on New Year's Eve 1970 for Southampton, installing an experiment aboard. The following season our new ship,[119] the RRS *Ernest Shackleton*, came into service.

---

119 RRS Ernest Shackleton was not a new build for BAS and we did not own it. It had previously been the MV *Polar Queen*, built, owned and operated by Rieber Shipping of Norway, and the arrangement was a bare-boat charter with BAS staff crewing her. It was a highly capable ice-strengthened support and survey vessel used primarily for logistics support but occasionally for oceanographic research. But its unusual design, with its accommodation right at the bow, gave it such an unusual motion that it was universally known as the vomit comet. It has now been replaced by the RRS Sir David Attenborough, otherwise known as Boaty McBoatface.

One of the more unusual TV interviews in my career – Lawrence McGinty interviews me for ITV out on the Recovery Ice Stream in the Shackleton Mountains.

BAS Twin Otter at the Theron Mountains; note the amazing sedimentary layering in the cliff face.

15

COMNAP AND THE
ANTARCTIC TREATY

I became the UK representative on the COMNAP in the summer of 1998 and attended my first meeting in June, in Concepción, Chile. This meeting was in association with the SCAR scientific symposium. To understand why the two organizations met together and more generally about the association of COMNAP with the Antarctic Treaty System (ATS), I need to digress briefly to describe how COMNAP came to exist, and what role it plays.

COMNAP is something of an oddity in the family of international organizations. It does not fall into the category of an NGO,[120] nor does it have the status of a formal inter-governmental organization. But all of its national representatives are the managers (or their designates) of the National Antarctic Programmes (NAPs), so all of them are in one way or another employees of their respective governments. How, then, did it come into being? Its roots lie in SCAR – a true scientific NGO. But SCAR was unusual, in that as well as having a structure of discipline-based scientific working groups, it had a working group concerned with logistics and operations in Antarctica – the Working Group on Logistics (WGL). This did not sit easily within SCAR and had no direct connection with the ATS, hence was not particularly effective in coordinating the growing operational and logistical activities happening under the governance of the ATS. In the mid-1980s several of the heads of the NAPs concluded that a separate executive group was needed that could quickly bring together experts to decide on effective practical measures on SAR, environmental management, and coordination of major international science projects among other things; and have the executive authority to efficiently implement them in a timely manner. Things came to a head at the SCAR meeting in Hobart in 1988 (incidentally, the first one that I attended). It was a difficult birth, in which the WGL died and from its ashes rose COMNAP and its sister grouping, the Standing Committee on Antarctic Logistics and Operations (SCALOP).

---

120 non-governmental organization

The vexed story of its birth and early years is very well covered by its first executive secretary, Al Fowler.[121] Suffice it to say here that as part of the divorce settlement SCAR and COMNAP decided that they would 'federate' with each other, with their executives holding joint meetings, exchanging documents, and regularly holding their general meetings at the same time and place to assist liaison. But COMNAP did not (and does not) answer directly to SCAR or to any higher international authority. This is unlike SCAR, which is part of the International Council of Scientific Unions. In its early years, the relationship between the ATS and COMNAP was uncertain at best, with the ATS not quite sure whether COMNAP would intrude on what it saw as its turf. But by the time I got involved the ATS had accepted COMNAP as an essential source of practical expertise and hence made it one of its three observer organizations. The others are SCAR and CCAMLR. The observers are entitled to attend and fully participate in Antarctic Treaty meetings from the perspective of their specific areas of competence, providing advice and support to the treaty parties as required. COMNAP is now the highly effective arm of the treaty, providing advice on the practical implementation of governance measures introduced by the ATS to better and more safely govern activities in Antarctica while protecting the environment.

I greatly enjoyed my involvement in COMNAP, making new international contacts and friends as well as contributing significantly in my own small way to the better management of activities within Antarctica. However, I cannot say that I found my first meeting particularly riveting. In fact, the strongest emotion that stands out from my diary is summed up as 'boredom'. But I quickly found two areas where I could make a real impact. The first, perhaps rather obviously, was in health and safety, where the BAS approach to Antarctic safety management had become to be seen as somewhat of an exemplar. The second was not anything quite so obvious – liability for environmental damage, of which more anon. All of my involvement within COMNAP related indirectly or directly to matters under discussion within the ATS. It seemed therefore sensible for me rather than Chris to take a day-to-day lead in the BAS dealings with the Polar Regions Unit of the FCO – the group charged with representing the UK at treaty meetings. So now I need to say a little bit about the ATS and how it works in practice, to set the context for my involvement in its activities through the final six years of my career.

First, a little history. The period immediately post World War II was a fraught one for Antarctica, during which it could very easily have become a focus of discord and conflict – possibly even a second front in the Cold War. Seven countries had territorial claims on the continent, of which three (the UK's, Argentina's and Chile's) overlapped. The USA in public made no claims and recognized no claims, but reserved the right to make claims to large swathes of the continent. In the late 1940s the seven claimants

---

121   Fowler A.N. (2000) *COMNAP, the National Managers in Antarctica,* American Literary Press, Inc., ISBN 1-56167-619-5

and the USA did try to negotiate a condominium arrangement, but with no success. Meanwhile the Soviet Union made plain that no international agreement about governance would be successful unless it was fully engaged in shaping it.

So the future looked somewhat bleak; but then a different initiative reared its head. In the spring of 1950 British geoscientist Sir Sidney Chapman was invited to participate in a meeting on the upper atmosphere at Caltech. On his way there he stopped off to visit the Applied Physics Laboratory in Maryland and spent the day with James Van Allen, who headed the high-altitude group using rockets to study the upper atmosphere. Van Allen arranged a dinner for Chapman at his home, inviting a small group of eminent American geophysicists, notably including Lloyd Berkner, Ernest Vestine, S. Fred Singer and J. Wallace Joyce, all well acquainted with Chapman. Over a dessert of Abigail Van Allen's famous chocolate cake[122] the conversation turned to the opportunities offered by advances in such technologies as rockets, radars and computers, to really get to grips with the major questions in geomagnetism and ionospheric physics; it was perceived that applying them through coordinated studies in Antarctica might hold the key to major advances. Lloyd Berkner proposed the idea of an International Polar Year to coincide with the major maximum in solar activity expected in 1957/58, with its focus on Antarctica. Over the next few years this proposal caught the imagination of the international scientific community to the extent that it grew into what became the truly amazing and successful scientific undertaking known as the International Geophysical Year (IGY). The seven claimants all quickly realized that little notice would be taken of their claims by other nations, but they did not want to force the issue. So they all in their various ways let it be known that they gave blanket permission to any science programme to carry out research in their territory, provided it was under the auspices of the IGY, for the period of the IGY. Ultimately 12 nations did have research programmes on the ground: the seven claimants (the UK, France. Australia, New Zealand, Norway, Argentina and Chile) plus the USA, the USSR, Belgium, South Africa and Japan. The IGY was so successful that it created the potential for such an exciting scientific legacy that after it ended in 1958 the scientific community wanted it to continue. Meanwhile it had become clear that the USSR had no plans to remove itself from the continent or from any negotiations about its international status. Some have argued that it was the pressure from scientists that had led to the treaty, but the actual drivers were more complex and had much more to do with international power politics than science. However, it could be argued that the undeniable success of the IGY gave diplomats a unique opportunity to use science as an acceptable public face, allowing them to justify the power diplomacy to their publics. To cut a long story short, there was much secret diplomacy before the 12 nations met together in Washington in the autumn of 1959 to hammer out an agreement – and what an amazingly simple and successful agreement

---

122 Van Allen 1997, transcript of oral history interview, University of Iowa

MEMBERSHIP OF THE ANTARCTIC TREATY

There are two levels of membership of the AT: Acceding Party and Consultative Party. The APs are countries that have signed to abide by the terms of the treaty, but which have not been invited to be full consultative parties, and so do not take part in forming a consensus (or not) over what rules the treaty decides to adopt. The CPs are those countries that are either one of the original 12 signatories or countries that have been invited by the existing CPs to become part of the consensus mechanism by virtue of having demonstrated their interest in Antarctica by 'conducting a substantial programme of research there'.

it turned out to be. It was signed by the 12 in 1959, and came into force in 1961 after all the signatories (known as consultative parties or CPs) had ratified it through their parliaments.

What did the treaty consist of? Its main provisions were that the continent should be reserved for peaceful purposes only, with freedom for scientific investigation and exchange of data. A crucial article allowed for freedom of inspection of a signatory's activities by other signatories. That the USA and USSR agreed to this trust-building article at the height of the Cold War was both amazing and central to the success of the treaty. Then came what I like to think of as the territorial truce – Article 4 – which effectively froze the claims in such a way that the seven claimants could continue to maintain them for their own citizens, whilst other signatories did not need to take any account of them provided they adhered to the principles of the treaty. But if the treaty were ever to fail then the *status quo ante* would apply. It is a masterpiece of drafting. The treaty also banned nuclear explosions, nuclear power stations and the dumping of radioactive waste – the first international agreement of that kind. Its decision making is by consensus – which often means that progress can seem glacial, but also means that in general once a decision is made its provisions are fully implemented by all signatories. Finally, the treaty applies to all land and ice shelves south of 60°S. It has no temporal end point, but did include a requirement for review after 30 years of operation (of which more later). Initially there was no appetite amongst the seven claimants for there to be a standing secretariat, so all of the governance of the continent took place in what are called Antarctic Treaty Consultative Meetings (ATCMs), which initially happened once every two years, but are now annual and last for two weeks. These are formal diplomatic gatherings, carried out with simultaneous translation in the four languages of the treaty (English, French, Spanish and Russian). The business discussed and decisions made are recorded in the report, which is the formal record of governance activities. The latter has to be agreed line by line, in English at least, by the end of the meeting, and is then published in the four languages. This can make for some very fraught final afternoons, as I know from my own experience, when diplomats are desperate to get away to catch flights but must reach agreement first. And make no mistake, the report is no small thing – it will normally run to several hundred pages with many more appendices listing the measures, decisions and resolutions agreed upon. The main drivers of business are what are known as Working Papers. These are submitted by a CP, or group of CPs, with the intent to have significant discussion possibly leading to agreement on new measures, decisions or resolutions. They have to be submitted well ahead of the ATCM and be available in all four languages, and their content must be discussed in the full session of the ATCM.

The text of the treaty contains almost nothing concerning protection or conservation. The only reference is in Article IX, Para 1, which lays out how the treaty parties will conduct their work, where sub-paragraph (f) talks about the 'preservation and conservation of living resources in Antarctica'. But this quickly became a major part of the work of the ATCMs, producing a series of subsidiary agreements that together comprise the Antarctic Treaty System. In 1964 came the Agreed Measures for the Conservation of Antarctic Flora and Fauna, in 1972 the Convention for the Conservation of Antarctic Seals (CCAS), and in 1980 the Convention for the Conservation of Antarctic Marine Living Resources (CCAMLR). It is now a separate but associated convention with its own permanent secretariat located in Hobart. CCAMLR was very important, as it was essentially a fisheries agreement, but a very special one which took into account the needs of all predator and prey species – including humans. Emboldened by their success over fisheries, the treaty nations decided to tackle the much more knotty subject of mineral exploitation. As a result, many more nations rushed to adhere to the treaty and to quickly move on to become CPs, so that they could have their say in any final agreement. Through the 1980s the membership swelled from the original 12 contracting parties to 28 CPs, and in 1988, they agreed the Convention for the Regulation of Antarctic Mineral Resources (CRAMR). But then crisis hit the treaty system.

Two nations, Australia and France, decided not to ratify CRAMR, causing a schism. Why they did this is an interesting topic in itself – they would claim that it was because they saw the writing on the wall as regards conservation, but it is notable that

GOVERNANCE OF ANTARCTICA

The main outcomes of ATCMs as regards governance are: measures which are regulatory with legislative intent; decisions which refer to internal organisational matters; and resolutions which are non-binding hortatory statements. Unsurprisingly, there are generally few measures compared with resolutions, as the former have to be brought into the various countries' national law to take effect.

MAIN PROVISIONS OF THE MADRID PROTOCOL

Bans mining and prospecting for minerals

Requires Environmental Impact Assessment

Provides comprehensive protection for fauna and flora

Requires sound waste disposal and waste management

Requires prevention of marine pollution

Provides for area protection and management

Imposes liability for environmental damage (at the time of writing, not yet ratified)

both are claimant nations, with a much more nuanced view of the issue of minerals than non-claimants. Meanwhile, the non-aligned nations in the UN, led by Malaysia, became very unhappy about the rich nations of the world carving up the resources of Antarctica for themselves and began agitating for action in the UN. And to top this, the review point of 1991 was rapidly approaching. At this point the treaty could easily have failed. But the CPs very rapidly negotiated a new agreement to provide comprehensive protection of the Antarctic environment and dependent and associated ecosystems, including a total ban on mineral extraction – or even prospecting for minerals. This Environmental Protocol to the Treaty was agreed and signed in Madrid in 1991 within a few days of the deadline for the Treaty Review, so it was taken to be the outcome of the review. Thus the crisis was averted. It is often referred to as the Madrid Protocol, and entered force in 1998 once the national parliaments had ratified it. In British law its measures were enacted as the Antarctic Act 1994.

The FCO had for many years looked to BAS for expert advice and support for its activities at the treaty; indeed, part of the reason for our increased funding from the 1980s had been to raise the UK's profile on the international stage. The Polar Regions Unit (PRU) at the FCO was regarded by the international community as a prime mover in Antarctic diplomacy. This, I believe, is because, uniquely within the FCO, the PRU is not staffed by short-term career diplomats who move on every two years, but by a small team of permanent experts who have built up an incredible level of knowledge and 'group history' which is the envy of the other Antarctic nations. This makes them a very formidable force at treaty meetings. There have only been four heads of PRU since 1945, and three of those had had long-term direct experience of living and working in Antarctica. The expertise provided by BAS was one crucial element in maintaining that reputation.

So with that rather lengthy but necessary piece of scene setting, we can now return to my small part in the international governance of Antarctica. As far as delegations to the treaty go, the UK was then quite small, consisting normally of a head of delegation, a deputy, a legal advisor (all from PRU), an environmental expert provided by BAS, and from 1999 me as a more general expert advisor on policy, science and operations. During my period of involvement, the head was Dr Mike Richardson, his deputy was Dr Neil Gilbert (to begin with and then Dr Jane Rumble, who subsequently succeeded Mike as head in 2007) and the legal advisor was Tony Aust (succeeded by Jill Barrett), whilst from BAS Dr John Shears was the environmental expert. I have to say, with the benefit of many years of hindsight that of all the activities I relinquished when I retired, participating in treaty meetings is the one I miss most. They were fascinating, though sometimes there were long interludes where watching paint dry would have been more rewarding – and then a delegate might say something controversial that set the meeting alight.

The Madrid Protocol had major impacts on the way the treaty parties conducted their business. One of the very significant ones was the creation of a standing committee of the treaty to act as an expert advisor on environmental matters – the Committee for Environmental Protection (CEP). Up until that time advice on environmental protection had been provided by a SCAR group known as the Group of Specialists on Environmental Affairs and Conservation (GOSEAC). Though SCAR was still looked to for a wide range of scientific expertise by the treaty parties, the CEP took over much of the role previously provided by GOSEAC and became a fundamental part of the parties' relentless drive for better and better environmental protection. Another major advance has been the explicit involvement in treaty meetings by representatives of the Antarctic tourist industry and by a consortium of non-governmental environmental groups: the International Association of Antarctica Tour Operators (IAATO) and the Antarctic and Southern Ocean Coalition (ASOC), both of whom attend as invited experts.

There were several hot topics in play when I got involved. One of particular focus for the UK was the vexed issue of a permanent secretariat for the treaty system. Argentina had offered to host this in BA, and there was a growing consensus for this, but the UK

INVITED EXPERTS

This is a specific class of attendees at ATCMs. They can participate in discussions and make written submissions, but only in the form of Information Papers; they are not entitled to submit Working Papers. This distinguishes them from the observers, who are encouraged to submit Working Papers

was refusing to join this consensus, so the idea was stalled. I cannot say that I was party to the inner thoughts of the British government on this issue – but one of my first acts in the diplomatic arena was as a walk-on attendee in bilateral discussions between Britain and Argentina held at the FCO in February 1999. This meeting was a consequence of a significant softening of relations between the two countries which followed President Menem's successful visit to London for talks with Tony Blair the previous October. The latter had laid the foundations for the 14 July 1999 agreement on access, air service and fishing with regard to the Falklands. Britain was now pushing for Argentina to improve its performance regarding Antarctica from a political, physical and scientific point of view. Specifically, we were looking for demilitarization of the Antarctic operation, a credible scientific programme, and a stop to illegal fishing and obstruction within CCAMLR. There seemed to be some optimism around the table, but my diary noted 'we got jam tomorrow', even though the Argentine delegation claimed that decisions had been taken in principle. But then we adjourned to the Argentine ambassador's residence in Belgrave Square for a really good lunch without any further progress.

Another hot issue was Antarctic tourism, and more specifically the problem of big ships. The traditional model for Antarctic tourist trips was the use of small ice-capable vessels carrying up to 200 passengers. But now, increasingly large cruise liners carrying 1,000 or more passengers were dipping into Antarctic waters around the peninsula as part of longer cruises. These ships were not designed for ice, the waters through which they sailed were poorly charted, and there was no effective SAR capability available to them. So there was a worry that a major environmental and human disaster was waiting to happen. The problem was succinctly summed up at a meeting I attended in April 2004 involving BAS, the Department for Transport, the Marine and Transport Agency and the FCO, to prepare the UK position for the ATCM meeting to be held in Cape Town later that year; the April meeting was held in Whitehall, and in it a senior DfT official stated that DfT didn't give a fuck for the environment – that was for the FCO to worry about – what the DfT worried about was a cruise liner with 700 British pensioners on board going on the rocks. So make certain that it doesn't happen. I will not record the official's name nor the name of the ship he had in mind. But the UK delegation became prime movers, pushing for legally binding measures to reduce the risks posed by and to the big ships. The fruits of that labour did not appear until after I had retired, but in 2009 a measure was passed that denied the right to ships carrying more than 500 passengers to make any landings in Antarctica. Then in 2011, as a result of pressure from the treaty parties, the International Maritime Organization (IMO) introduced a new regulation banning the carriage and use of heavy fuel oil[123] in Antarctic waters, and finally in 2014 IMO introduced a mandatory Polar Shipping Code, which covers the full range of design, construction, equipment, operational, training, SAR, and environmental protection matters relevant to ships operating in waters surrounding the two poles. It entered force in 2017.

A third big issue, and one in which I became seriously engaged, was that of liability for environmental damage. Article 16 of the protocol provided for the parties to

---

123 Heavy fuel oil (HFO) was routinely the fuel of choice for the big cruise liners, but if spilled it is a serious hazard to the environment. Ships from then on had to use marine gas oil (MGO), which is less harmful to the environment. Several of the big ships were withdrawn from use in polar waters because the cost of conversion was too great.

The MS *Zandaam* near Couverville Island, close to a beach which is part of a Specially Protected Area, home to a very large colony of gentoo penguins. The *Zandaam* has a capacity of over 2,000 passengers and crew.

'elaborate rules and procedures relating to liability for damage arising from activities taking place in the Antarctic Treaty area and covered by this Protocol'. Legal experts had been pushing this topic around the table at ATCMs and inter-sessionally for upwards of a decade, trying to shape an additional annex to the protocol. Little progress had been made, even in defining what the scope of such an annex might look like, with visions ranging from 'comprehensive' to 'environmental emergencies only' with no real agreement even as to what 'comprehensive' might encompass, or for that matter the definition of an environmental emergency. Worse, as their meetings had continued to specifically exclude experts on the practicalities of operating in Antarctica, they had no real feeling for what could actually invoke a liability question. Only in 1998 did they decide to bring in such outside experts.[124] COMNAP had already established a Working Group on Monitoring the Liability Annex (MOLIBA) whose aim was to try to understand what any emerging agreement might mean for the national operators. Any agreement would have significant ramifications for the UK presence in Antarctica, depending on exactly what was finally included. We had many abandoned facilities and field dumps, and were already under an obligation to remove/clean up that legacy, but

---

124 Decision 3 (1998) Liability, ATCM 22 Tromsø

might potentially be at risk stemming from a Liability Annex. So it was natural for me to get involved with MOLIBA during my first COMNAP meeting in 1998, and by 2002 to have become its chair.

The first ATCM that I attended, in Lima, Peru, in May and June of 1999, was also the first one to involve more than lawyers in the liability discussion. Little progress was achieved, and I contributed relatively little. It was really a fact-finding and familiarization event for me, plus a chance to make informal contacts with my COMNAP colleagues who were present as part of their country's delegation. But the meeting did pass a resolution[125] requesting detailed advice from COMNAP and SCAR in the form of a Working Paper on the operational and scientific aspects of preventative measures and response action (to environmental accidents). For me the meeting was notable for three other reasons: firstly on the positive side, it saw the beginning of the move by the treaty parties to involve IMO in defining a polar code; secondly, and less positively, Argentina apparently had walked away, at least in public, from the understandings developed in February in London concerning the siting of the secretariat; the third notable thing was the remarkable way the delegates were transported to and from the congress centre and social gatherings. This was a convoy of coaches preceded by: a police escort of motorcyclists to clear the roads and to close junctions ahead of us so we

didn't have to stop; a cordon of motor cyclists around the coaches; and a truck with a SWAT[126] team of highly armed troops – and an ambulance bringing up the rear. But the country was suffering from an outbreak of internal terrorism at the time, and I suppose we were a very embarrassingly tasty target.

COMNAP met later in the year for a week in Goa, India, where we discussed the COMNAP part of the task set by the ATS, but didn't actually do any work on it. COMNAP met again in Tokyo in July 2000 where we agreed to hold

One outcome of the Lima Meeting was that I was invited to visit the US programme the following Antarctic Season. A very useful but also fabulous trip resulted, during which I flew from Rothera in a BAS Twin Otter to visit the South Pole. Then from South Pole I was flown by an NSF C130 to the US station at McMurdo and from there to New Zealand.

125 Resolution 5 (1999) Advice from COMNAP and SCAR, ATCM23 Lima
126 Special Weapons and Tactics

a workshop to draft a COMNAP response later that year, to be hosted by the French in Brest. And we were lucky to have a bit of a reprieve on the timescale for delivery. The ATCMs are supposed to be hosted in turn, in alphabetical order, by the consultative parties at the host CP's expense; for 2000 it should have been Poland hosting. However, the Poles were unable so to do, withdrawing at short notice. Instead the Dutch hosted a one-week meeting in September in The Hague, consisting of the CEP, a meeting of the group of legal experts and a one-day SATCM[127] essentially just to consider the CEP report but also to allow the lawyers to continue their negotiations on liability. I and other key COMNAP folk attended the meeting, and for convenience we scheduled our liability workshop straight after it, in Brest, when we got to grips with what the treaty parties were looking for and how to deliver it.

From then on much of my focus at successive ATCMs (St Petersburg, 2001, Warsaw, 2002 and Madrid in 2003) was concentrated on the developing discussions and what was being sought from COMNAP, and from July 2002 I took the lead in delivering its response. Basically what it required was firm and quantitative information on what sort of environmental accidents might happen in practice, whether their impacts could be dealt with, and at what cost. The St Petersburg meeting defined the questions to address more precisely.[128] In summary: for the purposes of establishing limits on financial liability, compensation and insurability, what are the worst case and less than worst case scenarios for environmental emergencies, including the probability of occurrence and estimated cost for response action? And what scenarios might occur where no response action was possible? My diary records that the actual text of the ATCM request was drafted by Erik Chiang (USA) and me, thus making certain they were questions we could actually answer.

It was these questions that drove MOLIBA's work from then on. We delivered an interim offering to the Warsaw ATCM in September 2002.[129] This was a work in progress, and was seen as such by the ATCM attendees. As a result, I convened a small group of key people to complete the work in Washington DC in January 2003 at the invitation of the Office of Polar Programs where, after two intensive days, a final draft was produced. This was a crucial meeting both for COMNAP's input and for the ultimate success of the negotiation of the annex, so I should identify the people who made it happen: from the USA, Erik Chiang (OPP); from Australia, Andrew Jackson (Antarctic Division); from Germany, Hartvig Gernandt (Alfred Wegener Institute); and from Chile, Patricio Erberhard (Chilean Antarctic Institute). This final draft identified the likely land-based and marine-based accidents; listed them in order of a

---

127 Special Antarctic Treaty Consultative Meeting: an informal gathering of the treaty, normally held with a particular topic in mind. But in this case it was an emergency measure to keep the work of the CEP on track.

128 The final report of ATCMXXIV para 75, p. 19

129 ATCMXXV/WP25 Working Paper on 'Worst Case' & 'Less than Worst Case' Environmental Scenarios.

semi-quantitative parameter we called 'environmental significance'; identified whether response action would be possible or not; and estimated what that response action was likely to cost. The bottom line was that the worst case environmental accident for which response action should be possible would be a ship foundering and releasing oil near an environmentally sensitive area such as a penguin colony. The worst case for which no response action would be possible would be the pollution of a sub-glacial lake. I presented the outcome[130] at the Madrid ATCM in June 2003. The paper was greeted with great appreciation and satisfaction by the ATCM, and the paper, together with a presentation from the secretary of the International Group of P & I Clubs[131] on how ships are insured and what liability is covered, had a profound and lasting influence on the course of the negotiation to agreement on the annex.

I continued as chair of MOLIBA until 2005, but as far as the Liability Annex was concerned my focus now switched to working with the FCO legal advisor (now Jill Barrett) at the ATCM in Cape Town, and then at a special meeting held in New York in April 2005, where agreement was reached on the content of the annex. The COMNAP paper was particularly influential in shaping Article 9 on the limits of liability. I found it a great pleasure to work with Jill, who was both an excellent lawyer and a very pleasant person. She was also a very accomplished tango dancer – not that she ever managed to get me up on the dance floor!

And finally the Liability Annex to the Environmental Protocol was signed at the Stockholm ATCM held in June 2005. But even there its passage had a bit of a hiccup. At the end of the first week of the meeting it looked as though all the loose ends has been squared away. But then the Argentine chief delegate announced that Argentina would not be joining the consensus at this meeting. Some significant back-room diplomatic pressure was brought to bear – concerning what I know not – and on the following Monday consensus was reached. Sadly, however, 17 years on the annex still hasn't formally come into force because insufficient countries have thus far ratified it. I do not think this is because they are unhappy with it; more that it is a complex matter to set in their national law. A group of countries were only prepared to accept this somewhat limited annex provided that discussions on a 'comprehensive' annex would be given priority. Where that has got to at the time of writing I do not know – but probably not very far.

I had retired by the time the ATCM took place in 2006, but this was to be hosted by the UK to be held in Edinburgh, so for two years leading up to it I had been deeply involved with the FCO, as part of the planning committee. And then the FCO asked me if I would take on the role of chief rapporteur at the meeting, to oversee the writing and delivery of the meeting report. I was pleased to do this, so had a very enjoyable if

130 ATCMXXVI/WP09 Working Paper on 'Worst Case' & 'Less than Worst Case' Environmental Scenarios.

131 Protection and Indemnity; essentially the confederation of organizations that provide insurance for ships at sea.

intense three weeks or so in Edinburgh at FCO's expense, with a team of eight bright young FCO staff doing the hard work of report drafting. We produced an excellent report on time by the end of the meeting.

This meeting had very important long-term consequences for me – some more serendipity in my passage through life. On the US delegation was a lady named Victoria Wheatley who was deeply involved with the Antarctic tourism industry, and whom I had got to know quite well from previous ATCMs. Over lunchtime she suggested that I might like to come on an Antarctic trip as a lecturer – and, more importantly, that I would be able to bring Helen with me. As Helen had never had the chance to share my passion this was an offer that I seized upon, asking Victoria what role I might play. Her answer? 'Well, you've been around for a long time and know lots so we'll call you the historian.' And now, upwards of two decades later, I have made a second career as a historian/guide on Antarctic tour ships, and can reasonably think of myself as a budding historian, having several peer-reviewed papers to my name and co-authorship of two books – and Helen has been five times to Antarctica with me (my daughters, twice each). More about all that later, but it really is a funny old world sometimes.

16

RETURN TO SOUTH
GEORGIA AND HALLEY VI

As mentioned earlier, BAS had been forcibly ejected from South Georgia in early April 1982 by the Argentine invasion, and the island had then been retaken by British forces in late April. A small military garrison was established in the buildings at King Edward Point, formerly occupied by BAS. And this was how the situation remained until the end of the 1990s. During 1997 Dougal Goodman (as acting director at the time) seems to have had some initial discussions within government on the possibility of the garrison being withdrawn and BAS returning in its place. I was not party to these, nor in any preliminary discussions within BAS which may have taken place with senior biologists about what BAS might do if we returned. As I took up the reins as deputy director there appeared to be some interest in Whitehall in proceeding. But there were many different parties involved, each with their own agendas – the Cabinet Office, FCO, the Overseas Territories Directorate (OTD), Falkland Islands government (FIG), the government of South Georgia and the South Sandwich Islands (GSGSSI), the OST, NERC, MoD, the commander in chief of the British forces in the Falklands (then known as CBFFI), and lastly BAS. Then there was MRAG Ltd (Marine Resources Assessment

THE GOVERNMENT OF SOUTH GEORGIA
AND THE SOUTH SANDWICH ISLANDS

South Georgia was formally brought under the jurisdiction of the Falkland Islands in 1908 by Letters Patent which made it part of the Falkland Islands Dependencies. This situation persisted until 1985 when it was deemed politically appropriate to separate it and the South Sandwich Islands from the Falklands, by making it a separate Overseas Territory with its own legal system and tax arrangements. Its main sources of income are the sale of fishing licences and tourism.

Group), a commercial spinout from RRAG (Renewable Resources Assessment Group) at Imperial College. MRAG already provided data gathering and expert advice on the South Georgia fishery under contract to FCO/GSGSSI.

The discussions about a military withdrawal from South Georgia continued through the summer of 1998, and by autumn key government departments had agreed in principle, allowing the MoD to make a public announcement that BAS would replace the garrison in 2000. BAS would then carry out environmental research, particularly to help development of sustainable fishing in the seas surrounding South Georgia. A budget of £5.35 million was set for capital expenditure, with a further £1 million per year to cover running costs. Most of capital (£4m) would come from MoD, with the balance from GSGSSI (£0.75m), FCO (£0.35m) and FIG (£0.25m). The running costs would come from the MoD (£0.5m) with the balance spread between other stakeholders, including potentially GSGSSI, FIG and FCO. This funding model came with its own problems, as we shall see. On the day of the MoD announcement Chris Rapley asked me to take the executive lead and establish a project board to carry the project through. I readily accepted – only to find myself sinking into a hornets' nest of irate biologists before the day was out. I was confronted by deep-seated enmities, exposed by the project, between several senior staff, who saw themselves as having some expertise/ownership concerning South Georgia and its fishery, what should happen there, and who should or should not be involved. For a while I was trying to herd angry cats. I will not name names; those involved will know to whom I am referring, particularly as the lobbying for position was taken outside BAS into Whitehall in the hope of bringing pressure to bear on Chris to modify his stance. Suffice to say that Chris and I held some robust meetings during the back half of September with a few folk, when they were invited to start behaving themselves. The situation was finally stabilized sufficiently for me to convene the first meeting of the South Georgia Project Board on 7 October with at least the semblance of agreement on participation.

Part of the heat that had been generated arose because folk either didn't understand or didn't like the remit BAS had been given. From the end of the whaling era in the mid-1960s until 1982 BAS had provided the political presence at South Georgia, but otherwise had been free to do whatever science it wished within its funding envelope, in line with our operation elsewhere in Antarctica. But the new project would be different. Now we would be contracted to deliver a service to the GSGSSI – the customer – to fit into a particular funding envelope, carrying out such applied research as it specified, as well as providing the political presence. The waters around South Georgia – part of the CCAMLR-managed fishing area – were a rich source of income for GSGSSI from the sale of fishing licences, particularly for the very lucrative and much sought-after Patagonian toothfish. GSGSSI apparently needed logistical support for the resident marine officer, for the whaling museum at Grytviken, and for a programme of applied fisheries research aimed at providing the scientific underpinning for long-term sustainability for the fishery. We were required to negotiate a practical programme within the overall funding envelope, and arrange the design and construction of the required facilities (living accommodation, laboratories etc), then staff and operate them to the agreed requirements as a fixed price contract. And all of this had to be operational by the 2000/01 summer season. There were lots of really good basic science projects that folks were keen to start, so they were naturally disappointed that they could not be accommodated. But there was an added twist, which was that GSGSSI had no real idea what science it needed done or whether it really wanted any – an expert customer it certainly was not. In fact, my suspicion in the early days of our negotiations was that it preferred just to maintain the *status quo* with MRAG providing what was needed for fishery management. So it fell to BAS to create an appropriate applied fishery programme and then convince GSGSSI that it needed doing, whilst being very careful not to tread on MRAG's toes.

Having got the team in shape in BAS, I could be forgiven in supposing that we would then steam ahead with what, by any stretch of the imagination, was a tight schedule. But it was not to be. We immediately ran into problems with NERC, who did not want any of the BAS science vote budget used in support of the project. This was understandable from NERC's point of view, but it meant we would need to account for, and get paid for, everything associated with the project out of the budget allocated – including staff time for the planning phase. A complication for sure, but not a problem, surely? Yes it was, because the various stakeholders were slow to agree how to make the money available to us for 'technical' reasons. We also found it very hard to get agreement in principle to an MoU (which would give us authority to start spending), let alone a Statement of Requirements (SoR) from GSGSSI on what it wanted.

By October 1999 things were becoming critical. We had finally reached an agreement on the content of the SoR, but there still remained significant issues amongst the stakeholders regarding the MoU, and we had run out of what little seed money we

A Patagonian Toothfish, *Dissostichus eleginoides*,104 cm long, pictured at South Georgia. These fish can grow to over 2 metres in length. (Credit Tony North, UKRI/BAS)

had received up to then. We therefore could not start turning the SoR into a technical specification, and certainly could not start recruiting the necessary staff. So it was now my duty to raise the red flag and stop the work. Such was the wall of indifference and even obstruction we seemed to face that Chris and I spent the afternoon of Friday 15 October drafting a letter to all the stakeholders, announcing that we had ceased work and that consequently completion could not be guaranteed before 2002/03. The letter, firmly worded, finished by saying, 'BAS now awaits instruction from HMG on how to proceed from here.' My diary records on the following Monday that:

> the crisis button of Friday has produced very remarkable results – a letter from the FCO giving us all we want. Amazing! So it looks like we are back on track for a March 2001 handover.

The logjam on the funding disappeared almost immediately, and we were also allowed to use single tender action to a contractor (Morrison), which was already in a partnership agreement with FIG, to design and build the accommodation, saving a great deal of time.

But it was still not plain sailing. It wasn't just a matter of procuring and building a station on an easily accessible and pristine site. South Georgia is 800 miles from anywhere, accessible only by sea; there was only a short summer season when construction work is possible; there was no local infrastructure upon which to call; and it was hardly a clean site. There was the legacy of the old whaling activities and the old settlement at King Edward Point (KEP), where the most significant issue was the abundance of asbestos that needed removal. Then there was the legacy of the conflict, which required specialist work by the military to find and remove old explosive devices before any work on site could safely start. There followed a series of multi-departmental meetings, sometimes in the Falklands, sometimes in the UK, as we shaped the plan for BAS to return, dovetailed into the military departure and clean-up. I found the senior military officers (mostly at one-star general level) a pleasure to work with: very positive, can-do and efficient. But there was still yet one more difficulty to emerge out of the woodwork.

The running costs of £1 million were supposed to be provided jointly by GSGSSI, FCO (on behalf of MoD) and FIG. But there was tension in the Falklands about the project, stemming from the decision in the 1980s to make South Georgia and the South Sandwich Islands (SGSSI) a separate overseas territory, independent of the Falklands. But, in a typically British sort of fudge, the governor of the Falklands also remained the commissioner for SGSSI. In late November 2000 – when construction was well under way and we were just a few months away from commencing operations – I was in Stanley for yet more meetings. I had agreed to give a public lecture entitled 'Return to South Georgia', which outlined what was planned and who was paying for it. The talk seemed to be very well received – but it turned out that one of the members of

The base that BAS built: the South Georgia Fishery Research Laboratory, which replaced the old BAS station and military garrison at King Edward Point.

the Falkland Council was in the audience, who had been unaware that FIG would be contributing to the costs. For her it was quite a personal and sensitive issue, as she had spent much of her childhood at KEP. So the breakup of the FID was not to her liking. The result was a very robust meeting between me and the governor/commissioner of the time, Donald Lamont, when I pointed out that as far as BAS was concerned the funding arrangements had been set in stone for a considerable time and were not confidential. I do not know the truth of what information had or had not been passed one way or the other, so I will not speculate. We agreed to differ, and I subsequently had a much more convivial meeting with the members of the Falklands Council. But the outcome was that the FIG did not make a contribution to the running costs; those fell upon FCO and GSGSSI alone. My own view is that there was nothing in the project to benefit FIG so there wasn't really any reason why it should have put up the money.

We delivered on the project on time, with the formal handover taking place on 22 March 2001. Early on there was talk of a big opening event, possibly including a royal. But the late 1990s were a period when relations between Britain/Falklands and Argentina was softening, with some really important steps forward, such as the commercial air service via Chile. Consequently, the opening ceremony was low key, involving Chris, the CBFFI and the governor.

What did we deliver in the end? We built a brand-new station capable of housing up to 18 people in nine ensuite twin study-bedrooms, with a separate annex to house the marine officer and family. Then there was a research complex with a biology laboratory, a controlled environment facility (an aquarium to the uninitiated) and offices, plus all the facilities required to make the place self-supporting (vehicles, power generators, workshops, storage and a medical centre). The jetty was upgraded to allow ships of the size of *JCR* to berth, and there were two powerful RIBs[132] to provide the transport

132 rigid inflatable boats

for the marine officer to carry out his official duties. There was also a small inshore research trawler for the fishery research. The normal permanent complement provided by BAS for the station was eight staff: base commander (and magistrate), boatman, scientists, doctor and facilities engineer. The research programme was aimed entirely at underpinning the fishery and GSGSSI's stance within CCAMLR, looking at such important topics as stock abundance, population structure, annual variability, feeding ecology, reproductive biology and the effects of fishing on non-target species.

The handover brought the work of the project board to an end – but not my involvement with the project. Management and development of the facilities, and of the science programme was overseen by a liaison committee, which brought together BAS, GSGSSI and FCO twice a year, with meetings alternating between the UK and the Falklands. I led the UK delegation. In fact, one of my last acts as deputy director in January 2006, just a couple of weeks before I retired, was to take part in a meeting of the committee in Stanley.

In the span of my time with BAS up to the turn of the century, the organization had moved from a band of happy amateurs to a highly professional and efficient operation, seen as an exemplar by our international peers. As just one part of this transformation we now maintained a business plan, which was our working bible. It was a living document, revised and updated each year, part of which involved a review of all our assets (buildings, ships, aircraft, bases, major equipment) to assess the need for replacements, new investments etc. We laid out planning assumptions for when, say, a ship would need a major overhaul and the like, so that a structured plan could be presented to government for our future investment needs. In 2000 it had become clear that Halley V was a considerable success. Its original design life had been put at 15 years and it had already been in operation for 10 years. By then we had developed a great deal of practical expertise in how to efficiently maintain the station above the snow surface, to the extent that it remained fully operational throughout the annual jacking process. More than once I had sat in the dining room nursing a coffee or eating my breakfast while accessing the local internet as the station slowly but majestically rose above the surface. We had also learnt to manage the annual build-up of snow by careful grooming, and had a fleet of big bulldozers and snow blowers to do the job.

There was little doubt that the station could be kept fully operational for long after its design lifetime, and the business plan assumption was now for a lifetime of 20 years. But there was one irresistible force that stood in the way of that. And this was the steady march of the station westwards at around 1 to 2 metres a day as the Brunt Ice Shelf flowed out toward the sea, where its seaward edge regularly calved to release icebergs. Mostly these were small, so the edge eroded slowly, meaning that the coastline appeared to stay roughly in the same place whilst the station slowly moved towards it. But, episodically there would be a major calving when the edge might break back several or many kilometres, releasing one massive berg which reset the coastline.

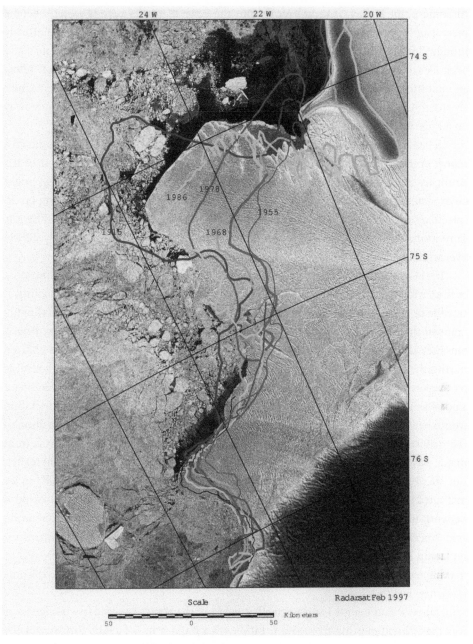

A satellite image of the shape and location of the Brunt Ice Shelf, taken in 1997. Also shown are historical locations of the ice front for 1915 (blue), 1955 (thin red), 1958 (thick red), 1968 (green), 1978 (purple) and 1986 (yellow) The square feature at the top of the image is the snout of the Stancomb-Wills Ice Stream, while the nose-like feature below it is where Halley Station is located. The Lyddan Ice Rise is in the top right-hand corner. The nose has yet to calve, and now protrudes much further westward than has been seen before. (Credit C.S.M. Doake (2002) Report on the Lifetime of Halley: risk of Brunt Ice Shelf calving. UKRI/BAS)

At some point Halley V would move into the coastal zone, where it would become increasingly vulnerable to such a major calving. The slow regular erosion had already brought Halley III to the coast, and for several years parts of the Armco tunnels had been clearly visible at the base of the coastal cliffs. We would of course never allow an operating base to get so close to the coast to be at serious danger from the regular erosion; the real danger was that of a sudden massive calving, taking the station away on a huge iceberg.

In late 2000 Alan Rodger, now head of the Physical Sciences Division, produced a report pointing out that there was insufficient knowledge about the behaviour of the Brunt Ice Shelf for a reliable risk assessment of when and how a major calving might be expected. As a consequence of this I established a multidisciplinary working group (glaciologists, Halley experts, logisticians and environmental experts), chaired by me, to re-evaluate the hazard posed due to calving and thereby establish the likely period over which it would be acceptable to plan for the occupation of the station.

The starting point was to identify the historical behaviour – location and motion – of the ice front. For the modern era that was relatively easy because of the availability of satellite imagery, but prior to that there was very little to go on: Shackleton had roughly mapped the coastline as he drifted past, trapped in the ice in 1915 on the *Endurance*, but after that there was nothing further until 1955, when the coastline was charted during the Royal Society expedition in preparation for the IGY. That 1955 coastline plot was crucial, since it showed the biggest eastwards break-back, and hence provided a possible geographical limit for where the risk of a major calving impacting the station would become large. It gave a starting point from which, given the current position of the station and the daily motion of the shelf, we were able to estimate that the risk from major calving would be low up to 2010 but rapidly become very significant thereafter. But we needed much more information on the current behaviour of the shelf, so we instituted a comprehensive programme of monitoring and measurements using a network of GPS stations and strain gauges, which has been maintained in operation ever since. We also refined the basic risk assessment, but the planning horizon for replacing Halley was set firmly as 2010. BAS now embarked on the long process of making a case for the investment required to build what (surprise, surprise) become known as Halley VI.

Halley V had been so successful that we took the time to consider whether there was merit in attempting to re-site it rather than build a new facility. But we quickly concluded that it probably was not practical, and even if it was we would not save much money and would not be able to optimize the accommodation for current and future needs. Successive Halley stations had always been located on the Brunt Ice Shelf within a few kilometres of each other, But I was keen to consider whether there was a more suitable place for Halley VI. The one place that offered some real advantages was the Lyddan Ice Rise, about 230 km north-east of Halley. This was a three-pointed star-shaped island of ice, rising to about 220 metres above sea level. It had two very significant advantages over the Brunt. The first was that the dome of the Lyddan was stable and essentially unmoving, so a station built there would not require re-siting regularly. The second was that it was to the north of the Stancomb-Wills glacier tongue. The latter had to be rounded to reach the Brunt, and was often a significant barrier because pressured pack ice regularly built up near it. On the negative side, access to the Lyddan from the sea was an unknown quantity. The site was a further 230 km from Rothera, reducing payloads that could be carried by air from there, and being at 220 metres altitude would be more prone to fog (which down at Halley might be low, but operable, cloud). Also the change of site would have an impact on the interpretation of the long-term data sets accumulated at Halley. Even so, for a while – even as late as 2004 – Lyddan was looked at as the prime site. However, we finally decided that the negatives outweighed the positives – basically better the devil you knew – and we settled on a site 20 km or so east of Halley V. That this was a fateful decision was to become clear about a decade after I retired – but more of that below.

The new station would be a very major project as regards UK spend on science facilities, so there was a lot of groundwork to do in making a case and scoping the likely cost. But the case did not rest only on the quality, importance and timeliness of the science that was planned. There was an equally important political dimension. As long as the government saw Britain's presence in Antarctica, and in the international fora associated with Antarctica, as important, then the BAS footprint of activity had to be maintained at least at the current level. Halley Station's geographical position was politically sensitive, as it sat close to the eastern border of British Antarctic Territory. It was for the FCO to decide on the political priority, but as in the past, we continued to have an unwitting ally, in the shape of the government of Argentina. Curmudgeonly noises from there over the Falklands tended to focus the FCO on the need to maintain the UK presence in the South Atlantic and Antarctic, so the way the Kirchner government was behaving in the early 2000s did us no harm at all.

We developed a strong scientific case and budget, based on what we believed would be the cost of building an updated version of Halley V. We first got in principle agreement for these from NERC (and its advisory committees) by the summer of 2003. It was then crucial to get the umbrella organization overseeing the research councils (known then as RCUK) to include the necessary funds in their bid to the upcoming government spending review (SR2004). So at the end of August 2003 we asked the BAS review group to endorse our overall concept and proposed budget, confirm the need to replace the station, and stress the priority seen as regards SR2004. This went well, resulting in a very positive letter from the FCO to RCUK. We had also set up a project board under my chairmanship to oversee delivery of the project – both delivering the new station and removing the old one under the requirements of the Madrid Protocol. But given the size and importance of the project, this board had a much more formal and structured manner of working than the board I chaired for the South Georgia project. Now, a standard government model called PRINCE[133] was employed. We had also recruited a full-time project manager by the end of 2003.

All previous Halley stations had either been entirely designed in house or had very strong in-house involvement in the nature of the structure. We had much expertise in what would and would not work in Antarctica within our style of operation, and given the success of Halley V could have just built on that concept for Halley VI. However, we had in the past given little thought to the ergonomic side of design; our accommodation was generally utilitarian, particularly that on the Brunt Ice Shelf. Given the very austere environment where sensory deprivation was a big issue, having a home that is a pleasure to live in makes a very big difference. Also we were toying with the idea of building a station designed from the outset to be relocatable. Consequently, and also because the organization had become much more public relations savvy, we decided to launch an international design competition in association with RIBA[134] to see what exciting ideas the world of architecture could come up with.

This was launched with an open worldwide call for expressions of interest (EoIs) which produced a very considerable response – 86 bids in total. An independent jury of experts was created to judge the bids, chaired by Sir Nicholas Grimshaw, then president of RIBA (particularly known for the Eden Project and Waterloo International Railway Station). Chris was also a member; but as I was chair of the project board there needed to be a Chinese wall[135] between me and the panel's deliberations so that it could deliver the final chosen design for my committee to take forward. The panel whittled the longlist of EoIs down to a shortlist of six proposals. The six candidates were given an honorarium of £10,000 each to develop concept proposals. From these a final shortlist of three was selected, to develop complete costed proposals including forming partnerships with contractors who were to be drawn from a shortlist created by a similar call for EoIs. And then the last step was to choose a winner from the three teams. All three finalists were strong contenders. One design I found particularly intriguing was a fully self-contained structure designed to walk itself to a new site when it required repositioning. But in the end, in July 2005 the jury opted for a somewhat more conventional but still highly innovative design from a consortium consisting of Faber Maunsell, Hugh Broughton architects and contractor Morrisons. This was a modular design with the modules joined together like railway carriages with flexible but weatherproof linkages. The modules were designed to be individually jacked, with their legs mounted on big ski pontoons which allowed them to be towed when the station needed relocating.

---

133 PRINCE (Projects in Controlled Environments) is a structured project management method which divides projects into manageable and controllable stages separated by 'gates'. There is a requirement to review the viability of the project at each gate before embarking on the next stage.

134 Royal Institute of British Architects

135 a virtual barrier: an ethical device to block the inappropriate transfer of information

The design had the advantage that it allowed great flexibility in both the layout of the modules and their number, offering opportunities for site development as needs changed. The consortium was offered an enabling contract to develop a costed tender by November 2005. (Although I had been quite taken by the self-propelled station idea, it would have been unwise to have gone for such a revolutionary, but rather inflexible, concept in such a harsh environment.)

Meanwhile there was the Antarctic Treaty dimension to be dealt with. There were two requirements that stemmed from the Environmental Protocol to be addressed. The first was the need to clean up the Halley V site – basically, to return the environment to its pristine state once the station was closed. But given the extreme nature of the environment and the fact the site would ultimately become part of an iceberg which itself would decay and disappear, there needed to be some sensible and pragmatic decisions about what 'clean up' really meant. Though the structures above the surface (buildings, antenna systems etc) could be removed relatively easily, there was a lot of buried infrastructure – building foundations and legs, fuel storage, water melter, Armco service tunnels, sewerage waste etc. To recover/remove these would require a truly herculean effort involving digging some very large and very deep (tens of metres) holes in the ice shelf. This would be environmentally damaging in itself because of the volume of atmospheric pollutants that would be released from the heavy plant involved, as well as being inherently a dangerous and very costly undertaking. In the end we got approval from the FCO to limit the clean-up to removal of all the above-surface facilities and as much hazardous material from sub-surface as was practicable. What would be left would ultimately end up on the seafloor somewhere as an artificial reef.

The Environmental Protocol also requires that before a party to the treaty embarks on any activity deemed to have 'more than minor or transitory impact' on the environment, a Comprehensive Environmental Evaluation (CEE) should be carried out. This CEE then has to be presented at a treaty meeting for review and comment. Depending on its reception at the ATCM, there was a requirement to take account of any substantial issues raised and revise the CEE accordingly for presentation at the next treaty meeting. We quickly decided that although a key design requirement of the new station was a considerably reduced environmental footprint than that of Halley V, it would still have more than a minor or transitory impact, so we opted to produce a CEE. In this we strongly argued that the value of the science conducted at Halley for the wellbeing of humanity greatly outweighed the environmental impact the station would have. The BAS environmental officer, John Shears, had the primary responsibility for drafting the CEE. Once we had got it approved by the FCO, John and I jointly presented it to the Stockholm ATCM in June 2005, where it was very well received and endorsed by the meeting.

So as the autumn of 2005 began things appeared to be proceeding on track, and we awaited the final tender from the consortium. The next step for the project board would be to assess whether the project could pass Gateway 3, the point when the crucial investment decision had to be made. But in early November a bombshell arrived – in the form of the tender with a ticket price of roughly double the available budget. The board, at its meeting on 9 November, had no choice but to conclude that the project was unaffordable in its present form. It was then my job to inform NERC, OST and the FCO of the situation, handle the inevitable questions as to why, and provide the first look at how the whole operation could be de-scoped to fit the available budget. And that was effectively my last act as far as Halley VI was concerned, because I retired from BAS at the end of the following January, leaving my successor, Robert Culshaw, to pick up the pieces.

The problems with this project made my last few months at BAS somewhat less comfortable than they might have been, and represented the start of a wider malaise within NERC and consequently in BAS. In my opinion NERC has ever been an organization searching for an identity and purpose. In 1965, when it was created, its name sounded grand and forward-thinking, but actually it came into existence not with some grand vision of unifying environmental research, but simply as a construct under which several pre-existing government institutes could be bundled to make their combined budget of similar weight to that of the Medical Research Council (MRC) in the eyes of the Treasury. The institutes that were brought together within NERC were very distinct from each other, each with their own long lineage, culture and operating mode. They did not need to be brought together to help them in their missions; the only advantage was that funding could be argued about with the Treasury on a more even playing field versus the MRC than if they had been on their own. Successive secretaries and later chief executives had tried throughout NERC's life to find a unifying purpose – with, in my view, little or no success. Fundamentally NERC had one purpose: to dish out money and audit that it had been spent wisely.

But in the final few years of my career, first to some extent with John Krebs at the helm, and then, much more effectively, John Lawton, NERC did grasp the nettle of what its role should be. At the same time Chris, JP and I had developed BAS into a finely tuned machine with excellent governance, management and science delivery, which was the envy of our peers. Lawton recognized that NERC needed the same sort of corporate approach, where accountability should rest where it would be most effective. This meant that the directors of the institutes should be accountable for them, but also those directors should play a full role in the corporate management of NERC. Thus the NERC Executive Board (NEB) was born, made up of the chief executive and the institute directors. And along the way it meant that the Halley Project Board was placed entirely within the BAS director's sphere of responsibility, using the PRINCE methodology for assurance and audit.

By 2005, however, we had a new chief executive, Alan Thorpe, and NERC director of finance, David Bloomer. They had a different, more intrusive – and, to my mind, much

The latest BAS station on the Brunt Ice Shelf, Halley VI, in all its glory. (Credit Peter Bucktrout, UKRI/BAS)

less helpful – approach. They saw the budget problem that arose in the Halley project as a failing of BAS management, and tried to use it to inject themselves into the minutiae of the management of the institutes. Actually, the way that the board had operated was precisely the way it had been supposed to operate; rather than rushing headlong into what would have been an unaffordable scheme, the formal gateway system required that the board took a timely decision to pause and review. But Thorpe and Bloomer made our life very difficult, seemingly trying to identify a scapegoat. Since I was retiring they focused more on JP, but made little headway against the rational and firm arguments that BAS produced. However, although my knowledge ceased to be first hand after January 2006, a war of attrition did seem to leave BAS management slowly emasculated after Chris and JP had retired, with consequences I will recount later.

Ultimately the project did proceed after de-scoping and accepting that there would have to be a significant reduction in activity at Halley V during the building phase for Halley VI. One major cost-saving measure was to use Halley V as the work camp, which had the added advantage of testing the relocatability of the new station. Each module was built at Halley V and then towed the 16 km or so to the new site. There was also a delay of several years on the original schedule, with the new station finally becoming fully operational in 2012. It turned out to be an outstanding success, both operationally and as a (very nice) place to live. It even has a mezzanine level in the lounge with a transparent roof dome, where folk can sit in comfort to watch the night sky and auroral displays. I only wish I could have got to Halley one more time to visit such a magnificent station.

What about the fateful choice not to build on the Lyddan Ice Rise, but near Halley V instead? Well, as we had expected might happen, a large crack began to develop from the southern coastal edge of the Brunt towards the northern grounded region, presaging a major break-out. With just such an eventuality in mind, we had designed the station so that it could be moved, and in summer 2016/17 BAS decided to move it 23 km inland. The job was successfully carried out in just 13 weeks – demonstrating the robustness of the design. But then something entirely unexpected happened – a new crack (known as the Halloween Crack, since that was the date it was first noticed) began to form to the north and east of the new site. How this new crack might develop was uncertain, so the decision was taken to close the station for the winter while the behaviour of the crack was assessed. Since then the station has been reopened every year successfully for the summer season, but closed again for the winter. Had we chosen the Lyddan it would still be operating year round; 20:20 hindsight is a wonderful thing.

Nowadays, though, it is none of my business, I muse as to whether I would be able to write a risk assessment that would allow a wintering research station to be sited on a floating ice shelf in Antarctica. I think it highly unlikely. When Halley was established back in the 1950s, though, such long-term considerations would not have figured in people's thinking, and as our tenure continued we thought we understood the environment sufficiently to be safe. Well, it seems that we didn't. Whether Halley VI will ever act as a wintering station again is a moot point; BAS has now made great strides in automating the science programmes there, using a revolutionary unattended micro-turbine power unit that has proved to be highly reliable. But of course there remains the political dimension – what the FCO considers to be meant by 'occupation' of the eastern side of British Antarctic Territory. This may require a year-round presence of some sort; maybe on the inland ice?

17

'EVENTS, DEAR BOY, EVENTS'

Harold Macmillan, British prime minister from 1957 to 1963, is reputed to have said this in response to a question about what was most likely to knock a government off track. By its nature, BAS has had its fair share of events over the course of its long history. One, which I have already recounted in detail, was what I had to cope with whilst BC at Base F. Another was the crash of the Borek Twin Otter at Rothera while I was acting deputy director. Later, when in that role substantively, my first major (but not last) event was the destruction of the Bonner Laboratory by fire.

The Bonner Laboratory, named after the zoologist Nigel Bonner, was a highly sophisticated research facility built at Rothera and costing £2 million, which opened in January 1997. It housed chemistry laboratories, a research aquarium and a year-round scientific dive support facility with a hyperbaric chamber. It was thus a major jewel in the BAS crown, and the envy of other national operators.

At 6.30 am on 28 September 2001 I was woken up by my bedside phone at home. It was JP informing me that the Bonner was on fire but that thankfully there were no

The Bonner Laboratory at Rothera Research Station on fire in September 2001. (Credit UKRI/BAS)

casualties. I was immediately off to the office, where the well-rehearsed BAS incident response plan was in operation, with John Hall (operations manager) coordinating the tactical response and liaising with the base. Chris being out of the office that day, I led on the strategy and communications with the outside world. We quickly learnt that within 8 to 10 minutes of the fire alarm sounding at 4 am BST, personnel had been mobilized to locate the cause of the alarm, and a team equipped with breathing apparatus was sent to examine the interior of the building. Within 13 minutes of the alarm, electrical power was disconnected; 15 minutes after the alarm the seriousness of the fire was correctly assessed and the team was withdrawn from the building. A little under an hour later (5.28 am BST) the base commander telephoned John Hall. From then on, Rothera personnel, in consultation with us, took steps to identify the source of the fire and to contain it. These involved using the Air Unit fire tender spraying water and a snow blower spraying snow. In the event these measures had little impact, and were abandoned by mid-afternoon in deteriorating weather conditions with the wind blowing in excess of 70 knots. Steps were taken to protect both the fuel supply system to the rest of the base and the seawater supply to the reverse osmosis plant which supplied the base's fresh water. These measures were successful. The main response on the station was then to keep all team members a safe distance upwind of the fire, as there were multiple hazards: toxic smoke, dangerous chemicals and exploding gas cylinders producing shrapnel. Once the fire had burnt itself out and the wreckage was deemed safe to approach, the base members secured the site as far as possible to preserve evidence ahead of a formal inquiry into what had caused the fire.

The fire had destroyed a major UK asset. The British government does not use commercial insurers to cover such infrastructure; instead it 'self-insures', which means there is no guarantee that money will be made available for a replacement. It was therefore incumbent upon BAS to determine what had caused the fire before we could move to making a case for replacement. We quickly recruited a professional fire assessor, James W. Munday, who travelled to Rothera as soon as the summer season started. He was a consummate professional who delivered a very detailed report by 3 December. In the meantime I had established a formal Board of Inquiry tasked with reporting to the chief executive of NERC with me as chair and two members: Bruce Smith, our non-executive board member, and Colin Read, an ex-FID who was now finance director of NERC. Our role was to review the findings of the fire investigation,

The remains of a gas cylinder which exploded in the Bonner Laboratory fire at Rothera.

look at how BAS had handled the event and make recommendations on any issues that came to light as a consequence. That board had its first meeting on 6 December in BAS, where we took evidence from BAS personnel, and a second meeting on 19 December in London, where we interviewed James Munday.

His report demonstrated beyond reasonable doubt that the fire had been caused by faulty electrical wiring to an outside light above the main door. This had caused arcing inside an insulated wall panel, setting the insulation alight. His view was that the fire had been able to get a firm hold undetected inside the wall panels and had spread into the loft space before it triggered the fire alarm. Checks of other similar installations at Rothera revealed the same error, which was quickly dealt with. Before delivering our final report I travelled south to Rothera and Halley in late January, returning home in early March. This enabled me to talk to the base members, and inspect the site of the fire and the work being done to clean it up by a commercial contractor. Its team had been able to locate a radioactive source, which was part of one of the scientific instruments used in the lab, and also had removed the risk from toxic chemicals. However, there were a number of 'cooked' gas cylinders that had not actually exploded, which were deemed to be too unsafe to be shipped out. So we got a special dispensation from the FCO to bury them at sea (in 500 fathoms of water) a few miles off the station. This in itself was a pretty hazardous undertaking, but thankfully went off without incident. I completed the inquiry report while south, and released the executive summary to base members at Rothera, as well as a copy of Munday's report. There were quite a few detailed technical recommendations – but in essence: the fire had been caused by faulty electrical wiring installed during construction, and the response of the base to the fire was professional

The operation to relieve Halley V by air from the Drescher Inlet. Two Twin Otters wait on the sea ice to be loaded with stores from the RRS *Earnest Shackleton*.

and sound, as was the incident response at BAS Cambridge. The government decided in its largesse to stump up the money to replace the laboratory – and the new one, with lessons learnt, was opened only 18 months later.

There were two other events to be handled that same summer season, both of them involving Halley Station. The first problem was that there was very heavy ice in the Weddell Sea that summer. The RRS *Ernest Shackleton* found progress very difficult to make, and by New Year's Day things were not looking good. I received a phone call at home from John Hall, wanting to discuss the way forward. Both he and the captain advised that the prudent course of action would be to retreat north to Stanley to refuel and then try again later in the hope that the pack ice would have eased. I concurred, so the ship turned back. By late January it was southbound through the Weddell ice again, with the wind more favourable for easing the pack. But by the end of January it was clear that there was no chance of it getting past the tongue of the Stancomb-Wills Ice Stream, and therefore had no access to Halley. So its captain turned north again, looking for a place with good enough sea ice for it to moor and with enough stable flat ice to establish a skiway from which the BAS Twin Otters could operate. This turned out to be the Drescher Inlet in the Riiser-Larsen Ice Shelf, about 300 km north-east of Halley. From there it was possible to at least get personnel transfers done, plus mail and high-priority cargo delivered. But we had never faced this situation at Halley before.

Around the same time, I flew overnight from Rothera to Halley, arriving there on the morning of 3 February. The weather at Halley had been uniformly bad through the summer and continued to be so for most of my visit. What with the consequent delay to the summer projects and the resupply problems, I found the atmosphere on base really quite flat, with morale not great. But actually we were carrying out a remarkable airlift from ship to Halley, with three Twin Otters flying a shuttle service with around a ton of supplies on each flight. I made several rotations as copilot and was astounded at the slick operation at the ship. The skiway, right next to the ship, was very busy with flights coming and going frequently. But there was new ice starting to form around the ship, so time was of the essence. There were also long periods when frustration mounted as the planes were grounded day after day by high winds and blowing snow. A comment from my diary for 12 February, during one of the extended periods of bad weather, sums it up:

> This is truly a silly place when the weather is bad. One quickly descends into a 'wait state' where the brain shuts down a bit. It is little wonder that people become lethargic and disengaged when the weather is bad!

Another from 14 February:

> the atmosphere here is very subdued – people sit in the lounge in silence a lot of the time, almost like a monastery!

Mining for water on a summer morning at Halley V; the main accommodation building can be dimly seen through the blowing snow. The spare shovel is waiting for me!

I made an effort to radiate a positive attitude, being outside every morning, no matter what the weather was like, to wield a shovel to mine ice for the water melter. It wasn't totally altruistic; as well as setting an example, it meant that I could have a shower every morning with a clear conscience.

I was involved in the final day of flying on 17 February, by which time we had moved all the people who needed moving and got sufficient supplies to the station for it to operate successfully over the coming year – but only by eating into the reserve supply of fuel. The next day the squadron of three Twin Otters, with me in one of them, departed for Rothera while the ship turned its nose northwards. I had a spectacular time flying the plane across the Southern Peninsula to Fossil Bluff on the coast of Alexander Island in beautiful conditions with the sun low in the west, bringing the snow-covered mountains and glaciers into sharp pink relief.

The second issue needing my attention at Halley was a major health and safety issue. The 45-metre masts that we had originally installed 20 years previously were still required for the AIS. However, as we had evolved from Halley III though Halley IV to Halley V they had been lowered and re-erected several times. Originally all the expertise in building and maintaining them had resided with my old ionospherics group. But as we had developed into a much more complex operation, so we had centralized the maintenance of all the heavy engineering work in an engineering group within the Logistics and Administration Division. The latter had by the turn of the century taken over responsibility for the masts, and had a designated mast officer. But it still fell to the wintering physical sciences staff to carry out essential maintenance.

On 22 January one of the two 45-metre masts collapsed whilst maintenance was being carried out. Luckily nobody was injured, but it could have so easily have been very different. So a formal inquiry was necessary, which I convened, to determine the proximate cause of the collapse; determine whether there were any predisposing factors that had led to the collapse; review BAS policy, procedures and training in regard to mast work; and make recommendations. Once I got to Halley and could inspect the collapsed mast and interview folk, it was quickly clear that the immediate cause had been incorrect adjustment of the stay tension. Tension builds up in the stays through the winter because of the accumulation of snow, which weighs them down at ground level. Very heavy snowfall in the previous few months had grossly over-tensioned them. The team had not been properly trained, and in particular were not aware of the need to slacken the stays from the top one downwards. Instead they had released the tension in the lowest stays, which allowed the mast below the first stay point to move out of alignment so that the downward force on the mast from the over-tensioned upper stays caused it to buckle and hence collapse.

We concluded that no individual was to blame, but that there had been a failure of process. A failure to properly implement the infrastructure, procedures, training and working practices that would foster safe and effective maintenance was the major systematic cause. A number of detailed recommendations followed to make the process much more robust in future. But there remained the problem of the second 45-metre mast, which was now highly suspect. There were professional steel erectors on site to carry out the annual raising of the platforms, and they devised a plan to safely topple it, which was done before I left for Rothera.

18

KIRSTY BROWN

It is a phone call that one dreads to receive when deputy director of BAS. It was 9.30 pm on Tuesday 22 July 2003, and I was quietly snoozing in my armchair at home when the phone rang. It was John Hall to report that there had been a fatality at Rothera Station. BAS had sadly suffered fatalities before, but this was the first one on my watch, and in fact the first for 21 years. We had a well-developed system for dealing with events, so I asked him to convene our incident response team (IRT) at BAS immediately, and arrived there myself at 10:30 pm.

Kirsty Brown ('Bang' to her family and friends), 28 years of age, was in her first winter at Rothera, employed as a research marine biologist, having graduated in geology. Her research programme, having to do with the impact of ice scour on the inshore benthic population, required year-round diving to inspect her study sites. Normally she would have been diving using full sub-aqua kit, but on this day, she and her dive partner had opted to snorkel as they were working just off the shore, where the depth was 5 metres or less, with a safety team of two on shore.

The bare facts as relayed to the IRT was that at around 3.25 pm local time she had been seized by a leopard seal and dragged into deep water (her dive recorder subsequently showed she had been taken to over 70 metres' depth). She and the leopard seal surfaced about six minutes later, by which time the shore support team had alerted the base, launched a boat, managed to thread their way through the pack ice, then beat off the seal with a shovel, recover Kirsty into the boat and immediately start CPR. The doctor quickly took over ashore, continuing efforts to

Kirsty 'Bang' Brown sitting in the right-hand seat of a BAS Twin Otter in Antarctica – something she loved to do. (Courtesy of the Brown family)

resuscitate, but they were to no avail and Kirsty was pronounced dead at 4.50 pm local time.

The IRT initially was made up of me, JP, John Hall, Mike Dinn (operations manager), our press officer, Linda Capper, and our personnel manager, Richard Hanson. Our immediate concerns were to provide what immediate support we could to the team at Rothera, while deciding who, when and how to break the news to Kirsty's family. Her parents, Tim and Judith, lived near Horsham in West Sussex. I dismissed the idea of a phone call, or asking the local police to call so late at night. Instead we decided that the best course of action was for me to be driven down to Horsham to arrive at a reasonable time in the morning to break the news personally. JP now provided a very valuable insight from his time in the RAF, where there were protocols for breaking news of fatalities. He pointed out that the person who broke the news was not generally the most appropriate person to try to provide follow-on support. Instead it was best to have a second team about 30 minutes behind the first, chosen for their knowledge of the victim. So once the news had been broken to the family, they could be offered the support of the second team if they thought it would help.

This was the plan we followed. I managed to get home for a brief sleep from about 2.30 until around 5 am, having agreed the next set of actions which would include contacting all the next of kin of the wintering team, a briefing to the BAS staff and a press release once the family had been told and given the opportunity to say whether/how they wanted the media involved. I had hoped to take the head of our medical unit with me for support and guidance on dealing with bereavement, but it was impossible for him to get from Plymouth in time, so instead I opted to take Fiona Brazil, our head of human relations, which turned out to be a wise move.

We had two hired limousines, one with Fiona and me, and the other to set off 30 minutes later with Paul Rodhouse (head of Kirsty's division) and David Barnes (her line manager in BAS). Fiona and I arrived at the Browns' household at around 7:30 am, chosen to be not too early, but also to minimize the possibility that they might have gone out. Breaking such news was not something I had any experience to call upon, and it is an understatement to say it was one of the more difficult jobs I have had to carry out. It was made somewhat easier by the fact that Tim and Judith were very level-headed people who coped with the news better than most. We offered, and they accepted, a visit from the follow-on team, and then we headed back to BAS, having initiated the follow-on actions by phone. We arrived back at BAS around mid-morning. I quote from my diary for the day:

> I am determined that BAS will be open and will give long-term support for the family – they are going to find it very hard to grieve properly til they have the body home.

And that is just what we did. We were open and proactive with the media, with both Chris and I doing interviews for radio and television. We also immediately suspended diving operations pending an inquiry into what had happened and a re-evaluation of our safety protocols.

We decided very quickly that we could not leave the folk at Rothera to cope on their own, with Kirsty's body there until the following Antarctic summer, as had invariably been the approach in the earlier cases of fatalities. So we began planning an attempt to fly into Rothera to give the team some support, take in a coroner to do the official work, and bring Kirsty home, thereby giving the base members some sense of closure. We also decided that the best way to ensure that the family felt included in our decision making would be for David Barnes to join us as their representative, to provide two-way feedback. The question quickly arose as to who should lead the expedition to Rothera. It was soon apparent that the base members wished it to be me, so I agreed to go. We also asked a female staff member, Laura Burrows, from Human Resources if she was prepared to volunteer to come with me. This was no small thing to ask, since there was a real possibility that even if we made it to Rothera the weather might stop us leaving again for an indeterminate time. But Laura rose to the occasion magnificently.

BAS had never attempted to make a journey into the continent in the middle of winter, so there was much planning to be done. First we had to get the Dash 7 and two Twin Otters from their winter quarters in Canada down to the Falklands. We planned that the Dash would make the attempt, landing on the runway at Rothera, but as it was a wheels-only aircraft we needed the Twin Otters as SAR backup. We would be tight on fuel because of the distance and the load we would be carrying, and it has to be remembered that in the event of any problems with the Dash (fuel or otherwise), there was no SAR apart from what we were laying on. Nor would there be alternate runways, so a forced landing would have to be a belly landing on the ice with the hope that the Twins would be able to come to the rescue. Of course the runway and hangar at Rothera had been closed down for the winter, so there was a major task for the base members in bringing them back into operation, which included clearing all the drifted snow that had accumulated. This also gave them a serious job on which to focus.

It took a fortnight or so to get things sufficiently under way for Laura and me to start our journey to the Falklands, from where the attempt would be made. We set off on Friday 7 August via Chile, had a day's layover in Santiago and arrived in the Falklands on Sunday evening. The Twin Otters arrived on the next day, followed by the Dash on Tuesday. I met the coroner, Nick Saunders, informally at a dinner hosted at Government House by the governor, Howard Pearce, and then had a more formal meeting with Nick the following morning at the town hall, followed by a working lunch with Howard on a variety of other matters. The next day or so was occupied in making certain that our plans for the flight were robust.

An RAF Tornado F3 from the Falklands garrison wishes us well on our journey to Rothera.

The weather dawned fair for the flight on Wednesday 13 August. We would be a party of eight: pilot and copilot (Doug Pearson and 'Ant' Tuson), two Canadian flight engineers, the coroner, with an accompanying member of the Falklands Islands Police Force (DS John Butler), Laura and me. We also – sadly – had to take a coffin, plus personal and survival gear, and some fresh supplies for the base. So, although we were not at maximum load, fuel would be tight, as we had to carry enough to reach Rothera, but possibly have to turn back immediately if the weather was too poor to make a successful landing – a round trip distance of 2,000 nm. The flight normally takes around five hours each way depending on the wind, but on this occasion the wind was against us, giving a six-hour flight time southbound. After about one hour of our journey we had unexpected visitors. Two RAF Tornado F3 fighter jets from the Falklands garrison, having hunted us down, joined us off our wingtips, one each side, just for fun. We had time to take some photos before there was a roar of the afterburners as the F3s departed – vertically upwards!

For the first couple of hours the weather reported from Rothera was fair, but then it started to deteriorate, and as we drew near falling snow was reported. Being above the cloud we could see the mountains of Alexander Island, picked out in Alpine glow, way to the south of Rothera – but at the station the snow was now falling steadily. I was sitting in the jump seat in the cockpit, so could see and hear what was going on as we started our approach. Doug indicated that we only really had enough fuel to make one attempt to land – possibly two – before we would have to abort and return to the

Falklands. The base personnel were asked to line up vehicles each side of the threshold to the runway (now with a covering of snow) and have flares ready to set off when instructed. We let down through the heavy overcast and broke out of the cloud over Ryder Bay to find poor visibility and without the threshold in sight. Our minimum for the landing was that we had to have visual contact with the runway by 1 nautical mile out – otherwise we aborted. As we started our final approach I sat there watching the DME[136] countdown – 1.3, 1.2, 1.1 … and just as Doug's right hand was on the throttles to abort, out of the gloom came a blaze of light and flares. A few seconds later and we were on the ground in a dense cloud of snow thrown up as the engines were put into reverse thrust to bring us to a stop. When the snow settled, I saw we were safely down – but not pointing exactly along the runway.

My first act was to go for a walk with the base doctor, Jane Nash, to give her a chance to talk if she wanted, or just be with somebody new. It was around minus 16° C with gently falling snow, and we strolled around the point for a while. She was open and forthcoming, willing to talk, seemed composed, on top of things, and happy to have the opportunity to chat. My impression was of a very competent and level-headed person. After that I had a similar session with the base commander, Andy Barker. I was already well acquainted with Andy; he had worked at BAS office as a computer wizard before becoming the BC. He also was well on top of a very trying situation. Laura was similarly engaged with other base members, while the coroner and John Butler were carrying out their more formal interviews. It was surreal for me to be thrust back into winter in Antarctica in such tragic circumstances, but a quote from my diary shows the place weaved its magic upon me pretty quickly:

> And now as night draws on the sky has cleared and I get that wonderful sense of cold cleanness and grandeur that brought me to love the place 35 years ago.

It was a bittersweet evening for one base member, Richard Burt; he had been in a relationship with Kirsty as well as her dive partner on the day, but it was his birthday, so we celebrated with a cake, after which I gave a short speech to the team to explain why we had come – the 'family' coming together at a time of tragedy.

With good weather to end the day, we were hopeful we could head home the next day. But the morning dawned very unpromising with a strong north wind and blowing snow. Both Laura and I spent the morning giving folk an opportunity to talk one on one if they wished, something I found Laura to be excellent at. Then just as I had sent an email back to JP to say we were not going to be flying that day the wind dropped and we prepared a little ceremony to mark Kirsty's departure. Her

---

136 Distance measuring equipment, a radio aid that measures the distance of an aircraft from the runway threshold on final approach.

coffin, draped in the BAT[137] flag, was sledged to the runway apron by a procession of base members. At the side of the plane Andy Barker said a few words and I read the famous poem 'Death is nothing at all' by Henry Scott Holland. 'Ant' filmed the little ceremony for the family. Then all too soon we were strapped into our seats, off down a very snowy runway and into the clouds. Thankfully we had a tail wind so were back to Stanley in under five hours. We took Richard with us so he could join Kirsty's family for her funeral. The next day gave us chance to catch our breath in Stanley as well as put the arrangements in place for repatriating Kirsty. And finally we set off on Saturday courtesy of the RAF airbridge, to get home the following Monday. Must be the shortest winter trip to Antarctic ever!

Kirsty was buried in the local churchyard across the fields from her home on 5 September. It was a lovely late summer day, and the service was a simple one, with well-known hymns that all could sing. I found it all very emotional, and Chris gave a very nice little toast and eulogy at the wake afterwards, likening Kirsty to the flash of a kingfisher. A formal inquest was held in Stanley in November where the judgment was accidental death by drowning, with considerable praise from the coroner for the performance and behaviour of the base members. The family established a research fund in Kirsty's honour, and she was awarded a posthumous PhD by the University of Adelaide. There is a monument to Kirsty at Rothera Point with the inscription

Kirsty 'Bang' Brown, 27/9/1974–22/7/2003. In such a short time she achieved so much and lived life to the full.

and a few miles south in Ryder Bay lies Kirsty Island. The fund provided money in collaboration with BAS to carry out essential research into the interactions between humans and leopard seals. Meanwhile, within BAS I instituted a review and risk analysis of diving operations, to inform a decision on when/if we could recommence our scientific diving programme. The two efforts resulted in a comprehensive publication[138] which will be of lasting importance to folk around the world who dive in Antarctic waters, and new protocols which allowed us to safely recommence scientific scuba diving but not snorkelling

I would like to record my appreciation of the efforts made by my colleagues to ease the pain of Kirsty's passing for her family and friends. The operation does stand the test of time as a model of how to cope if, heaven forbid, there is another winter fatality for BAS to deal with. It was a tragedy for Kirsty's family, but one they bore with great dignity and courage. Subsequently her parents were able to visit Rothera by ship in the company of several old fids.

---

137 British Antarctic Territory

138 Muir S.F., D.K.A. Barnes and K. Reid (2006) Interactions between humans and leopard seals, *Antarctic Science* 18(1) pp. 61–74

Above: The Rothera Base members escort Kirsty to the waiting plane.

Left: Laura with me about to board the Dash 7 for home.

19

TO THE MOON AND MARS
BUT NOT BEYOND

And now for something completely different. At the end of November 2004 I was quietly sitting at my desk when a surprising email request popped up in front of me. It was from the Royal Astronomical Society (RAS), inviting me to be part of a commission the RAS planned to establish in order to review the scientific case for human spaceflight. But the UK government had long had a firm policy of not engaging with, and not spending any money on, anything associated with human spaceflight. Also, as far as I had been aware the RAS had not in the past shown any positive interest in the topic. There was of course the major ESA programme, Aurora, which aimed to explore the Moon and Mars using both machines and humans, and the UK would be making a decision in December 2005 on whether and if so in what way it wished to be involved in this programme. The science minister at the time, Lord Sainsbury, had let it be known that he was open to hearing a well-argued case. So the purpose of the commission was to help frame the advice that RAS would provide him. Thus we had a deadline of autumn 2005 to deliver our findings if they were to be influential.

But why ask me? It is true that I had been a fellow of the RAS since the early 1970s, but I had no expert interest in human spaceflight. However, once I reflected for a while I could see that there were significant parallels between humans conducting science in Antarctica and humans conducting science in space; both environments were very hostile and isolated, and for both the costs and risks of putting humans in the field were high. Also in both cases there was a big role for automated data collection systems. So maybe I would have something valuable to contribute.

The commission was to consist of three people; the other two were Professor Frank Close FRS, who would be the chair, and Professor Ken Pounds FRS. Frank was then professor of theoretical physics at Oxford University, an eminent scientist specializing in particle physics and a renowned communicator of science through broadcasting, books, lectures and other activities. Ken was then head of the Department of Physics and Astronomy at Leicester University. He had been the founding CEO of the Particle Physics and Astronomy Research Council (PPARC) and a former president of the RAS. So I was being asked to join some august company. None of us had previously taken any public position on the importance of human spaceflight.

I must admit that my first thought on seeing the invitation was to conclude that the scientific case was weak, and that the real case rested on the human desire to explore – which for me was justification enough. It also turned out that when Frank, Ken and I got together at the RAS over a sandwich lunch for an initial chat their first response had been much the same: scepticism. I had a feeling that a significant proportion of the RAS Council (and membership) had expected – even hoped for – that outcome.

Our first meeting took place on 10 December 2004 with much fanfare and a press release. It was timed to coincide with a one-day RAS discussion meeting entitled 'The Scientific Case for Human Space Exploration' which brought together speakers from ESA and NASA, and scientists from UK and US universities, plus one speaker, Charles Cockell, from BAS, all of them making the positive case. We commissioners spent the day listening to the presentations as well as planning how to proceed with our investigation. But why was there a BAS scientist speaking? Well, there was a developing field of science, astrobiology, relatively new at the time, whose aim was to search for and understand the life cycle of lifeforms surviving under the extreme conditions likely to be found in extraterrestrial environments, in particular on the planet Mars. There was thus interest in studying lifeforms that could survive in the most extreme conditions found on Earth. One such environment is of course Antarctica, where combinations of very high desiccation, very low temperature, seasonal (rather than diurnal) illumination and high UV radiation exist, particularly in the dry valleys in the Ross Sea sector. So BAS had an astrobiology programme using our own, more local, dry valley – the Mars Oasis on Alexander Island.

There was a further dimension in which Antarctica was an excellent analogue: it provided an opportunity to study the effects that long-term isolation in harsh environments had on the psychology and performance of people, and therefore how best to build and support teams that might be sent on long-duration space missions, such as a trip to and from Mars. I, of course, had direct personal experience of long periods of isolation and sensory deprivation from my winters at Base F and subsequent long summer seasons on the Brunt Ice Shelf, as well as a great deal of experience in managing folk in such situations. Given also my background in carrying out complex experiments in harsh environments, and in using automation, actually I came to the table with considerable relevant experience.

The brief from the RAS was quite specific; it came down to answering the question 'Will having people in space materially advance our knowledge, especially of astronomy and geophysics, in ways otherwise impossible or less certain?' We felt, however, that this question was much too narrow, and early in our deliberations we concluded that as the costs of any involvement by the UK would be likely to exceed a reasonable fraction of the national science budget we would need to explore the wider science context; the benefits for public inspiration, outreach and education; the commercial/industrial dimension; and the overall political and international environment.

I found the commission a challenging but really enjoyable activity, this was partly because my two colleagues, Frank and Ken, were both very able individuals as well as being good and amiable companions. I think we were an effective team – and we needed to be, because of the quite tight deadline (effectively only nine months) by which we had to report, and also because of, as it turned out, the controversial result of our investigations. I had expected to retire on 6 March (the day before my 60th birthday),[139] but the first attempt to replace me, in autumn 2004, had not produced an acceptable candidate. So I ended up having to stay on while a second search was conducted (ultimately for a further year or so, to 31 January 2006). So whilst I had expected to have lots of free time to devote to the commission, instead my life was rather full on through that final year; but to some extent the commission work was a bit of light relief.

We conducted our research through regular meetings (approximately once per month), reading papers and reports, taking evidence and interviewing key experts, and creating a questionnaire to elicit the views of the membership of the RAS. We also took the opportunity of a major international astronomical meeting held in Cambridge in September 2005, to organize an evening session when three eminent volunteers were invited to debate the issue in front of a large gathering. In addition, such was the interest generated by the establishment of the commission that in June 2005 the BBC carried out its own online survey of the public attitude; around 20,000 votes were registered, with a majority favouring Britain engaging with human spaceflight.

We concluded early on that scientific missions to the Moon and Mars could address questions of profound interest to humanity. Key amongst these were the origins and history of the solar system, whether life was unique to Earth and how life on Earth had begun. We then asked ourselves the question: could these questions be adequately addressed by robotic missions alone now, or on a 25-year time horizon? To answer that we needed to consider what sort of measurements might be required. It was soon apparent that a wide range of samples would be required from spatially and geologically diverse settings on both the Moon and Mars, and this would include taking rock cores up to maybe hundreds of metres long and perhaps drilling through the Martian ice caps to obtain a climate record, as had been done in Antarctica with such great success. So could an expedition to drill and recover to Earth significant rock and ice cores be mounted robotically?

---

139 Throughout my career in government service it had been an immutable rule that individuals retired the day before their 60th birthday. By 2005 things were beginning to change because of the rising cost of pensions, but I was still expected to depart on that date. At the time of writing, however, the opposite applies – work until you drop!

None of us were experts in what is now referred to as artificial intelligence (AI) so we spent a day at Oxford University talking to world experts in the subject. They were keen to concentrate not on AI or on robotics, but on automation and the mean time between failures in automated systems. How long could an automated system be left to carry out its task before human intervention would be required? The more complex the task the shorter the time, and also the more remote the human from the instrument the shorter the time because of the increasing delay in communications (between 4 and 24 minutes each way for Earth to Mars). To cut a long story short, the answer to drilling an ice core robotically was a very conditional yes, if you were prepared to keep on trying many times to get it right – but it would go much better if there was a person with a spanner there to fix it when it went wrong. We were particularly struck in this regard by a comment made by Steve Squyres of Cornell University, one of the three speakers at our debate. Steve was principal investigator on a Mars rover project, and therefore somebody that one would naturally expect to speak in favour of using machines alone. But far from it. He wrote:

> we are many decades away from robots that can match humans even in the lab. Laboratory state of the art tends to be some 20 years ahead of what can be tolerated in space where one has to attempt 100% success.[140]

It became pretty clear to us that the wholly (as things stand) human characteristic of lateral thinking and responding to the unexpected was not going to be reproduced in AI in the foreseeable future – if ever. The power of humanity to adapt to circumstance in a way impossible for a machine (then, and still as I write) was summed up very nicely by Charles Cockell in what he called the Christmas Present Effect. He recalled that he went into a large shop in Cambridge to buy some paperclips, but came out with them plus a famous board game. How did this happen? It was close to Christmas, his sister was a keen player of the game and had a close association with Cambridge, and the version of the game on sale was set in Cambridge (which he had not known before the shopping trip). So he bought it for his sister as a Christmas present.

His story illustrated a number of human facilities that make us uniquely capable scientific explorers: pattern recognition; libraries of information on all sorts of topics collected over many decades and instantly available; the rapid acquisition of samples; and an ability to recognize new circumstances and opportunities not part of a prearranged plan. In summary humans can think and act laterally in ways that machines cannot – yet. But of course, machines can happily operate in environments

---

140 Steven Squyres is a world-renowned professor of physical sciences at Cornell University, specializing in planetary sciences. The quote is from the Report of the Commission on the Scientific Case for Human Space Exploration 2005, Close F. et al, published by the Royal Astronomical Society. Available from http://www. star.ucl.ac.uk/~iac/RAS_Report.pdf

that are too extreme for humans. This led us to the broader conclusion that the ideal for some classes of research was human and machine working together, and that certainly for Mars, and probably for the Moon, the human would need to be local to the machine because of the long delays in communication to and from Earth.

We considered missions to the outer planets as well as to Mars and the Moon, but here the question of duration in the face of a hostile radiation environment had to be addressed. We were well aware that the radiation environment of our solar system is not healthy for humans. There are two main types of radiation: the solar wind, and highly energetic cosmic rays from outside the solar system. Advice we received from experts suggested that whilst sufficient protection might be possible against the solar wind (provided there are no really major solar events), there was as yet no reasonable expectation of shielding from cosmic rays. So, with reasonable estimates of dose, and the likely travel times, given known types of propulsion, Mars seemed to be about the limit – and even then humans could expect to get a whole-life dose[141] on one trip. So we did not consider the advantages that might come from having humans visit the moons of the outer planets, Jupiter onwards.

Then there were the wider societal issues. The way ESA operated, member countries could pick and choose the project they wanted to invest in. Contracts for industry and academia to carry out the necessary development and construction work were then awarded, matched to the proportion of the cost the country put forward: no investment, no contracts. It was generally acknowledged that the industrial gain from the expertise acquired and the wider spin-off commercial opportunities far outweighed the initial investment. So we concluded that there were significant advantages to British high-tech industry from involvement in human space flight. We also had representations from the medical world about the importance of Britain having its own programme of research into the effects of spaceflight on the human body. At first we took this to be a rather circular argument – no need to worry about the effects on humans in space unless you plan to send humans into space. But it was impressed upon us that research on human physiology in various gravity regimes gave very important opportunities to better understand how the human body functions – and malfunctions – here on Earth. Last but not least, there was the power of human spaceflight to inspire children into a career in mathematics, science and engineering. And here we looked into a Scottish initiative, 'Blast off to Science', where NASA astronauts participated in summer schools to great success. This Scottish experience inevitably raised the thought of how much more impact would be created by having British astronauts doing the same thing.

Much to our surprise, and I imagine to that of many fellows of the RAS, our conclusion was, to quote from our report, 'that HMG re-evaluate its long-standing opposition to British involvement in human space exploration'. We even had the

---

141 The average dose of radiation a human suffers on Earth as a result of the background radiation from all sources.

temerity to suggest what level of funding the UK should be prepared to commit: £150 million per year over 15 years, being a 15 per cent share.

Towards the end of our work we were under a lot of pressure to finalize the report in time for the RAS council meeting to be held on Friday 15 October. We made it by the skin of our teeth, and all three of us attended the meeting, where Frank gave a formal presentation of our findings. My diary for the day notes:

> The council actually received the report much more positively than I expected and Frank did a good job with his presentation. The Council seemed (almost) unanimous in their praise. Anyway (they) accepted the report and agreed (a) to send it out to such worthies as the Science Minister etc, and (b) consider how to follow up.

British astronaut Tim Peake talking to primary school children at the Farnborough Air Show in July 2014. (Credit Kulvinder Johal)

This meeting was followed up on 18 October by a lively but good-natured press briefing, during which I gave a live interview with BBC Radio 5. However, the outcome of the meeting was controversial, with some scions of the UK astronomical hierarchy, who I will not name, rubbishing it. But the report was surprisingly influential. The government commissioned its own investigation, inviting Frank and Ken to participate, and – glory be! – decided to put some money up for a British astronaut to fly on the International Space Station. Thus Tim Peake got his six months in space, launching on 15 December 2015 and returning to Earth on 18 June 2016.

I had the good fortune to attend the Farnborough Air Show in July 2014 as helper for Helen, who by then was deeply into outreach work to inspire school children into science and engineering. I found myself acting as warm-up man (spouting on about Antarctica) to a large group of primary school children. And who was I warm-up man for? Tim Peake. So I had the great pleasure of watching a *British* astronaut inspiring a group of British school kids. It was also made clear to me by a senior official from UKSA[142] that it was our commission that had really been the catalyst for the shift in government thinking and funding. A very satisfactory ending to the story as far as I was concerned – but whether the British involvement was a flash in the pan or will lead to something much more exciting and long range remains to be seen.

142 United Kingdom Space Agency

20

RETIREMENT LOOMS

My official retirement date had for many years been set as 6 March 2005. But that was a Sunday, so the date would actually have been Friday 4 March. However, the recruitment of my replacement moved somewhat slowly and unsuccessfully. Also, as mentioned earlier, the rules were becoming more flexible as the full costs of non-contributory final salary index-linked pensions were becoming apparent to the government. So by September 2004 I had agreed to stay on until the end of August 2005; then there was a further delay, so my actual final day turned out to be Tuesday 31 January 2006. My replacement was a senior diplomat from the FCO, Robert Culshaw, who had neither a science or hands-on polar background, but had been the director (Americas) at the FCO, which role had included the Antarctic portfolio. So he was well versed in the political dimension to the job, and well connected in the right government circles.

I had started actively planning for my retirement back in 2002, but this became a rather protracted process as the date receded and work priorities intervened. I did however manage to attend a pre-retirement course organized by NERC in April 2003. This turned out to be a very relaxed residential event in a splendid setting by the Thames in Abingdon. It left one abiding message stuck in my mind ever since which has underpinned my outlook on life: 'use it or lose it', whether it be physical or mental agility.

Those last few years were very full and very busy, with a very wide-ranging set of responsibilities; the health and safety portfolio alone was verging on a full-time job. Not only did BAS operate a number of laboratories covering a wide range of sciences including the use of radionuclides and a variety of dangerous chemicals, but also it had a fleet of ships, a small airline, a scientific diving programme operating year-round from Rothera, and an active programme of geophysical work requiring the use of explosives. And we did all this in an objectively hazardous environment. A hazardous environment for which there were no government guidelines. We endeavoured to follow the requirements of the Health and Safety at Work Act (1974) and the codes of practice that flowed from that, but they had not been written to take account of the very harsh and isolated environment in which we worked, so for our overseas operations it just had to be guidance on best practice.

I like to think that my lasting legacy here was to engender a proactive learning culture, which I did through a safety management system built on four distinct pillars. These were: risk assessment; training and equipment; accident, incident and near miss reporting (AINMR); and comprehensive accident investigation and open reporting. I tried to make the culture 'no blame'; only in cases of wilful negligence or malign intent would this not hold. It was very important that we knew the objective risks of carrying out complex operations in such a hostile environment, and matched our corporate appetite for risk taking accordingly. We also had to embrace the possibility of accidents generating legal action as one of the results. In all this I was largely successful; the AINMR approach in particular was very helpful, teaching us about holes in our approach before any major accident happened. We also got some very memorable AINMs. One in particular sticks in my mind. Two guys were on Sunday cook at South Georgia, and because a recent ship visit had delivered some fresh chillies they decided on a beef chilli for dinner. They were both involved in chopping the chillies, then one needed to urinate – but forgot to wash his hands first. He exited the loo in some discomfort, causing the second chap to laugh so much he had to wipe his eyes. They both ended up in pretty smart order being treated by the young lady doctor to remove chilli juice from eyes and penis. Hugely funny for all concerned, but also providing some serious and valuable lessons in good kitchen practice and hygiene. It showed, too, that there was a good sense of humour as well as good adherence to the requirement to report.

There was always the vexed issue of how much freedom we allowed our field staff to enjoy the environment in which they found themselves. I made certain that we didn't have a draconian policy to limit recreational activities such as field travel, boating, diving, skiing, snowboarding etc, but I did enforce a strict regime of certification of competency. The BAS 'four pillar' system came to be seen as an exemplar both within NERC and within the community of national operators through COMNAP. We did have accidents – no operation such as ours could possibly be entirely free of them – and we were sued on occasion. But our processes were sufficiently robust and well documented to make such events very rare. Overall I am very proud of my contribution to making BAS as safe as possible.

In 2004 I made two trips to Antarctica, both in their own way valedictory tours, but as things turned out actually very premature. The first, in January and February, took me to Rothera and Halley via Santiago de Chile and the Falklands. For many years BAS had kept one staff member in Port Stanley to look after our affairs; Myriam Booth had held this post with great distinction, but had recently retired to be replaced by a young Falkland Islander – Pauline Sackett. Pauline was an ex-FI police officer, and one of her first important jobs was to meet the deputy director from the plane on arrival. She had a brand-new Land Rover in which to do this. But the computer said 'no', with the Rover stopping and refusing to start again. So after an hour of waiting I bummed a lift the

The BAS Dash-7 aircraft touching down on the gravel airstrip at
Rothera Station at the end of a flight from Stanley.

40 miles or so into town with somebody else, to be met by a very forlorn Pauline. She
was actually very effective in her new role, serving BAS extremely well for many years.
But this event became a standing joke between us thereafter and we have remained
friends since then.

I was to fly to Rothera on the Dash 7, but before I that had a meeting of the South
Georgia Liaison Committee with the governor at Government House. At the time, it
was Howard Pearce who held that position, a very capable man but also very good
company. Once the business was done he held a dinner in my honour at GH. I also
managed to have a day of relaxation – trout fishing – when, as usual, I caught my
supper. Then by Dash 7 to Rothera where I got to inspect (and enjoy) the new Bonner
Laboratory, built with new fire safety features but also with lots of extra little touches
which came from having the opportunity to learn from the mistakes of the first version.
On to Halley by Twin Otter, which was a bit of a Cook's tour with a stop at Fossil Bluff
(in King George VI sound) and Berkner Island (in the Ronne Ice Shelf), where we had
a project to recover an ice core down to bedrock, to provide a high-resolution climate
record for the last 60,000 years or so.

As this was my last visit to Halley, it was filled with nostalgia. I did the usual things:
reviewed health and safety practices, ran Q & As for the staff etc. But I also had a chance

to do an aerial survey of the Lyddan Ice Rise, which at that time was our first choice for the site of Halley VI. This survey flight and discussions with the BAS pilots started to raise the first significant doubts in my mind. We had to wait several days for the weather to be suitable at the Lyddan (fogged in by low cloud) even though at Halley it was perfectly flyable – a point that, as mentioned earlier, was not lost on me. The other point that particularly hit home was that the extra distance from Lyddan back to Rothera would mean that we would be unable to carry out a direct non-stop medevac using our Otters. My visit to Halley was somewhat cut short by the demands on aircraft, so I just had a couple of hours' notice to get packed and jump on a plane – and thus my last visit to Halley came to a somewhat abrupt end.

Once I was back at Rothera the medevac issue was brought more sharply into focus. We had a joint operation between the Navy (*Endurance*) and BAS (*Ernest Shackleton*) to replenish a fuel depot on the Ronne Ice Shelf. One of the Navy Lynx helicopters crashed while moving fuel drums, resulting in three casualties – two of them seriously injured. All three were quickly medevacked to Rothera by Otter, then the two very poorly men were flown immediately to Punta Arenas by Dash 7 for hospitalization. Had the accident been on the Lyddan, the logistics would have been much more difficult.

My final day at Halley. The PACE antenna array is in the horizon, and the Piggott Building, which housed all the UASD facilities, is on the right in the background.

At Rothera there was another curious event to be dealt with. An American pilot attempting to fly a small single-engine plane from Ushuaia over the South Pole and back had made an emergency landing there, creating a headache for us and for him. British government policy was that the Rothera airstrip was closed to private operations except when danger to life and limb was involved or the operator was supporting a National Antarctic Programme. Also, all expeditions were supposed to be approved and permitted by the relevant government – in this case the USA – before being undertaken. Part of that process would have been to ensure the plan was practicable, and had adequate emergency equipment and contingency arrangements.

Once in the vicinity of Rothera the pilot requested permission to land. This was refused. A little while later he declared an emergency, claiming he had run into heavy icing and the plane had no de-icing capability (a fundamental requirement, one would have thought, given the likelihood of cloud with icing conditions). So he landed. But then with the fuel load he was carrying he would have needed a full gale down the runway to have any chance of getting airborne again. He appeared to have no emergency equipment whatever, and little or no food.

I arrived at Rothera just after he had landed and been provided with basic humanitarian assistance: food and a bed for the night. The next morning there was quite a bit of back-and-forth discussion with the powers that be in the UK about what to do with him and his plane. He was threatening to dump excess fuel on the ground to lighten his plane, so we finally agreed to help him decant it into drums, and he then departed back to Ushuaia – but not before I had talked at length to him, and gained the impression that he had little idea of the extreme environment he was in.

The unwelcome visitor on the apron at Rothera. The pilot was attempting a non-stop flight from Punta Arenas to the South Pole and back, but gave up near Rothera due to airframe icing.

While I was at Rothera I had lots of issues to deal with, some of which radiated out of the BAS office in a way inconceivable a few years earlier, when communications were sufficiently rudimentary to allow an almost complete break from the outside world; we were now trialling a new BAS-wide satellite-based system to bring seamless email, phone and internet to ships and bases.

But the most notable thing about my stay at Rothera – my last visit there, too – was the manner of my departure. I left by Dash 7 on a glorious sunny day. The captain for the day – Geoff Porter – invited me to travel in the jump seat, and instead of just climbing to 20,000 feet or so and flying straight to Stanley he took me at low level all the way up the peninsula. We orbited Vernadsky at low level while I chatted to the team there by radio, we flew through the Lemaire Channel and through Neptune's Bellows at Deception Island, and we flew past the windows of the control tower at the Chilean airstrip on King George Island. All in all, a most splendid flight out from Antarctica. I don't think that JP was at all impressed, but fortunately he limited himself to a grumble about the amount of fuel burnt.

My second trip south in 2004 was in October–November, taking in the Falklands, the South Orkney Islands and South Georgia, sailing from the Falklands on the *JCR*, and using the RAF airbridge flight to and from the UK. Howard Pearce was getting married in Stanley Cathedral, an event to which I was invited, as well as the evening wedding party at the town hall. I also got a day out fishing, again catching my supper. Then once installed on board the *JCR*, the captain, Jerry Burgan, and I hosted a lunch on board for Howard and his bride, Caroline. One of Howard's old FCO buddies also came – Hugh Bicheno, a rather larger-than-life character who turned out to be an ex-secret service officer in Argentina in the run-up to the Falklands Conflict, and who was then researching a new history of that nasty little war.[143] It was an excellent event, and we sailed the next day for Signy Island in the South Orkney Islands to open our summer-only station there. From there we headed for Bird Island, where I got involved in helping with the relief operation; it was here that I rolled my last 45-gallon oil drum for BAS. Then came what I thought would be my final visit to South Georgia with a visit to the BAS station at King Edward Point, before turning west for the voyage back to Stanley.

That westward voyage was memorable for three reasons. We had by now got our comprehensive communications system fully operational, so on my trips south I could no longer escape the office – it came to me by email, phone calls and weblinks. The lovely sense of cutting off the outside world was gone. Two phone calls during that time stick in my mind. The phone in my day cabin and the one by my bunk were both direct dial, as though they were local Cambridge phones. One night the phone rang by my bunk, and it was one of my daughters calling for a chat. She had apparently got the local

---

143 The book was subsequently published as *Razor's Edge: The Unofficial History of the Falklands War* (Weidenfeld & Nicolson, 2006) ISBN 0-297-84633-7. It is a unique and fascinating look at the conflict.

The last oil drum I ever rolled for BAS. This one is on the jetty at Bird Island.

time difference backwards – but it brought home to me just what a profound change had happened since my wintering days, when I could send my family just 100 words once a month. What a profound difference these communications would make to the experience of travelling to Antarctica; even out in the remotest field camp satellite phones allowed direct dialling home. The second phone call was from Helen to inform me there was a letter for me from the Cabinet Office – should she open it? It turned out the Queen was minded to award me the Order of the British Empire (an OBE) for services to science, and wanted to know whether I would accept it. *Would I?* Of course I would! The protocol for such awards is that the recipient never sees what is in the citation, and is not supposed to make the award public until it is formally announced at the next release of the honours list. So I know not why I was deemed a worthy person, and I had to hold the news in until 31 December.

The third reason it was a memorable voyage was because of what happened when I did my usual Q&A session for the ship's company, to give them a chance to make their points to the top of the shop. I was somewhat surprised to see how many folk had turned up, but it all became clear at the end when the captain, Jerry, stood up. It turned out they were all there to mark my retirement. I now have a very fine brass statue of a whale's fluke mounted on a plinth that sits in my office at home, and on my wall is

At Buckingham Palace with my daughters Liz and Clare, to collect an OBE.

a super picture of the *JCR* in ice, signed by all the ship's company. Things to treasure.

Back in Stanley I had a weekend to wait for the airbridge flight home, so there was a chance to tie up a few loose ends, but then Howard marked what was expected to be my final visit as deputy director with a reception and dinner in my honour at Government House.[144] This was also a rather special and emotional affair for me, with lots of folk – old friends, and colleagues going back to my first visit in 1966 – invited to attend. My emotions the next morning as my plane overflew Stanley homeward bound were complex indeed.

Although my final full year at BAS – 2005 – did not involve any trips south, it was nevertheless very busy. I have already dealt with some of the big issues – the Liability Annex, Halley VI, human space flight etc, but there was also a lot of official travel, covering

The reception at Government House. Old friends and new wishing me the best for my retirement. The governor is on my left, and his wife Carolyn just behind and between us. David Walton is standing behind her. Captain Gerry Burgan is on my right, and on my far right is Doug Bone, who sailed south with me on *John Biscoe* in 1966.

144 As I have already pointed out, Howard had to do this all again in January 2006 when I came back for my last South Georgia liaison meeting

the USA (twice), Singapore, Tasmania, New Zealand, China (twice), Bulgaria, Belgium and Sweden. I was also now taking the advice from my retirement course to actively plan my future for Day 1, Month 1 and Year 1 post BAS.

There was a feeling amongst my colleagues that after 40 years in BAS I would find retirement difficult. I had decided early on that it would be a clean break as far as BAS was concerned – nobody wants a very senior ghost hanging around – so I did not attempt to have an honorary position at BAS. This would anyway have made my successor's life very difficult, coming as he did from outside. I had already been asked to be chief rapporteur for the 2006 ATCM in Edinburgh, and late in 2005 was invited to lead an international commission to evaluate Finland's Antarctic research programme. So the first few months would be busy with just these projects. David Walton and I had also decided that we would work together on a book. This project had started life as a sequel to Sir Vivian's history of BAS, *Of Ice and Men*, but quickly developed into something quite different – more of a study of the interplay of science and diplomacy in the story of Antarctica. I had also started planning two grand adventures – one, starting the day after retirement, would be an extended trip to New Zealand with Helen, and the other would be to walk the South West Coast Path, a 630-mile trail around the coast from Minehead in Somerset via Land's End to Poole in Dorset. Then in November I had a chance meeting in the BAS canteen with an old fid – David Fletcher – who now worked in the Antarctic tourism industry. I let it be known that I would consider any invitations that might be forthcoming from that sector for guest lectureships, not thinking that anything much would come of that (little did I know …). So I thought I was well set up for the start of my retirement – and as things turned out, I had sown the seeds for a very rewarding time, but as has often been the case with me, serendipity played a very major part in pushing me in a direction I would have never dreamt of – a second career as an Antarctic historian, about which more later.

On the Friday before my actual final day, the following Monday, there was a formal goodbye reception. This was quite an emotional event with gifts and fine speeches with a very sizeable attendance of old lags from my past. Alan Rodger had put together a very funny, flattering and embarrassing slide show which went down very well, and Chris gave a more formal thank you. I made a short speech, but goodness knows what I said.

The final day was more relaxed, when I spent much time wandering around the building saying goodbyes to folk. This was very emotional, particularly the little personal gifts and cards I was given. I think my diary for the day should have the last word:

> Not quite sure how I feel about the act of retirement. The one thing that has really moved me is the number of people from all round BAS who took the time to thank me for helping them with their careers. That is something I will treasure. So a new start and a new adventure tomorrow.

21

NEW ADVENTURES

From the first moment of retirement my life has been very busy and very rewarding. I am very lucky to have a final salary index-linked pension – a parasite on the hide of the taxpayer I hear you cry – but it has meant I haven't had to worry where my next mouthful will come from. Instead, I have been able to occupy myself with just those things that interest me. I have found myself with two unexpected but interlinked careers as a historian of Antarctic affairs and as a lecturer-guide with a number of Antarctic tourism companies. I have also been involved in scientific publishing as a director of Antarctic Science, a charitable organization which publishes a learned journal of the same name and uses the revenue to provide support for early career scientists engaged in polar research. I found this highly rewarding, finally retiring from the board in 2016. But that first year was much taken up by four activities. There was the Edinburgh ATCM (see Chapter 15), the review of the Finnish Antarctic Programme, the South West Coast Path and the book project with David Walton.

I started on the South West Coast Path in April 2006, walking from Minehead to Barnstaple, approximately 100 km in five days. I found this a really enjoyable experience: the scenery was stunning, the weather reasonably kind (for the most part) and the walking, though energetic and challenging at times, really satisfying. On that first outing, however, I made one big mistake– I decided to carry my bed on my back: full camping kit, plus food and cooking stove. On Day 3 – from Lynmouth to Coombe Martin – the mistake was borne home on me. This is one of the toughest sections of the whole path, only 21.5 km in length but with much up and down from sea level to clifftops and back, amounting to a total ascent of 1,150 metres. It had the highest point on the whole route – Great Hangman at over 300 metres – and when I got to the top of that I realized that my backpack was so heavy that I was flattening my feet. So from there on I decided discretion was the better part of valour and planned my route to end at a comfortable inn or guest house each night, which more than halved the load I carried. I had two more sessions of walking the path that year: Barnstaple to Bude, and Bude to Rock (near Padstow), by which time I had completed a total of around 270 km with a total ascent of over 10,600 metres. This set the pattern for the next three years.

The South West Coast path on the north coast of Cornwall between Hartland Quay and Bude.

I had three sessions in each of the next two years and two in 2009 to finish the whole route – a total of 1,015 km with a total ascent of over 35,000 metres (a little short of ascending Everest from sea level four times). It was one of the most satisfying projects of my life.

The review of the Finnish Antarctic Programme occupied much of 2006 on and off. It was commissioned by the Finnish Ministry of Education and organized under the auspices of the Academy of Finland. The review panel's task was to evaluate the Antarctic research performance for the period 1998 to 2005, looking at both the quality of the output and the functioning of the associated logistic and administrative support. The evaluation panel consisted of an international group of three scientists: myself as chair, together with a Canadian physicist, Professor Peltier, and an Italian glaciologist, Professor Navarro, both eminent in their field. We were very ably assisted by Dr Mikko Lensu from the academy, who acted as coordinator and hence did much of the legwork and administration on our behalf. The panel did most of its work remotely, with much documentation and analysis very ably provided by Dr Lensu. But we had one extended visit of several days to Finland (8–11 May) when we toured various institutes in Helsinki and Oulu. Then I returned in November to deliver our findings to the academy.

As an Arctic Rim country, Finland has a large and nationally important portfolio of polar research covering many disciplines, but for obvious reasons almost all was then focused on the Arctic. But the country had also acceded to the Antarctic Treaty in 1984 and had become a full consultative party in 1989. The primary reason for Finland becoming involved in Antarctica was the possibility of mineral exploitation. The failure to agree the minerals convention and the subsequent about-face, with the successful agreement of the Environmental Protocol, effectively removed that primary policy requirement for a Finnish presence in Antarctica. Our panel concluded that there had never been a comprehensive rethink of why Finland had a presence in Antarctica, and as a result the science programme was incoherent: it underperformed compared with the majority of other national Antarctic programmes, and it also underperformed compared with other Finnish research programmes funded by the academy. Our report ran to over 50 pages, but I will not go into the details here; if you have an interest it is publicly available.[145] Suffice to say that it did not make comfortable reading. with a top-level recommendation that:

> Finland carry out a review of why it is carrying out a research programme in Antarctica and whether the current programme meets its national aims.

In November I gave an uncompromising formal presentation of our findings to a meeting of the great and good at the Academy of Finland, which was followed by responses from the main players. It was a hard message for them to swallow, but the responses and the subsequent discussion were by and large positive. After the meeting I had one very surprising moment. I had expected that the meeting would be a closed one – which probably would have been the case for a similar occasion in the UK. But such is the openness of Finnish society that I immediately found myself giving a live interview on Finnish radio to a reporter who had been present for the whole event. Then the Finns went even further, by tabling two papers at the 2008 ATCM which gave the summary of the findings and what they planned to do about them.[146] Would that other CPs would do the same. In fact, I am embarrassed to say that while I was BAS deputy director, although we had regular international peer reviews of our performance, all uniformly very positive, we never made them public.

The findings of this review set my mind ticking over on how well other CPs were doing, in terms of both scientific output and political influence within the treaty system itself. Over the next few years I devised an empirical way of measuring both, and in 2012 published a paper,[147] co-authored by David Walton, which caused quite a stir: the national operators that performed relatively well were able to crow to their governmental masters, whilst those that were less effective had their inadequacies brought out into the cruel light of day. The United Kingdom turned out to be pre-eminent, having more political influence (by my measure) than any other country, and in science output second only to the USA. It was also fascinating to see, perhaps not too surprisingly, that claimant nations and the two that reserved the right to claim (USA and Russia) occupied the top of the list. I understand that during a time of crisis for BAS the National Security Council, chaired by the then prime minister, David Cameron, had our results before it as part of the evidence for supporting BAS into the future – and it worked!

---

145 Antarctic Research in Finland – International Evaluation https://www.aka.fi/globalassets/awanhat/documents/tiedostot/julkaisut/13_06-etelamannertutkimus.pdf

146 ATCMXXXI/IP003 Antarctic Research in Finland 1998–2005 International Evaluation, and IP040, Finland's Antarctic Research Strategy

147 Dudeney, J.R. and D.W.H. Walton (2012) Leadership in politics and science within the Antarctic Treaty, *Polar Research*, 31, 11075, DOI:10.3402/polar.v3110.11075

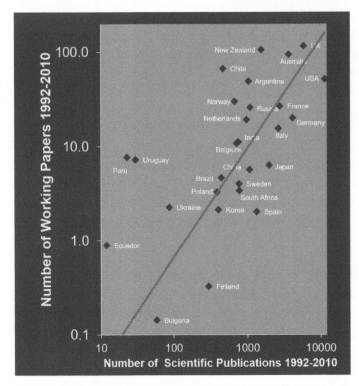

Appraisal of influence within the treaty. The graph shows the political influence estimated by counting the number of Working Papers each CP produced over the period 1991 to 2010, and the scientific output by the number of peer-reviewed papers that each nation published on Antarctic-related subjects over the same period. Note this is a snapshot and is not necessarily relevant today. For more details, see Dudeney & Walton (2012).

In May 2006 I was contacted by an Antarctic tour company, Peregrine Expeditions, asking if I would be interested in joining its cruises as a guide during the coming Antarctic season. Contact having been made, there the matter rested until August, when I had a telephone contact with a senior member of its staff – a Canadian, Aaron Lawton by name. This turned into an informal job interview, at the end of which I had been offered participation in two cruises for February 2007. (As I have already mentioned, Victoria Wheatley had by then invited me to participate in cruises in 2008 with Abercrombie & Kent, with Helen as my guest, but at this point nothing had been agreed formally.) So now the first steps on my new career as an Antarctic tour guide had been taken. I will return to Antarctic tourism and my part in it in the next chapter.

I also took my first steps in what has become a major part of my life – researching, lecturing on and publishing on Antarctic political history – though I didn't realize it at the time. It was the book project with David Walton that started me on that road. By the end of 2006 we had decided on a book about the interplay of politics, science and governance of Antarctica in the framework of the Antarctic Treaty. David seemed very keen to be the lead author on the project, and rather than start the project in a bad atmosphere by disagreeing, I accepted his wish. This was not a good decision, but its consequences were ultimately very positive for me. David sadly passed away in 2019, and I miss him greatly as we were both friends and colleagues throughout our long careers at BAS. He was a very clever and broadly based scientist and book publisher; he had his fingers in all sorts of projects, and that did not ease up when he retired shortly after me. He had too many things on his agenda – and one fatal weakness, which he would have been the first to admit. He had no interest in meeting deadlines. He would happily sign up to deliver something by a particular date and then just as happily completely ignore it. In this we were polar opposites, and having worked with him at BAS during my time as deputy director I should have known better. I will come back to what happened. But before that I should mention two other activities that I have found very rewarding in my retirement.

When Dougal Goodman left BAS he became the director of the Foundation for Science and Technology (FST). The best way to introduce the FST is to quote what it says about itself:

> The Foundation for Science and Technology is a UK charity, providing an impartial platform for debate of policy issues that have a science, research, technology or innovation element. Established in 1977, the Foundation brings together Parliamentarians, civil servants, industrialists, researchers, learned societies, charities and others. It convenes discussion events, publishes a journal three times per year, and hosts a podcast. It also organises the Foundation Future Leaders Programme, supporting the next generation of professionals from universities, industry and the civil service. In addition, the Foundation provides guidance on governance issues to Professional and Learned Societies[148]

BAS was a corporate member, which allowed BAS staff to attend FST meetings. These took the form of a series of presentations on a particular topic, followed by debate and a dinner, at which the debate was continued, hosted at the Royal Society. The meetings operated under Chatham House Rules[149] and thus very senior people from all walks of life were prepared to present and/or participate in meetings even when the topics were highly controversial. During my time as a HoD and then deputy director I had attended these meetings regularly. Dougal was indulgent enough to allow me to continue attending in an individual capacity for quite a few years after I retired, only requiring me to sing for my supper by hosting tables at the dinners, charged with stimulating further discussion on the topics in hand. I greatly appreciated this opportunity to have my say on many diverse topics and to interact with the great and good from a wide spectrum of government, academia and industry.

It was at an FST meeting in November 2007 that I got talking to a retired geologist, Professor Peter Simpson, who had been a colleague of my brother at Imperial

---

148 https://www.foundation.org.uk/

149 The content of a meeting may be discussed widely but no individual may be quoted

College. He was by then the executive secretary of a different but equally interesting organization called the Parliamentary and Scientific Committee (P&SC). It is an associate parliamentary committee; it was in fact the first such grouping, founded in 1939 to bring scientists, industrialists and parliamentarians together to aid the war effort. It is cross-party, is chaired by an MP, and has a president chosen from the House of Lords. Organizations (learned societies, academic and industrial) pay a subscription to be members and attend meetings. It is a major focus for scientific and technological issues, providing a liaison between parliamentarians and scientific bodies, science-based industry and the academic world. It also has a small number of individual members – currently there are 14 – who are invited to join. To cut a long story short, Peter Simpson asked me whether I would be interested in having my name put forward to become an individual member (IM). I jumped at this of course, and have been an IM ever since. The P&SC normally meets once a month when Parliament is sitting, using one of the committee rooms for an evening debate on a scientific topic about which there are national or international policy implications. I find it both an honour and also a great opportunity to be able to sit at the heart of such an important organization and to put my twopennyworth into issues as diverse as antibiotic resistance and the impact of space weather.

22

ANTARCTIC TOURISM AND
ANTARCTIC HISTORY

My contact with Antarctic tourism goes back half a century, to my year as a base commander, when there was almost no tourism to Antarctica. While I was there I was 'blessed' with two direct encounters: the first is covered in Chapter 2, and the second I will relate here. It occurred in January 1969, just before I headed home. This involved a Chilean ship, the *Aquilles*, which brought about 120 tourists to visit one afternoon. This went well, but just as with the visit of *Navarino* back in 1968, I felt that there had been insufficient prior contact with us to arrange the visit. I had made this point to Sir Vivian in March 1968, and repeated it in my Base Annual Report in 1969. Little did I know that I was reigniting an existing controversy between BAS and the FCO on the one hand and Lars Eric Lindblad on the other. Lindblad is rightly seen as the father of Antarctic tourism, his first cruise, from Ushuaia to the Antarctic Peninsula, having taken place in January 1966 using the MS *Lapataia*. This cruise had visited the then active British base at Deception Island. Then in 1968 the *Navarino* had visited Deception Island before going to Base F, by which time the BAS base had been closed because of the volcanic eruption. The controversy was whether or not its crew had broken into the base and looted it. There was strong circumstantial evidence that they had, which had soured relationships between Lindblad and BAS/ FCO. I then stepped into the story by criticizing the lack of adherence to the agreed communication protocols on the visits of both the *Navarino* and the *Aquilles*. This caused a pointed exchange between Sir Vivian and Lindblad, when the latter (who had been on the *Navarino* at the time of the visit to Base F) painted a very different picture from mine. One of us was obviously confused, and I don't think it was me. These early encounters between BAS and the tourists probably coloured the BAS official position regarding tourist visits to the BAS stations, and certainly when I was deputy director we still limited visits to just two a season to Rothera, with a requirement to set the dates months in advance to limit disruption.

The MS *Aquilles* in Penola Strait, off Base F in January 1969.

My next encounter with tourism was at Antarctic Treaty meetings where the treaty parties were much exercised by the issues surrounding it. Different parties had different agendas, ranging from wanting to ban or seriously limit it, through support for controlled and environmentally sound activity, to participation in it – sometimes somewhat covertly. But by the turn of the century Antarctic tourism had matured and now based its business plan on an environmentally benign and educational approach, aiming to comply fully with the Environmental Protocol. A trade association – the International Association of Antarctica Tour Operators (IAATO) – has coordinated almost all tourism activities since 1991, with the primary aim of advocating and promoting the practice of safe and environmentally responsible private-sector travel. IAATO has a seat at the table of the treaty as an invited expert, as mentioned in Chapter 15. Over the years IAATO has developed a very comprehensive set of rules and guidelines to ensure that its members carry out their activities in as an environmentally sustainable way as possible, so the treaty parties have often picked up on these rules and guidelines, to make them part of the treaty system for managing tourism.

Nowadays there are several strands to IAATO-based tourism. By far the largest part is ship-based, on small (60–500-passenger) cruise ships, from which landings at points of interest are made; this is defined as an expedition-style undertaking. Almost all of this operates out of South American gateway ports – primarily Ushuaia and Punta Arenas, focused on the Antarctic Peninsula, South Orkneys, South Shetlands and South Georgia. There is also a small operation into the Ross Sea, based primarily out of Hobart. Much larger vessels are active too, but those carrying more than 500

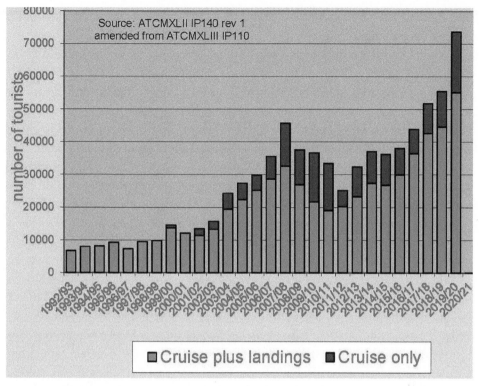

The growth of shipborne tourism over the past 25 years. Note the steady growth followed by the impact of the 2008 financial crisis, and then rapid growth until Covid-19 brought the industry to a halt in 2020/21 (data values are from IAATO reports presented at ATCMs as identified on the plot).

passengers are not allowed to make any landings. There is also a small operation of inland adventure tourism which makes use of blue ice runways to fly tourists into the continent, based mostly out of Punta Arenas and more recently from Cape Town. Finally, there are small yacht operations; almost all of the operators, except for private yachts, are members of IAATO.

So let's turn to my experiences within the tourism industry. They started in February 2007 when I arrived in the Argentine port of Ushuaia on the shores of the Beagle Channel to spend about a month as a presenter/guide aboard the Russian vessel *Akademik Ioffe*. The *Ioffe* had been built in Finland as an ocean-going marine research vessel in the dying days of the Soviet regime and, together with its sister ship, the *Akademik Vavilov*, had been designed to carry out active marine acoustic research. Both ships were capable ice vessels and were very manoeuvrable, having bow and stern thrusters. As I found out, they were also very sea kindly in heavy weather – unlike some of the BAS ships. Both were still nominally science research platforms, but had been chartered by Peregrine for cruising in the Arctic and Antarctic. They carried a maximum of 100 passengers or so – but in spartan conditions compared with vessels designed as passenger cruise ships.

When I joined the ship the tourism business was pretty opaque to me, and it was not obvious that the expedition leader, 'Dutch' Wilmot, had been briefed on what my role was expected to be. I had no idea how I was even supposed to get into the port to join the ship until I happened upon an old hand, Peter, the morning I was to join; he took me under his wing. Apart from Peter's help, though, I was basically left to either sink or swim in the first few days as I slowly worked out my role within the team. This was quite different from the care that BAS management gave its field staff. Another big difference was that I was now on the bottom rung of the hierarchy: instead of a fine suite of rooms to myself (as I was used to on the *JCR*) I was now assigned a small cabin without facilities and sharing with two others, one of whom – thankfully – was Peter. I leaned on him quite a lot in the first couple of days as I oriented myself and got kitted out.

The officers and crew of the ship were Russian and, except for the handful who waited at table in the dining room, they kept pretty much to themselves, with little or no interaction with the passengers. The expedition team of 19 had been contracted by Peregrine to provide for all the passengers' needs, both on board and on excursions, and included three chefs; the Russians had their own chef. The Peregrine team came from a wide variety of backgrounds, but fell into four broad categories: boat/kayak guides, presenter/guides, hotel staff and medical staff. The ship offered an expedition-style operation, so there were none of the entertainment facilities normally found on cruise ships; there was, though, a bar, a lounge, a dining room and a presentation room. There was also a small gym and sauna. Most of the staff (including hotel staff and some of the presenters) were required to drive the Zodiacs – these were RIBs capable of carrying 12 passengers, used for making landings and cruising close to the ice and wildlife. The presenter/guide's main role was providing information in the form of formal talks and informal chats, and assisting managing the passengers when making landings. The ship had a Russian doctor, but Peregrine provided another one for the passengers and to provide emergency response ashore.

There were presenters who specialized in wildlife, in geology/glaciology and in history – then there was me, who didn't really fit neatly into any of these categories at the time. I had talks prepared on the international diplomacy of Antarctica, on why Antarctica was important as a global base for science, on BAS, and on my own experiences. But it became obvious that my role was really 'old Antarctic hero' – wise old man of Antarctica. I was not on this cruise as a historian. Anyway over the first day or so I got to grips with what I saw as my duties, and started to work to fit into the team. I found it a pleasure to work them; they were all highly motivated and excellent team players. All were prepared to go the extra mile to provide the passengers with a 'once in a lifetime' experience. They were a very mixed bunch with a broad range of backgrounds, so working with them had many parallels with my earlier life at BAS. It was the same goal-driven activity in the same difficult and demanding environment – though of course the goals were very different. I got a great deal out of this first encounter with the industry, visiting places which I would have never had reason to in my working life, and having truly close encounters with the wildlife, which would not have been possible either. I also found that the passengers were for the most part a lively, intelligent bunch who were very keen to hear what I had to say, and to learn from the experience.

I thought I had done well as a guide; all the onboard feedback was very positive. So after I had got home I was somewhat surprised not to hear anything from the company. But it turned out that Peregrine had been bought out by a larger travel company, and the folks who had been running its operation had left for pastures new. But they will reappear in the story. So I turned my attention to the offer that Victoria Wheatley had made for me to travel as historian/guide on the *Explorer II* (later renamed *Minerva*) with Abercrombie & Kent. This ship was significantly larger than the *Ioffe* and much more luxurious, having been built as a luxury cruise liner. It had the capacity to carry over 400 passengers, but for its Antarctic operation was limited to a maximum of 200 so that the product could still be seen as an expedition, albeit somewhat more luxurious. But for me the really important aspect was the invitation for Helen to accompany me. For both of us, though, there was some nervousness: Antarctica had been my life, but Helen had had to put up with my long absences without the opportunity to experience the place herself. So her view of Antarctica was somewhat jaundiced. Two serious questions arose: would she fall in love with it as I had done? and would she be a good sailor?

I had obligated myself to be a historian, so I had a lot of homework to do in the lead-up to the voyage to prepare myself, and as we shall see it was the start of something really quite unexpected but which now dominates my retirement. I joined the *Explorer II* in Ushuaia on 21 January 2008, and we sailed that day for the Falklands. The operation was similar to Peregrine's; there was the same sort of expedition team of interesting and committed folk, one of whom was an ex-BAS boatman, Russ Manning. But now the expedition team was not involved in the hotel side of the operation – for that, there was a marching army of professionals on the ship. I was quickly (and more effectively) inducted into the team, and gave my first presentation on our first day at sea. The first cruise went really quite well, and again my real pleasure was in working with the team. Then at the beginning of February back to Ushuaia, where Helen was waiting to join the ship.

We set sail on a pretty comprehensive cruise which would include the Falklands, South Georgia and the peninsula, before returning to Ushuaia. And the first test was passed as we sailed across the Scotia Sea towards South Georgia – Helen *was* a good sailor! It was clear very quickly, too, that she was captivated by the experience

Helen and me aboard the *Explorer II* in 2008 off Point Wild, Elephant Island.

of South Georgia and the Antarctic Peninsula – particularly the penguins and their chicks. She also enjoyed life on board, mixing with the expedition staff, passengers and ship's officers – the latter, unlike the Russian crew on *Ioffe*, were expected to dine with the passengers. So this first trip was a success for her, and she has joined me for four further trips, including being with me at Vernadsky to mark 50 years since I first went there: a lovely moment for us both.

I did the next two seasons with A & K, making some good friends amongst the expedition team, but then a combination of the financial crash and the withdrawal of the ship from polar service left me beached for a year. The crash had a sizable impact on the polar tourism sector, which contracted for several years before beginning to recover in 2010/11. The folks who had run the Peregrine operation had started up their own operation – again using the *Ioffe* and the *Vavilov* – and again running the simple non-luxury operation. So I found myself back in contact with Aaron and working as historian/guide for the new operation, now known as OneOcean. I really felt at home with OneOcean's field operation, and this company provided an excellent expedition experience for its passengers. It was also always kind and helpful to me, allowing me to bring both Helen and my daughters on cruises with me. My younger daughter, Clare, even travelled as artist in residence on board for two seasons. But the back office was never a well-found operation and the company seemed always to be running close to the edge financially; I worked every season up to 2019/20, when the company went rather spectacularly bust.

I had also done a couple of cruises on a super-luxury ship, the *Seabourn Quest*, but found the over-indulgence on it not at all to my taste. In the 2019/20 season I managed to get a berth with an Australian company, Aurora Expeditions, on a brand-new ship, the *Greg Mortimer*. I really enjoyed it – finding it much more like the field programme of OneOcean, but with the bonus of not having to wait months to be paid. However, when I got home from the cruise on 6 March 2020 it was just before Covid hit and brought the polar cruising industry to a halt. As I write, the industry is trying to re-establish itself with the possibility of a full season ahead, depending of course how the nasty little virus evolves.

What do I make of the Antarctic tourism industry now? I have to say that I have a rather nuanced view. There is no doubt that it is very well organized and operates

The adventures of Peter Penguin. He made three trips with me to Antarctica. On the third trip he brought my daughter Liz along. But he spends most time with my grand-daughter Kira.

in the most environmentally benign way possible – and much of that success has been produced by self-imposed constraints, which the Antarctic Treaty has formalized *post hoc.* The industry has up to now had a business model that relied upon wealthy well-educated customers who are environmentally conscious and want to learn more about the continent. It has argued that the small environmental impact that it has had is more than outweighed by the large number of influential Antarctic ambassadors that it produces. While the industry was still small I largely agreed with this position, and I believe it was true. But by 2019 I had started having doubts, because of the sudden rapid growth – not only in the number of the ships but in their increasing size. It seemed like the tragedy of the commons was going to destroy the essence of what made the experience special. I certainly felt that a crisis was approaching.

But then Covid brought the industry to a dead stop. After two lost seasons it is now (August 2022) in the process of arising phoenix-like from the ashes and will probably quickly recover and then exceed its previous size. Whether this can be managed in a way that both protects the environment and the essential essence of the wilderness experience for the passengers is a moot point, and the human species does not have a good track record for dealing with such dilemmas. We must look to the treaty parties and IAATO to find a way forward. But I have been invited to participate again by two companies, so before I am too old and doddery, I plan to go again, even if I do have to wrestle with my conscience. I am truly grateful to the tourism industry for the opportunities it has given me to take my family south – a small recompense for the long winter nights when they were stuck at home while I was playing in Antarctica.

I have recently been involved in a book proposal sent out for review, and was somewhat amused, dazzled and self-satisfied to see myself referred to as a Polar Historian of Repute by one of the referees – though they didn't specify whether it was good or bad repute. So now I will tell you, dear reader, how I progressed, and you can

Enjoying some boating on a summer day out with my younger daughter, Clare, in Cierva Cove on the Antarctic Peninsula (Credit Steven Rose).

draw your own conclusions as to that statement's veracity. I have already mentioned the project that I had begun with David Walton. This got off to a really positive start, so that by 2008 we had put together a book proposal entitled *Politics in a Cold Climate: Antarctic Science and Governance*. This was planned to address and understand the interactions between national political agendas and international science in shaping the regulations for the governance of Antarctica. We pitched it to Cambridge University Press, which accepted it. We also applied, and received, emeritus fellowships from the Leverhulme Trust, which gave us travel money to visit various overseas national archives, and a small grant from the Trans-Antarctic Association. I used my travel grant to visit the US National Archives in Maryland and to make two visits to Hobart, where I was also a visiting fellow at the University of Tasmania, for a few weeks by kind invitation of Tony Press. who hosted me at the ACE CRC.[150]

---

150 Antarctic Climate and Ecosystems Cooperative Research Centre. Dr Tony Press had been the director of the Australian Antarctic Division, Australian representative on COMNAP, a member of the Australian delegation to the treaty and chair of the CEP during my time as deputy director of BAS, so we had interacted quite a bit over the years. He had retired to the University of Hobart to head up the Antarctic Climate and Ecosystems Collaborative Research Centre based there.

I started out researching the US and Australian governments' attitude to the governance of Antarctica in the immediate post World War II years, which I found fascinating. I had not taken much interest in Antarctic history up to then, but this research, coupled with my developing interest in Antarctic politics from my time on COMNAP and at the treaty meetings, started to lead me along a path which emphasized the political history more than the coupling of governance and science. Enter Dr John Sheail.

David and I had decided we needed to know more about the British attitudes and policies post war, and particularly how BAS had ended up in NERC. The obvious place to start would be the NERC Archives, and here David remembered a retired staff member of CEH (Centre for Ecology and Hydrology, then another component body of the NERC), who had knowledge of the archive. That person was John Sheail. David arranged for John to meet us at BAS in May 2009. It is no exaggeration to say that meeting John was to change my retirement completely and lead directly to my new job description. John is an outstanding historian but a very quiet modest man. He was happy to talk to us about the NERC Archive, but opined that what we really needed to do was to search the official record held at the National Archives (TNA) at Kew. John had spent a lot of his career researching in TNA, becoming a wizard at uncovering important documents there. Although he had no specialist knowledge in Antarctic matters, he offered to go digging in TNA for us, provided we could steer him on what we were looking for and cover his travelling expenses. We did the latter first from the Trans-Antarctic Association grant and then from a grant from the British Antarctic Territory administered by the FCO. So commenced my collaboration with John, which continues until today.

Slowly over the next few years the emphasis of the collaboration shifted from David and me with John acting as a research assistant, to John and me working on material from TNA with David slowly fading into the background. John would make regular visits to TNA with a digital camera, photographing documents he thought would be of interest. Over the years these images have accumulated into a formidable collection of government material on or about Antarctica, the Falklands, and Southern Ocean whaling, covering the period from around the 1890s to post World War II, currently comprising around 42,000 images. It has become a hugely rich source of research material.

To begin with I worked hard on the original book, drafting several chapters, and doing quite a lot of analysis. But slowly, frustrated by David's lack of engagement, I began to become more motivated by the unfolding political history of Britain's involvement in Antarctica as revealed in TNA material. This led me, in collaboration with John, to write research papers based on what we were finding. Our underlying purpose has been to debunk deep-rooted myths that have arisen partly because the official files have remained closed for so long. Regarding the original book, we persistently fed on the patience of the commissioning editor at CUP while we missed deadline after revised deadline, until my embarrassment grew strong enough for us to withdraw at the end of 2014 with as much grace as we could muster. But by then John and I were embarked on a different book, with David as sleeping third author, which concentrated on how and why Britain had become involved in a territorial claim to Antarctica. This was finally published in 2019 with the title *Claiming the Ice: Britain and the Antarctic 1900–1950*,[151] by which time David had withdrawn completely from the project. Sadly, he died just before its publication.

Along the way our myth busting produced three new and quite distinct contributions, which resulted in peer-reviewed research papers – and also, indirectly, in another book. The first paper concerned Operation Tabarin. This operation had led to the foundation of what was to become BAS, and I had always held to the accepted wisdom that it had been a secret military operation to establish observation posts to look out for Axis surface and submarine raiders which might use anchorages in and around the peninsula as safe havens. I never questioned this, even when the most superficial analysis should have raised red flags concerning the stupidity of the idea. But John's ferreting in TNA slowly revealed a very different story: the operation had had nothing to do with war and was all to do with protecting the British claim in Antarctica against encroachments upon it by Argentina and, to a lesser extent, Chile. The British were occupying the territory because the legal advisors at the Foreign Office had asserted that without occupation the British claim would wither. John and I also traced the origins of the dispute between Britain and Argentina back to the Scottish National Antarctic Expedition of 1902–1904 led by William Speirs Bruce. The paper was intended to be published under all three of our names, but for reasons I will not enter into here John Sheail decided to take his name off the paper[152] – something I regret to this day, because without his diligent research in the archives the work would not have seen the light of day.

The Tabarin paper kindled my interest in Bruce and the myths that surrounded him, not least why his expedition had never been honoured with Polar Medals. The myth here was that this had been due to the malign influence of the then president of the RGS,[153] Sir Clement Markham. John and I showed that this was indeed a myth; the rules for the award of the medal simply meant that Bruce and his men were not entitled to it. This finding resulted in a further publication.[154] I was then invited to give

---

151 Dudeney, J.R. and J. Sheail (2019) *Claiming the Ice: Britain and the Antarctic 1900–1950*, Cambridge Scholars Publishing, ISBN 978-1-5275-3048-5

152 Dudeney, J.R. and D.W.H. Walton (2011) From 'Scotia' to 'Operation Tabarin' – Developing British Policy for Antarctica, *Polar Record*, DOI: 10.1017/S0032247411000520

153 Royal Geographical Society

154 Dudeney, J. R. and J, Sheail (2014) William Speirs Bruce and the Polar Medal: myth and reality, *The Polar Journal* DOI: 10.1080/2154896X.2014.913915

a talk on Bruce at a meeting of the Devon Polar Society in Plymouth, a group that had a sizeable membership of serving and retired medical people from the BAS medical unit housed at Derriford Hospital. Through this medical link a retired NHS consultant, Isobel Williams, heard of my interest in (and apparent deep knowledge of) Bruce. She had already written a couple of polar biographies (one on Edward Wilson and the other on Edgar Evans), and was planning one on Bruce. So she contacted me for advice on her project. To begin with I helped by providing information from TNA files, but it soon became apparent that co-authorship would produce a much better product than either of us could produce alone. And so the biography *William Speirs Bruce, Forgotten Polar Hero* was born, and was published in 2018.[155]

Perhaps the piece of research of which I am most proud concerned Sir Ernest Shackleton and his attempt to cross the Antarctic. I had been a great admirer of Shackleton since my early days as a fid, so what we discovered in TNA was shocking to me, and made me reappraise the man. Once again the story would not have been told but for John's uncanny skill and perseverance at following a paper trail in an archive. We were deep into studying Britain's territorial claim to parts of Antarctica (which ultimately became British Antarctic Territory) and its consequent dialogues and discords with Argentina. John unearthed a Foreign Office file entitled 'Argentina 1916', which he imaged and then thought little more about, not having the context to see the amazing story it told. But when I took a look at it I had one of those spine-tingling moments which happen rarely in research, when you know you are looking at something game-changing which nobody else has seen. For in this file there was a long letter written in early June 1916 by Reginald Tower (the chief minister in the UK legation in BA) to the foreign secretary, Sir Edward Grey. In it Tower revealed that the whaling company that Carl Larsen had established at South Georgia had an unusually powerful and ice-strengthened whale catcher that it was offering to use to rescue the 22 men marooned on Elephant Island, but that Shackleton – then in the Falklands – had turned the offer down! This finding led us into a paper trail which told of the very comprehensive efforts and expense that the British government went to – with the help of the Australian and New Zealand governments – to search for Shackleton and his men, and then to attempt recovery of both the Elephant Island party and the so-called forgotten men stranded on the shore of the Ross Sea. We told this story in yet another publication[156] in 2014. The story that unfolded, and how it reflected on Shackleton's character, was sufficiently surprising – shocking even – for it to be covered

---

155 Williams, I.P. and J.R. Dudeney (2018) *William Speirs Bruce, Forgotten Polar Hero*, Stroud: Amberley Publishing, ISBN 978-1-4456-8081-1

156 Dudeney, J.R., J. Sheail and D.W.H. Walton (2014) The British Government, Ernest Shackleton, and the rescue of the Imperial Trans-Antarctic Expedition, *Polar Record*, DOI:10.1017/S0032247414000631

    Dudeney, J.R. (2018) The British Government, Ernest Shackleton, and the rescue of the Imperial Trans-Antarctic Expedition, CORRIGENDUM, *Polar Record*, doi:10.1017/S0032247418000281

by a feature in the *Independent on Sunday*[157] but that was partly because my daughter Clare's partner, Paul Bignell, was the journalist involved. There was also a slight blot on the landscape, in that in the original paper we had wrongly ascribed the offer as having come from Carl Larsen, when actually it had come from one of his brothers. So in 2018 I published a short corrigendum to make this plain.

One thing leads to another, so I will return to the referee's comment on my latest project. This is a book about the Southern Ocean whaling industry and the part that Britain played in it with John, and Paul Rodhouse, an old colleague from BAS. As I write in summer 2022, we have a contract from a publisher and have much of a first draft written. So has all this effort made me a Polar Historian of Repute? If it is true, then it is only so on the coat-tails of John Sheail. None of it would have happened without him. I am honoured to have been able to fly in his slipstream.

---

157 https://www.independent.co.uk/news/uk/home-news/ernest-shackleton-put-media-his-men-refusing-sturdier-ship-lucrative-newspaper-deal-9746416.html

23

NERC MESSES WITH A
NATIONAL TREASURE

On a fine sunny morning in October 2012 I arrived at my local GP's surgery for my annual flu jab. Such occasions are strictly orchestrated – a jab a minute, straight in and straight out. But not this time. When my turn came, my GP brought the whole process to a sharp halt so that he could interrogate me at length as to whether or not I was going to save BAS. I realized at that moment that NERC would probably not get its way with BAS. If even such as my GP knew about BAS and was concerned about it, this was no longer a spat about the future of an obscure research institute. NERC had taken on a national treasure, but seemed not to have realized it. And so it turned out. Within less than a month NERC had changed course – but it was a hard battle. This chapter will tell the story of my part in it.

By 2012, there was a new senior management team at BAS: Professor Nick Owens had succeeded Chris Rapley as director in 2007; Robert Culshaw was deputy, following on from me; and John Pye had been replaced by Ian Dunn. There was also a new head of NERC, Professor Duncan Wingham. I have talked about the tensions between BAS and NERC already, but I do not know what actually sparked the conflict at the end of 2011. However, it appears that Nick Owens and Duncan Wingham fell out in a big way over the need for serious spending cuts, such that Nick was invited to no longer come to work. My first intimation of trouble was when I met Dr Ed Hill at a reception at the FCO on 20 February 2012. Ed was director of another NERC-funded institute – the National Oceanographic Centre (NOC) based in Southampton. Ed and I had interacted on many occasions on NERC business, so it was natural for us to gossip, and he told me that Nick was on long-term sick leave. But when I was visiting BAS in early March I found that Nick was on what was termed 'gardening leave', and that Ed Hill had actually been made interim director of BAS whilst retaining his role at NOC. Not long after this (on 29 March) I met Nick himself looking hale and hearty at a centenary event (of Scott's expedition) at St Paul's Cathedral, where I learnt that he had effectively been dismissed because he had defied NERC over the funding issue. But oddly there seemed to be no intention of having Robert (as deputy) step up, whilst the director's post was advertised. The following day I happened to be at BAS again to celebrate a staff member's retirement. Afterwards I noted in my diary that Ed Hill was not going down well there, with the view being – 'has no interest in learning about BAS, no intention of travelling overseas on BAS business or going South'. A very senior member of BAS staff opined that a bit of investigative journalism might find out what NERC's real aims were. Enter my daughter's partner Paul Bignell and the *Independent on Sunday* (*IoS*).

That day I gave Paul a summary of what I knew, and a few names of folk whom it might be interesting for him to talk with. Being a rather good journalist, he also had his own contacts, whom he quite rightly kept to himself. He approached NERC on 6 April, eliciting the following response:

> It is the case that the director of BAS, Professor N.J. Owens, is currently on special leave. In his absence NERC has appointed Professor A.E. Hill as interim director, recognizing the considerable skills and experience of Professor Hill in leading complex scientific and logistical activities. This is part of NERC's commitment to ensuring that BAS maintains its focus on delivering excellent science. Professor Owens has not been sacked and NERC has no intention of advertising for a new director for BAS. It is not true that Professor Hill is unenthusiastic about visiting Antarctica; it is true that he is rightly focussing on finalizing BAS's financial plans to resolve any uncertainty some staff might feel.[158]

This odd response caused Paul to dig deeper into the story. This led to a major article in the *IoS* the following Sunday, 8 April, which was deemed of sufficient interest to devote the front page and a full two-page spread inside to the story, under the headline 'Frozen Out, British Polar Research in Crisis'. It was excellent journalism, which revealed that NERC had attempted to enforce a cut of £13 million on a budget of £48 million. It reported that Owens had gone over the heads of NERC officials to alert the FCO that BAS would no longer be able to deliver the presence required in Antarctica, and that FCO officials had been so concerned that they had raised the issue at a National Security Council meeting in January chaired by the prime minister, David Cameron. The *IoS* reported that the PM had pledged support for BAS and told officials to sort the funding issues out. But the victim of the spat was Nick Owens, who it seemed had fallen on his sword for BAS. The next day, NERC responded with a piece in the daily *Independent*, in which it announced 'level' funding for BAS for the next three years.

Over the next few days I learnt from sources in BAS that the *IoS* article had caused serious waves in NERC and BAS, and had forced NERC into announcing the funding

---

158 Email exchange between Paul Bignell (then a journalist with the Independent on Sunday) and NERC dated 6 April 2012. Paul Bignell has given permission for it to be reproduced here on the basis that it was intended for the public domain.

decision before it had been properly scrutinized internally. A subsequent chat, on 10 May, with senior BAS staff revealed that Owens was moving to a new job at Plymouth Marine Laboratory, and that there were no plans to search for a replacement. The first intimation that something like a merger or takeover was in the air now came with the suggestion that NERC had serious intentions of calving off the engineering/logistics part of BAS to NOC and running down the rest. Another little snippet was that the *IoS* article had caused the State Department of the USA to seek clarification and reassurance from the FCO as to the UK's commitment to its Antarctic presence, the apparent uncertainty no doubt causing some concerns in that department.

On 7 June the news came that NERC proposed to merge NOC and BAS. A curious and somewhat contradictory announcement was put up on the NERC website: on the one hand it stated that both centres would keep their premises and identities with minimum staff transfers – but on the other there would be great savings and synergies from the formation of an Institute of Marine and Polar Sciences. I could not see how this could possibly work, but the statement made clear that final decisions would not be made until the NERC Council Meeting in December. Then on 31 July, BAS lost its top management team (except Ed Hill), with the resignation of Ian Dunn and the departure of Robert Culshaw. The circumstances under which Robert was invited to leave were obscure, and he was bound to silence at the time. I attended the little goodbye ceremony, when it was suggested that somebody should make a Freedom of Information (FoI) request for a document entitled 'The Future of BAS', which had figured at the May NERC Council Meeting. Paul immediately proceeded to do so but after several months, including making a formal appeal, he failed to move NERC from its argument that disclosure would not be in the public interest. Julian Hubbert MP also tried to gain some access to the document via a Parliamentary Question, but was equally unsuccessful.[159]

Having apparently decided on the case for the merger, NERC consulted merely on the modalities of how the merger should be carried out. The consultation document[160] was released on 11 September 2012, open to national and international organizations and interested individuals, with a closing date of 10 October.

My response was delivered to NERC on 20 September. It comprised a detailed paragraph-by-paragraph critique of its plans, and ran to nine pages. Not only did I disagree with the strategic aims (such as they were), but also I expressed my amazement that there appeared to have been no staff work done to establish what the real cost/ benefits, if any, would be. I pointed out that both NOC and BAS were high-performance organizations with highly respected international and recognized brands. Each had its own culture and traditions, with highly motivated staff who identified very strongly

---

159 For the wording of Hubbert's PQ and the minister's response see Hansard (Citation: HC Deb, 15 October 2012, c244W)

160 https://nerc.ukri.org/about/whatwedo/engage/consultations/merge/bas-noc-merger-consultation/

with that brand. BAS, which I knew much more about, had a unique culture; its staff were very highly motivated with a strong can-do attitude in which multidisciplinary teams routinely delivered complex cutting-edge projects safely in highly challenging circumstances. So there needed to be a very strong argument for disturbing such storming teams if as a consequence that disturbance robbed them of their identity. Changing the name of an organization may not seem a big deal, but when identity and sense of purpose are bound up in it, it *is* a big deal. High performance takes years to build up – but can be lost in a day. My summary conclusion was:

> Overall the document has the smell of a done deal, but not one that has been properly thought through. I suggest that it is withdrawn and brought forward again once the necessary staff work has been done to give strategic reasons for the merger that stand up to critical scrutiny, identifies with some assurance what the costs/impacts/savings really are, what management structures are actually needed, how they will be staffed, and provides measurable criteria for success.

Having been a regular attendee at Foundation of Science & Technology meetings and an individual member of the Parliamentary & Scientific Committee, I had built up a wide range of contacts amongst relevant scientists, politicians and officials in science policy, so I made a point of circulating my response to them as widely as possible, as well as to my network of polar people. My document quickly developed a life of its own, as the recipients circulated it to their contacts. But in particular, I sent a copy to Andrew Millar MP, who was chair of the P&SC, and perhaps more importantly the chair of the House of Commons Select Committee on Science & Technology. He responded immediately, saying that he had circulated my document to the other members of the select committee. I would not wish you, however, to get the impression that my response was particularly influential; NERC was deluged with input – in total 364 responses from individuals and organizations, some of them from very influential people indeed, and almost all of them negative in one way or another towards the proposal. But my seizing the attention of Andrew Millar created a key step change in the external pressure on NERC, because he decided on 5 October that his select committee should hold an urgent inquiry into the issue as part of an ongoing inquiry into marine science. It also emerged that on the same day two members of NERC Council had visited BAS to meet staff, and that at that meeting it was reported that Ed Hill had admitted that NERC had not even prepared a business case for the merger. Not only that, but I learnt from another ex-colleague that Al Gore, former vice president of the USA, had written personally to NERC, expressing his concerns. This letter had also made its way into Paul's hands, giving him two nice scoops – the Gore letter and the fact that there was to be an S & T committee inquiry – for another major article in the *IoS* on 7 October. There was also a hard-hitting piece (in which I played no part) from the columnist

Charles Clover in *The Sunday Times*, with such wonderfully perceptive lines as 'the real reason is personal empire building'!

Through the autumn NERC suffered a steady trickle of negative comment in the press (such as the *Observer/Guardian*, *New Scientist*, *Research Fortnight*, the BBC webpage, and *Prospect* magazine) inspired by others. NERC responded by claiming that it had no intention of closing BAS – but it was still wedded to its proposed Institute of Marine and Polar Sciences. On top of that there now loomed what might be termed a perfect storm of exposure in Parliament, scheduled for October and November. The Upper Chamber was planning to hold a debate on 18 October under the title 'The Centenary of the Scott Expedition to Antarctica and of the United Kingdom's enduring Scientific Legacy and Ongoing Presence There'. A Library Note[161] had been prepared as background for the participants, with information on Antarctica's geography and environment; the history of its exploration; the international agreements that govern the territory; international scientific cooperation; and the UK's continuing role and presence. But it also gave a detailed description of the merger plan and the press responses to it. So the topic was bound to be part of the debate, particularly as many interested parties (myself included) had made a point of briefing members on our concerns. Also, and potentially more significant, important legislation – the Antarctic Bill, required to update the Antarctic Act 1994, to bring the Liability Annex into law – was before the House as a Private Member's Bill,[162] with its second reading scheduled for Friday 2 November. There was a danger that MPs could be inclined to 'talk it out' if they were sufficiently unhappy with the merger plans. And of course, there were lots of influencers waiting to make sure that they were well briefed in that regard. And then there was the planned inquiry by the S & T Select Committee.

On 10 October the clerk to the committee invited me to submit written evidence to it. My response was delivered on 15 October, but I could not circulate it more widely until the hearing had taken place. My evidence was made public on the parliamentary website[163] immediately following the hearing and release of the committee's report.

The first intimation that the NERC position might not be completely firm came on 10 October, when according to sources in BAS Duncan Wingham suggested to senior staff at BAS that he might be open to a Plan B. Perhaps it was no coincidence that this was the day on which the consultation closed; he would by then have been aware that out of over 360 responses only 3 supported the plan. It was around this time that I had the encounter at my GP's surgery.

Events now moved very quickly. The Lords' debate on 18 October was thoughtful and well informed, and was largely taken up with the merger controversy. Lord Wallis

---

161 https://researchbriefings.files.parliament.uk/documents/LLN-2012-034/LLN-2012-034.pdf

162 The Antarctic Bill, Neil Carmichael MP, https://commonslibrary.parliament.uk/research-briefings/rp12-63/

163 https://publications.parliament.uk/pa/cm201213/cmselect/cmsctech/699/699we07.htm

(chairman of NERC) attempted to make NERC's case, but there was clear cross-party opposition. Baroness Warsi, the Foreign Office minister, reaffirmed the government's commitment to the UK's dual mission in Antarctica in that the scale of operations would be maintained, and confirmed that the merger was not a done deal – but did not explicitly confirm that BAS in its current form would remain the instrument of delivery. I was asked by Chi Onwurah MP, opposition spokesperson on Science & Technology, what I thought of the debate. I expressed my concerns that Warsi's statement left open the possibility of breaking up BAS to leave just a rump, providing logistics.

On 22 October I learnt that NERC had decided to bring forward the council meeting when the decision would be taken to Thursday 1 November – the day before the second reading of the Antarctic Bill and well before the planned date for the S & T hearing! When Andrew Millar learnt of this (from Paul) on 24 October he was apparently spitting nails in anger, and the next day he brought the hearing forward to 31 October, inviting the minister for science, David Willets, Lord Wallis, Duncan Wingham and Ed Hill to appear before him. On 23 October Lord Wallis made a speech at a function associated with the passage of the Antarctic Bill through the Commons. In this he described much of the consultation responses as hype and hot air, and made a great virtue of changing the names of NOC and BAS. Needless to say, a recording of this made its way into the public domain!

So the last week in October was shaping up to be really busy for NERC. Paul previewed it with another excellent piece in the *IoS* on 28 October under the headline 'British Antarctic Survey saved as merger plan scuppered'. In this he predicted 'from key sources within Government and polar science ... though a final decision is still to be made, the plans are likely to be dropped'. He reported that the plans had been met with derision, critics saying that NERC had offered no business case, and that there had also been a public petition which had already garnered 3,000 signatures. Yet more bad news for NERC came on Monday 29 October from a group of NGOs (WWF, Greenpeace, RSPB and Friends of the Earth), which jointly challenged the legality of the consultation exercise and threatened judicial review if the plans were not dropped.

It was in this febrile atmosphere that the S & T committee convened for the public hearing at Portcullis House on the morning of 31 October. I attended it in person, as I was joining the annual lunch for the P&SC scheduled for that day, to be held in the Cholmondeley Room and Terrace in the House of Lords, where I expected to get pretty immediate feedback from the horse's mouth (Andrew Millar) over pre-lunch drinks. Paul too came to the hearing. Willets was very correct in emphasizing that ministers did not interfere in the internal activities of a research council. The trio of Wallis, Wingham and Hill put a positive spin on what was planned, but Ed Hill came under pressure on the grounds of conflict of interest. The committee also expressed its displeasure over NERC's calendar games. Then the committee went into private session. Over lunch Lord Jenkin told me he had been phoned by Wallis to say that NERC would withdraw the merger plan the next day – quite a different line from that of his evidence – and Andrew Millar told me that the report would be published at 4 pm that day! Another member of the S & T committee also opined that NERC would not like the outcome. That was indeed the case:

> The NERC council should not proceed with their current plans to merge the British Antarctic Survey (BAS) and the National Oceanography Centre (NOC) MPs have warned today.
>
> The Science and Technology Committee was not convinced that the Research Council had properly made a case for the merger in terms of science or cost saving. The Committee also had concerns about the process of consultation and the apparent lack of concern about sensitive geo-political considerations surrounding the South Atlantic operations.[164]

It was against this background that the NERC Council was convened the next day. At the time I viewed the step by NERC to move this meeting forward as indicating its desire to get the merger done and dusted before the S & T committee met and before the Antarctic Bill was debated. I think that this was a common worry amongst my many colleagues, not the least Andrew Millar. But NERC was under heavy pressure from all sides. Contrary to Lord Wallis's view of the consultation, it had received an almost universal negative response. So in retrospect a more charitable explanation could be that it brought the meeting forward so it could withdraw the plan before getting hammered by the S & T committee and so the second reading of the Antarctic Bill would not be disrupted. I would have loved to have been a fly on the wall at that meeting – but suffice to say that NERC did fully step back from the merger, yet even then somehow shot itself in the foot again. How?

Well, the next morning the second reading of the Antarctic Bill commenced. Here is a quote from my diary for that day:

> I was able to watch the second reading of the Antarctic Bill live on TV in the morning and great fun it was too. No announcement from NERC overnight or this morning, but just after the debate got under way the opposition foreign affairs spokesman intervened to announce that a ministerial statement had been made to say the merger was off! (turns out that Willetts realised NERC had done nothing so he did it for them! They heard from a journalist!!) Anyway all the right things were said from both sides of the house and I found myself in the midst of a mini press frenzy acting as a talking head as BAS were not allowed to speak to the press – another silly decision by NERC. So I expect to be all

164 https://old.parliament.uk/business/committees/committees-a-z/commons-select/science-and-technology-committee/news/1201031-nerc-report/

over the newspapers tomorrow – already quoted on the BBC news website and live on Radio Cambridgeshire in the early evening. Things take another twist against NERC in the evening when Andrew Millar writes an open letter to Wingham seeking clarification on some points and asks the specific question of why Culshaw wasn't made acting director when Owens left (thought put in his head by Paul).

Thus was BAS (and NOC) saved for the nation, and on 27 November I learnt (again from Paul) that my old friend and colleague, Alan Rodger, an ex-beastieman and now senior BAS staff member, had been appointed as interim director of BAS, replacing Ed Hill. Alan was a very safe and intelligent pair of hands, and thus the process of rebuilding morale and focus for BAS could begin.

But that wasn't quite the end of the story. On 11 November 2014 the P&SC celebrated its 75th anniversary with a reception at Buckingham Palace, hosted by the Queen and Prince Philip. It was in this rather unlikely setting that I had a bit of a run-in with Duncan Wingham. Here is what I recorded in my diary:

> I suggested that the NOC/BAS merger episode was not NERC's finest hour – He accused me of insulting him and also strove to re-write history by suggesting it was all part of his grand strategy to force BIS's[165] hand over funding!

But even *that* wasn't the end of the story. Very sadly, after retiring from BAS, having pulled the place together and handed over to his successor, Professor Dame Jane Francis, Alan Rodger contracted lung cancer, and after a remarkably brave and dignified response finally passed away on 3 January 2020. His funeral was held on 24 January with a wake at BAS afterwards. I ended up, at his wife's request, as informal master of ceremonies for the wake. Duncan Wingham approached me to ask if he could say 'six or seven sentences'. I assumed he wanted to say something appropriate about Alan's service to NERC and BAS – but not a bit of it. Instead it was in essence a repeat of what he had said to me at the Palace. This was hardly appropriate, and the looks on the faces of most of the attendees made that point very clear. And so the saga ended – for me, at least.

---

165 Department for Business, Innovation and Skills

24

WHAT DID IT ALL AMOUNT TO?

As I write this the world is in a very strange place in which we are all living in the aftermath of a global pandemic – Covid 19 – which has been dominating everything for more than two years. One of the very many consequences of this has been the cancellation of effectively all Antarctic tourism activity for the 2020/21 summer season, and much of that for 2021/22. Whilst this is perhaps not in the grand scheme of things a cataclysmic impact compared with the grievous loss of life that has occurred from the pandemic, it is something that has caused me to stop and reflect on my connection with Antarctica, even though I hope to travel there again. What did it all amount to?

Some folk seem to carefully think through and map out the course of their lives. I have never done that. All I have ever done is allow serendipity to have its way with me, by seizing on some of the opportunities it presented. When I embarked on my degree course I had no thought of engaging in such an unusual lifestyle; in fact as far as I can remember I had no thoughts whatever about what my future would hold, except that it might involve science in some way. But as it turned out my developing character was very well suited to the solitary isolated life of an Antarctic winterer. Psychological studies[166] of wintering teams from Australia and the USA in the 1960 and 1970s identified the ideal winterer as an 'educated isolate'. This is a person who is content with their own company and is less likely to seek comfort for emotional issues from others, but is also able to work effectively as part of a team. That sums me up pretty well, but whether my character was formed by nature or nurture there is no way of knowing – though in my childhood I was pretty well left to make my own way, particularly after my family broke up, which may well have a bearing on the matter. And, as is clear from the narrative so far, I am not one to have a large circle of close friends; the intimate friendships I have formed over my lifetime can be counted on the fingers of one hand. But those few people have been very important to me.

---

166 Strange, R.E. and S.A. Youngman (1971) Emotional Aspects of Wintering Over, *Antarctic Journal of the USA*, pp. 255–257

Palmai, G. (1963) Psychological Observations on an Isolated Group in Antarctica, *The British Journal of Psychiatry*, 109, pp. 364–370

There is no doubt that my year as a base commander had a fundamental effect on my appreciation of myself and my place in the world. As I look back from a vantage point of more than half a century, that young Dudeney seems to have been quite a separate person from me. I do marvel somewhat that he was able to cope so well in such challenging circumstances. I am not sure that I could do the same now. I do wonder how he did it; my one real memory is of him telling himself over and over again that there was no alternative but to rise to the occasion.

Even when I got home from my first trip to Antarctica I didn't actively aim to continue a career involving the continent. More to the point, I took the path of least resistance by accepting the chance of short-term employment with BAS and continuing to do so until it gave me a permanent job, all the while becoming more and more besotted with the place and the nature of the activities I was able to engage in. Many years later, during my interview for the director job, I was challenged as to why I had not moved out of BAS to gain wider experience, which would have made me more appointable in the eyes of the panel. My answer was why would I, when I was having such fun with all the logistics that BAS had, and the great team that I had created and

The Dudeney Nunataks (75°10'30"S, 69°35'30"W). These nunataks are part of the Sweeney Mountains in Palmer Land. I, amongst others, was honoured in 2020 to mark the 200th anniversary of the sighting of Antarctica with the citation: 'To honour those who have made an exceptional contribution to furthering the understanding, protection and management of Antarctica over the last fifty years, and whose achievements warrant highlighting alongside those of the early explorers'. (Credit Teal Riley)

with whom I had been able to realize my dreams? BAS has provided me with travel all over the world, innumerable contacts with highly able people both inside BAS and outside, and a licence to do wonderful things down south provided I could get somebody to pay for them – which I usually did. It has also, in retirement, given me a whole new and completely unanticipated career as a Polar Historian of Note and Antarctic Guide, which allowed me to continue to escape to the Antarctic almost every season until Covid-19 appeared. I use the word 'escape' advisedly, because fundamentally it is escapism pure and simple. Even with much better communications, as soon as I set off across the Southern Ocean all the cares and worries that dogged me at home just faded away.

What does it all amount to? Well, I have often been known to say that it has beaten having to have a job to make a living. It has been in some ways a lifetime of self-indulgence, a lifetime of major challenges, lots of fun, some loneliness and despair, and occasional moments of real danger and fear, but also lots of moments when I pinched myself with joy that somebody was actually paying me to have such sublime experiences. My one big regret has been the impact it has had on my wife and daughters as a result of my frequent long absences from home. I think I have left a respectable mark on Antarctic scholarship, Antarctic governance and Antarctic operations in my own small way, and recently I achieved a measure of Antarctic immortality by having a small group of nunataks named after me. But more than that: two of my highly valued and long-term colleagues (Alan Rodger and Mike Pinnock) were also honoured to have nunataks named after them in the same mountain range as mine. A lovely way to mark our collective achievements.

On occasions I have been asked to sum up my fascination with Antarctica in a single sentence. All I can say is that the continent is to me 'the sound of silence'.

INITIALISMS AND ACRONYMS

Initialisms are pronounced letter by letter (eg BBC) whereas acronyms are pronounced as words (eg OPEN SESAME).

Initialism/acronym	In full
ACE CRC	Antarctic Climate and Ecosystems Cooperative Research Centre
AGO	automatic geophysical observatory
AGU	American Geophysical Union
AI	artificial intelligence
AINM	accident, incident and near miss
AINMR	accident, incident and near miss reporting
AIS	Advanced Ionospheric Sounder
APL	Applied Physics Laboratory
ARA	Armada de la República *Argentina*
ASD	Atmospheric Sciences Division
ASMA	Antarctic Specially Managed Area
ASOC	Antarctic and Southern Ocean Coalition
ASPA	Antarctic Specially Protected Area
ATCM	Antarctic Treaty Consultative Meetings
ATS	Antarctic Treaty System
AWS	automatic weather station
BAS	British Antarctic Survey
BAT	British Antarctic Territory
BBC	British Broadcasting Corporation
BC	base commander
BIS	Department for Business, Innovation and Skills
BP	British Petroleum
BST	British Summer Time (UTC+1)
BA	Buenos Aires

C&N	Christiani & Nielsen
CAA	Civil Aviation Authority
CBFFI	commander in chief of the British forces in the Falklands
CCAMLR	Convention for the Conservation of Antarctic Marine Living Resources
CCAS	Convention for the Conservation of Antarctic Seals
CEE	Comprehensive Environmental Evaluation
CEH	Centre for Ecology and Hydrology
CEO	chief executive officer
CEP	Committee for Environmental Protection
COMNAP	Council of Managers of National Antarctic Programmes
CONICET	Consejo Nacional de Investigaciones Científicas y Técnicas or National Council of Science and Technology
COSPAR	Committee on Space Research
CP	consultative party
CPR	cardiopulmonary resuscitation
CRAMR	Convention for the Regulation of Antarctic Mineral Resources
CRREL	Cold Regions Research & Engineering Laboratory
CSIR	Council for Scientific and Industrial Research
CUP	Cambridge University Press
DC	Directors' Committee
DEM	diesel and electrical mechanic
DGRC	director general of the research councils
DLR	Deutsches Zentrum für Luft- und Raumfahrt, e.V., or German Aerospace Centre
DME	distance measuring equipment
DPP	Department of Polar Programs
DS	detective sergeant
EID	Environment and Information Division
EISCAT	European Incoherent Scatter Radar
EoI	expression of interest
ESA	European Space Agency
FCO	Foreign and Commonwealth Office
FI	Falkland Islands
FIBS	Falkland Islands Broadcasting Service
FIDS	Falkland Islands Dependencies Survey
FIG	Falklands Islands government

FIGAS	Falkland Islands Government Air Service
FIPASS	Falkland Islands Interim Port and Storage System
FRS	Fellow of the Royal Society
FST	Foundation for Science and Technology
GGS	Global Geospace Science
GH	Government House
GOSEAC	Group of Specialists on Environmental Affairs and Conservation
GP	general medical practitioner
GPS	Global Positioning System
GSFC	Goddard Space Flight Center
GSGSSI	government of South Georgia and the South Sandwich Islands
HAO	high altitude observatory
HEI	higher education institution
HF	high frequency
HMG	Her Majesty's Government
HMS	Her Majesty's Ship
HND	Higher National Diploma
HoD	head of department
HQ	headquarters
HSO	higher scientific officer
IAA	Instituto Antártico Argentino, or Argentine Antarctic Institute
IAATO	International Association of Antarctica Tour Operators
IAGA	International Association for Geophysics and Aeronomy
ICI	Imperial Chemical Industries
ICS	International Council for Science
ID	identity document
IDIG	International Digital Ionosonde Group
IGY	International Geophysical Year
IH	International Harvesters
IM	Individual member
IMC	Instrument Meteorological Conditions
IMF	interplanetary magnetic field
IMO	International Maritime Organization
INAG	Ionosonde Network Advisory Group
INPE	Instituto de Pesquisas Espaciais, or Brazilian Institute for Space Research
IoS	*Independent on Sunday*

IRT	incident response team
ISO	International Organization for Standardization
ISSTP	International Symposium on Solar Terrestrial Physics
IT	information technology
ITV	Independent Television
IUGG	International Union of Geodesy and Geophysics
JANET	Joint Academic Network
JCR	*James Clark Ross*
JP	John Pye
KEP	King Edward Point
LADE	Líneas Aéreas del Estado
LIARA	Laboratorio Ionosférico de la Armada de la República Argentina or Ionospherics Laboratory of the Argentine Navy
LP	long-playing record (they played for about half an hour)
LTS	Light Tower System
M&E	Metcalf & Eddy
MF	medium frequency
MoD	Ministry of Defence
MOLIBA	monitoring the Liability Annex
MoU	Memorandum of Understanding
MP	Member of Parliament
MRAG	Marine Resources Assessment Group
MRC	Medical Research Council
MY	million years
NAP	National Antarctic Programme
NASA	National Aeronautics and Space Administration
NATO	North Atlantic Treaty Organization
NCS	NERC computing service
NDB	non-directional beacon
NEB	NERC Executive Board
NERC	Natural Environment Research Council
NGO	non-governmental organization
NHS	National Health Service
NOAA	National Oceanographic and Atmospheric Administration
NOC	National Oceanographic Centre
NOZE	National Ozone Experiment
NRL	Naval Research Laboratory

NSF	National Science Foundation
NZ	New Zealand
OBE	Order of the British Empire
OPEN	Origins of Plasmas in Earth's Neighborhood
OPEN SESAME	OPEN Satellite Exploration Simultaneous with Antarctic Measurements
OPP	Office of Polar Programs
OST	Office for Science and Technology
OTD	Overseas Territories Directorate
P & I	protection and indemnity
P&SC	Parliamentary and Scientific Committee
PACE	Polar Anglo-American Conjugate Experiment
PBC	permanent base commander
PhD	Doctor of Philosophy
PI	principal investigator
PPARC	Particle Physics and Astronomy Research Council
PRINCE	Projects in Controlled Environments
PRU	Polar Regions Unit
PSO	principal scientific officer
RAF	Royal Air Force
RAS	Royal Astronomical Society
RCUK	research councils UK
RGS	Royal Geographical Society
RIB	rigid inflatable boat
RIBA	Royal Institute of British Architects
RMS	Royal Mail Ship
RN	Royal Navy
RRAG	Renewable Resources Assessment Group
RRS	Royal Research Ship
RRS	Radio Research Station
RSPB	Royal Society for the Protection of Birds
RSRS	Radio and Space Research Station
S & T	science and technology
SAIP	South African Institute of Physics
SANAE	South African National Antarctic Expedition
SANCGASS	South African National Committee for Geomagnetism, Aeronomy and Space Sciences

SAR	search and rescue operation
SATCM	Special Antarctic Treaty Consultative Meeting
SCALOP	Standing Committee on Antarctic Logistics and Operations
SCAR	Scientific Committee for Antarctic Research
SEL	Space Environment Laboratory
SES	Satellite Earth Station
SGSSI	South Georgia and the South Sandwich Islands
SHARE	Southern Hemisphere Auroral Radar Experiment
SoR	Statement of Requirements
SPA	Specially Protected Area
SPRI	Scott Polar Research Institute
SPSO	senior principal scientific officer
SRC	Science Research Council
SSB	Space Sciences Building
SSO	senior scientific officer
SSSI	Site of Special Scientific Interest
STAR	Solar Terrestrial and Astrophysical Research
STOL	Short take-off and landing
STP	solar terrestrial physics
SuperDARN	Super Dual Auroral Radar Network
SWAT	special weapons and tactics
TID	travelling ionospheric disturbance / thrasonical ionosphericists dining
TNA	the National Archives
TNT	trinitrotoluene
TOMS	total ozone mapping spectrometer
TV	television
UASD	Upper Atmospheric Sciences Division
UK	United Kingdom
UKSA	United Kingdom Space Agency
UN	United Nations
UPI	United Press International
URSI	Union Radio-Scientifique Internationale, or International Union of Radio Science
USA	United States of America
USAF	United States Air Force
UTC	Coordinated Universal Time

UV	ultra-violet
VHF	very high frequency
VIP	very important person
WBC	winter base commander
WGL	Working Group on Logistics
WWF	World Wide Fund for Nature (originally the World Wildlife Fund, and retains its original initials and panda logo)